The Bolivian National Revolution

THE BOLIVIAN NATIONAL REVOLUTION

Robert J. Alexander

RUTGERS UNIVERSITY PRESS, 1958

New Brunswick, New Jersey

Dedicated to

FRANK TANNENBAUM

Preface

This is not an impartial book; but I hope that it is objective. I am very frankly sympathetic to what has been going on in Bolivia since April 9, 1952. However, I hope that I have been able to see and understand the weaknesses and abuses in the revolutionary process, and to present them, as well as its strong points and triumphs, in the pages which follow.

Too little attention is paid in the United States to events in Latin America. The Bolivian National Revolution has suffered from this fact. There has been little serious discussion of the significance and progress of the widespread changes which have been in progress in Bolivia for the last six years. The most complicated minutiae of politics in the countries of Europe and even of Asia may be reported in the North American press, but little attempt has been made to understand one of the most significant events which has occurred in our own hemisphere in over a generation. Much, if not most, of the news and interpretation of the Bolivian National Revolution has come from sources antagonistic to the Revolution, and most particularly from the expropriated tin-mining companies. It is hoped that the present volume will contribute at least a little to righting this situation.

Much of the material in the present book is the result of six visits which I have made to Bolivia, over a period of ten years. My first visit, in 1947, followed by only a few months the overthrow of the regime of Major Gualberto Villarroel, in which the Movimiento Nacionalista Revolucionario first had its experience in government. At that time, I had a good deal of skepticism concerning the M.N.R., accepting to a considerable degree the description of this party then current in Bolivia, as a pro-Nazi and totalitarian group. However, even then, this description did not seem to fit the Movimientista trade union leaders whom I met during this first visit. Nor did it seem to apply to certain M.N.R. leaders and sympathizers whom I came to know as exiles.

My subsequent visits to Bolivia took place after the beginning of the Bolivian National Revolution. They were made during the North American summers of 1952, 1953, 1954, 1956, and 1957. I visited during both the Paz Estenssoro and Siles administrations. I spent the larger part of my time during all of these visits in La Paz, where I was able to talk with trade union leaders, politicians, businessmen, government officials—including people supporting the M.N.R. regime and those opposed to it. I was able to attend meetings of the Chamber of Deputies, several meetings of the Central Obrera Boliviana, and a meeting of the Cámara Nacional de Industrias.

My last visit to Bolivia, in 1957, was as a temporary employee of the International Cooperation Administration (Point Four). Through the kindness of members of the I.C.A. Mission I was able to glean a good deal of information concerning the operations of United States Government agencies in Bolivia since 1952, though no one in the I.C.A. is responsible in any way for my presentation of this information, or for its accuracy.

Aside from periods in La Paz, I was able to get out into the countryside and study at first hand conditions in different parts of the nation and different aspects of the revolutionary movement. I visited agrarian reform projects, a part of the United Nations' Misión Andina operation, and one of the principal mining camps, and saw other aspects of Bolivian economic and social affairs.

During these visits to Bolivia I became convinced that the social revolution which has been going on in that country since 1952 is a genuine attempt to carry out changes in the nation's society and economy which are long overdue, and that it is an attempt to lay a solid foundation for the development of real political democracy. I am much more inclined than I was a decade ago to accept the M.N.R.'s statements that they were never pro-Nazi, and to feel that although their nationalism made them unsympathetic towards the United States in the 1940's, their attitude on international affairs at that time is in any case of little relevance now.

What is important is what the M.N.R. regime is trying to accomplish, and how it is setting about to accomplish it. I hope that in the pages that follow I have been able to shed some light on these matters. I believe that they add up to an attempt to bring Bolivia into the twentieth century which deserves the attention and sympathy of all those North Americans of liberal inclinations who feel that there is merit in an attempt to end age-old tyranny and to provide the basis for a small nation such as Bolivia to make available to all its people a decent standard of living and full participation in the rights of citizenship.

My principal reservation with regard to the Movimiento Nacionalista Revolucionario and the government which it has directed since April 9, 1952, has to do with its treatment of

the opposition and its stubborn refusal to allow two newspapers representing the opposition to resume publication.
However, this attitude of the government is conditioned by
the fact that the opposition has never abandoned its belief
that the present government can and should be overthrown
by force. Furthermore, since becoming President in July, 1956,
Hernán Siles has sincerely tried to provide the widest degree
of freedom of speech and organization compatible with the
safety of a government faced with this kind of opposition.
Therefore, I do not believe that this reservation is sufficient to
justify withholding a favorable judgment of the M.N.R. regime as a whole.

Of course, I owe a debt of gratitude to all those to whom I
have talked during my various visits to Bolivia, a few of whose
names will be found in the footnotes. I also appreciate the
help of Dr. Edwin Lieuwen, of the University of New Mexico,
in reading and criticizing the chapter on militarism, and of
Dr. Carter Goodrich, of Columbia University, in doing the
same for the chapter on the United Nations' activities in
Bolivia. Naturally, they are not in any way responsible for
what I say in those chapters.

As authors usually do, I owe a great deal of gratitude indeed to my wife, Joan P. Alexander, who has borne with me
in the writing of this volume and has edited many of its
chapters, improving upon their style and making suggestions
drawn from her own observations on the scene.

ROBERT J. ALEXANDER

October, 1958

CONTENTS

Introduction

Since April 9, 1952, Bolivia has been trying to catch up with history. The National Revolution which began on that date, and which is the most profound movement for social change which has swept any Latin American country since the Mexican Revolution of 1910, has attempted to lay the foundations of a twentieth-century society.

Pre-revolutionary Bolivia was really two countries. One consisted of the Indian population, which made up three fourths of the nation, but which for all practical purposes played no role in its civic life. The Indians spoke their own languages, worshiped (under a thin veneer of Catholicism) their ancient gods, and in general had as little as possible to do with the white man, the man from the city.

The isolation of the Indian was the result of a long and

bitter historical experience. For four centuries, the aborigines had fought a losing battle against the Spanish conquistadores and their descendants, for their land, their culture, and their very soul. Experience had taught the Indians that their best protection was to draw as little attention as possible to themselves and to prevent the white man from knowing their real thoughts, or even understanding what they had to say.

In contrast to the Indian nation of Bolivia stood the Bolivia of the cities. La Paz, Sucre, Potosí, and other metropolitan centers were the domain of the white man. Many of the whites were not really of pure-blooded European descent, but culturally and at least in part racially they traced their roots to the Old World.

In the cities the beginnings of modern industry developed after World War I. In the cities, the political life of Bolivia took place. In the cities were the primary and secondary schools and the universities. In the cities, Spanish was the language of most of the people.

The link between rural and urban Bolivia, between the white, Europeanized civilization and the traditional Indian one, was the mining camps. Here there developed, particularly in the tin industry, modern enterprises which used relatively up-to-date methods. Here were congregated large numbers of Indians, who came to know Spanish and who became acquainted with at least the rudiments of modern technology.

The miners were the first largely Indian group to become discontented with things as they were. Through their trade unions they began to press for better conditions. Through various political parties they started to make their voices heard on the national scene. It was the miners who became the backbone of the revolutionary movement which reached its culmination on April 9, 1952.

Since its triumph, the National Revolution has sought to alter fundamentally the traditional pattern of social and economic and political relations in Bolivia. It has sought to

make the Indian a citizen and to give him land. It has sought
for the first time to make education available on a large scale
to the aborigines. It has sought to develop an economy which
would be more balanced than the lopsided mining and subsistence agricultural pattern which had hitherto predominated. It has sought to substitute the orderly processes of
elections for the traditional Bolivian method of changing
governments—the *coup d'état*.

All this has not been easy. Although Bolivia has had the
most stable government in its history since 1952, the revolutionary regime has faced a series of crises which would have
resulted in the downfall of a government less solidly based
on the support of the great masses of the people.

The mining industry, which provides virtually all of the
country's foreign exchange, and a large part of which was
nationalized by the revolutionary regime, was in a state of
crisis long before 1952. Little had been done to develop new
sources of mineral, and the percentage of ore in the mineral
being mined was decreasing rapidly. This situation was intensified with nationalization and the withdrawal of all the
foreign technicians employed in the mining industry.

Agriculture had also been in difficulties long before the
National Revolution. The part of the soil worked by the
Indian for his own account produced little more than enough
for his own subsistence. That which he worked for the landlord produced foodstuffs for the growing cities, but did not
produce them in sufficient quantities, so that for many years
before 1952 Bolivia had been importing needed food. This
situation was made worse by the agrarian reform policies of
the revolutionary government, since many of the new Indian
farmers saw no reason why they should produce any more
grain or potatoes than they needed for themselves.

Inflation had already started before the Revolution. The
boliviano, the national currency, had been sinking in exchange value since before the Chaco War of the 1930's.
Under the revolutionary government, the serious inflation of

pre-1952 became catastrophic. Money virtually lost all value, and the continuing existence of a legal rate of exchange and a "free market" rate which had no relation to one another gave rise to a great deal of corruption and a disjointed and completely unrealistic economic situation, particularly insofar as manufacturing industries were concerned.

Meanwhile, the measures of the revolutionary government were promising new problems, while at the same time presenting opportunities which the country had never known before. The entry of the Indian masses into the market for the first time threatened to create shortages in the immediate future which would be an unbearable strain on the country's small foreign exchange resources. This very same phenomenon, however, promised to create for the first time in Bolivia a market which would offer a real base for economic development.

At the same time, the energetic development program of the governments of the National Revolution paved the way for the opening up of the vast and untapped resources of the nation. Road building, agricultural development, and the expansion of the oil industry in the East promised to make available to the rest of the country resources which had never before been used, both in the Highlands (the Altiplano) and in the tropical and subtropical lowlands of the Eastern part of the country.

All this will take time. The story of the Bolivian National Revolution is the story of a race against time. The success of the Revolution will depend in large part on whether the measures of economic development can come to fruition before the full impact of the economic and social changes sponsored by the new regime begin to be felt. It will depend, too, in a vital degree, on whether the country continues to receive the help from the United States and from international agencies of the United Nations which it has received during the first six years of its existence.

The Bolivian National Revolution is a profound one, and

one which cannot help but have effects on Bolivia's neighbors. A perceptive observer can already see these results in Peru, and perhaps, too, in Ecuador. However, the effects of the National Revolution's granting equality to the Indian masses have only begun to be felt.

It is of importance to the future of the whole Western Hemisphere that the Bolivian National Revolution be successful. Not only is this so because this movement is bringing changes which are long overdue in Bolivia and several other countries of the region, it is also true because the Revolution represents an attempt to meet American problems in an American way.

Much has been said about "Communist" influences in the Bolivian Revolution. However, the plain fact is that the movement has been carried out by an indigenous Bolivian party, the Movimiento Nacionalista Revolucionario, by leaders who owe no allegiance to anyone except their nation and its people. The roots of the strength of the Bolivian Revolution lie in this fact. If the Bolivian Revolution were to fail, its failure would be widely interpreted as a defeat for those political elements in Latin America who reject Moscow and Peiping's dicta that the only way to carry out a successful revolutionary movement and to bring a backward nation into the twentieth century is to follow the road traversed by the Communist dictatorships of the Soviet Union and China. The failure of the Bolivian Revolution would be a triumph for the Communists and their fellow travelers.

Such a failure would also be a crushing defeat for the United States. Not only has the United States done nothing to interfere with this revolutionary movement, the actions of which have been much more profound than anything the ill-fated Arévalo-Arbenz regime did in Guatemala, but it has extended a great deal of help to the Bolivian revolutionary regime. Economically, politically, and morally, the United States has said to Bolivia and to the world that this country does not necessarily support the *status quo* in semifeudal underdeveloped nations. It has said that there *is* an alternative way to modernization, prosperity, and social justice to that preached by the Communists, and that nations—at least in the Americas—which seek this way can count upon the support of the United States.

It is thus not only to the advantage of the peoples of Latin America, who are seeking the fulfillment of their own destiny and who do not want to be subjected to anyone's tutelage—be it that of Uncle Sam or of the Communist totalitarians—but it is also to the advantage of the United States and its role as the principal spokesman for democracy in the world, that the Bolivian National Revolution succeed. This book is an attempt to study how the leaders of the Bolivian National Revolution have sought to make their movement a success.

The Bolivian National Revolution

1 . . .

Bolivia—The Beggar on a
Throne of Gold

Bolivians have long been prone to describe their country as "the beggar on a throne of gold." Although Bolivia is immensely rich in natural resources, its people are among America's poorest. Although the land possesses vast mineral deposits and untapped agricultural resources of virtually every kind, little of this great potential wealth has been developed. What development there has been has not served to benefit the vast majority of the people one iota. They remain in miserable poverty, in spite of the fact that "there would seem to be no material reasons to prevent the people of Bolivia from living a life of reasonable comfort and contentment for many generations to come." [1]

The United Nations Technical Assistance Mission *Report* of 1950 (the Keenleyside *Report*) summed up the state of

Bolivia before the National Revolution of 1952 when it said:

Agriculture is stagnant and foodstuffs and raw materials that could be produced at home are being imported. The mining industry has reached a point at which, unless confidence can be created and considerable capital invested, a period of serious decline seems imminent. Oil and hydroelectric energy cannot be adequately developed because the available resources have not even been surveyed. A large part of the population is illiterate and ill, and infant mortality is appallingly high. Existing highways and railroads are decaying for lack of maintenance, at the same time as ambitious new projects are being initiated. Meanwhile, the country passes from crisis to crisis and from revolution to revolution. . . .[2]

The reasons for these apparently paradoxical conditions are to be found in the economic and social institutions which have characterized the country since the Spaniards conquered it, early in the sixteenth century. Only with the National Revolution of April 9, 1952, was a serious attempt made to alter these conditions and to make available to the average Bolivian some of the riches with which he is surrounded.

Bolivia is the third largest country in South America in area, but the Census of 1950 showed it to have only about 2,704,000 people.[3] This is perhaps an understatement of the actual number of inhabitants—perhaps 3,500,000 would be a closer estimate. The great majority of the people, and virtually all the Indians, live in the high plateaus of the Andes which run like a spine through the Western part of the country, twelve to thirteen thousand feet above the sea, or in the valleys running down from the mountain chain. Altogether, the mountainous part of the country does not make up more than a third of the nation's area, but it is the center of most of the agriculture, contains the country's mineral wealth, has all but one of its major cities.

The Eastern section, or "Oriente" as it is called locally, has a sparse population, but it is the proverbial "land of the future." It is known to possess large amounts of oil, has vast cattle lands now inhabited largely by wild descendants of animals brought by the Spaniards, and has the possibilities of producing cotton, sugar, rubber, and virtually every other tropical product. However, until the National Revolution, little was done to put these potentialities of Eastern Bolivia to practical use.

The mountainous nature of part of Bolivia and the tropical quality of the rest have created very difficult transportation problems. Dr. Carter Goodrich, for several years of the United Nations Mission in Bolivia, has summed it up thus:

There are a few railroads, and an increasing number of trucks travel the precipitous roads. But on the Altiplano, the llama and the burro and the Indian's back still do much of the transport. The airplane is changing the picture, and it is now possible to fly over the Andes from La Paz in little more than an hour to places in the lowlands which before could be reached only by an expedition taking weeks on muleback. Yet at the landing strip the plane may be met by an oxcart, and dugout canoes still ply the tributaries of the Amazon, along with a few small steamers or "lanchas." [4]

Economically speaking, Bolivia has never ceased to be a colony. During the period of Spanish control of "Upper Peru" (as the country was then known), the Bolivian economy was characterized largely by the exploitation of rich mining reserves, principally silver. This was done through the use of forced labor, although in the later years of Spanish domination there was more humane treatment of the workers, and a sizable part of the returns from the output remained in or came back to Bolivia.

During the first fifty years of the Republic, things changed considerably. The government banks which had serviced the mining industry during the Spanish days were liquidated. Though the land remained in the hands of the same people who had owned it before, mining became disorganized as the result of the dissolution of the government banks, and there was a tendency to form private banks to help mining. The first of these was in Oruro, and others followed. There was still intensive exploitation of silver, which was used as currency, though at the end of the period several banks were established which issued paper currency. In 1862 the Banco Boliviano was set up as the bank of issue, and subsequently there were other banks established in various departments (the equivalent of North American states). All of these were authorized in 1870 to issue paper money to 150 per cent of the value of their capital.

The government participated in the returns from the mining industry. In 1831 it was taking 5 per cent of the value of silver and gold mined, and by 1870 this had risen to 6 per cent. However, gold and silver, though important to the economy, were not very important to the finances of the State, because of bad collection methods. Copper and other base minerals were dug to fill the country's domestic needs, but not for export. The government sought to stimulate the mining industry.

The government also tried to encourage agriculture, grazing, and manufacturing. Decrees of 1835 authorized money grants and medals for those establishing certain industries or making improvements in agriculture and grazing. In 1835, too, the Sociedad de Agricultura y Fabriles was established to represent the farmers' and manufacturers' interests. In 1839 the government authorized the establishment of a modern textile plant. At the same time, the government prohibited import of certain manufactured goods, as a means of encouraging industry. The government itself spent a good deal on the importation of machinery. It encouraged the growing of coca and quinine. It also gave land to both foreigners and migrants from within Bolivia who would open new areas to cultivation.

During all this period there existed a natural protection

of Bolivian industry because of the country's isolated geographical position. However, this same isolation often caused trouble, and in the 1870's, when there was a series of bad harvests, there was great distress in the cities, which were completely dependent on Bolivian agricultural production for their food supply.

The government engaged in considerable public works construction, including churches and some roads, during these first fifty years of the Republic. In 1873 a private group financed the building of a road from Tarija to Oruro.

Throughout the first half century of the Republic mining produced a considerable favorable balance of trade. In spite of this, the government continued during most of the period to have deficits. At one point, the government's financial situation was so bad that it had to deduct as much as 50 per cent from the salaries of its civil and military employees.

The most serious blow to Bolivia's economy during this period was the War of the Pacific in 1879. As a result of this conflict with Chile, Bolivia lost the valuable nitrate deposits on the Pacific Coast in the Province of Antofagasta.

The period from 1900 to 1950 was marked by growing commercial contact with the outside world because of the growth of tin mining. Tin constituted 71–75 per cent of the country's exports throughout this period. Minerals in general constituted 93–95 per cent of the exports, but the whole economy tended to move around the tin industry.

Between 1896 and 1930 imports into Bolivia rose from 12,000,000 *bolivianos* to 66,000,000 *bolivianos*. Exports rose from 26,000,000 to 126,000,000. The greatest exports were in the years 1916–1920, when the first World War greatly stimulated them. In 1900 the country exported 9,000 tons of tin and in 1930, some 40,000 tons. The value of exports was £280.7 per ton of tin in the 1916–1920 period, the highest price reached between 1900 and 1930.

With the world Depression came the decline in tin prices, and hence in exports. In 1927 the country sent abroad some

47,000 tons, but this dropped to 21,000 tons by 1933. Prices fell from $96 a ton in 1926 to $33.60 in 1933. After this, production rose, achieving an export figure of 43,000 tons in 1945, the highest since the 1920's; but even this was not back to the pre-Depression level. During the second World War there was an increase in both prices and the amount of tin exported. After the war both of these again declined.

Bolivia's balance of payments was favorable until 1930. However, this did not contribute to the wealth of the country as might have been expected. The government continued to have deficits, because of its tax liberalism. After 1908 the government began to finance public works, repay its debt, and maintain the gold standard largely by borrowing from abroad. Sometimes it had to pay as much as 50 per cent in discounts to those making the loans. This borrowing did not usually help much in the development of the economy, but merely tended to cover the government's deficit. An exception to all this occurred during World War I, when high demand and prices for tin, wolfram, and other products obtained and provided the country with an exceptionally large income.

A few years after World War I came the Chaco War with Paraguay. This hurt the economy of Bolivia. It increased the government's debt, both internal and external; during this period the government started the habit of borrowing from the Banco Central, the inflationary spiral commenced, and the government's deficits grew.

After the Chaco War there began a readjustment of tax rates. There was increased taxation of the mining industry, which had to pay part of its foreign exchange to the Banco Central. The government initiated a system of preferential foreign exchange rates. However, at the same time, the ability of the mining industry to pay increased taxes had begun to decline. Political instability made it impossible to handle the government's budget on anything approaching a scientific basis.

The post-Chaco War period was marked by an impoverishment of the mining industry and a failure to capitalize the mines. In 1938 the capital equipment of the mines stood at $160,000,000, and in 1950 it had increased virtually not at all, standing at only $161,000,000.

The government's mining tax policy over the years can be seen by the fact that from 1900 to 1905 the government took only 2½ per cent of the mines' income. In later years the percentage rose to as much as 13 per cent, and in 1920 a profit tax was introduced, but taxes were still very low. During the Depression the government was recapturing, as of 1931, only 3 per cent of the return from mining. In 1940 the tax return still stood at only 11.7 per cent.

There were relatively small changes in the other sectors of the economy between 1900 and 1950. About 73 per cent of the population continued to live in the countryside, where the land was cultivated by methods used since colonial times. Only from 1935 on did some landlords begin to use modern methods. On the Altiplano the large landholdings, the *latifundia*, reigned supreme, and semifeudal methods of cultivating the land were used by large, medium, and small proprietors alike. Only in the East had the use of wage labor taken the place of semifeudal sharecropping.

The peasant produced for his own use, and did not demand industrial goods. The landlords sent their part of the return from production to the city, where they sold it at large profits. After 1930 it became increasingly necessary to import foodstuffs to meet the growing demand of the cities and mining camps, while only rubber and a few other tropical agricultural products were exported by the rural sector of the economy. During the nineteenth century Bolivian agricultural production had been sufficient, but subsequently it was not, because of the rise of tin mining, which generated greater demand for food. Successive regimes were uniformly uninterested in encouraging agriculture, since the demand seemed small, and in any case there was plenty of foreign exchange to finance imports. The system of landholding, lack of initiative, bad health conditions, lack of capital and modern techniques, all held back agricultural development.

Transportation was one of the most serious bottlenecks preventing the expansion of agriculture. Until the end of the nineteenth century the government took relatively little interest in overcoming this lack of transport facilities. The growth of the tin industry made development of railroad connections with the outside world necessary. As a result, the country's first international railroad, the Guaqui-La Paz line, was completed in 1903, and the La Paz-Arica (Chile) railroad was started in 1904 and completed in 1913. By 1928 the government had a policy of building railroad connections with Argentina and Brazil.

The government also began to build highways at the end of the nineteenth century. Between 1900 and 1930 the road network was extended and improved. The peak of this activity was the beginning of the Cochabamba-Santa Cruz highway into the Oriente in the late 1940's. During the 1930–1950 period there was growing interest on the part of the government in building highways, schools, and electric plants.

The railroads were financed largely by foreign loans, as were the main highways. All centered on the needs of the mining industry. Railroad connections with Brazil and Argentina and the Cochabamba-Santa Cruz highway were the only projects of which this was not true.

Until 1920 Bolivian manufacturing was in the artisan stage. Afterward a number of firms of importance, such as breweries and textile plants, were established. The government adopted a moderately favorable attitude toward industry. The inflation after 1933 favored manufacturing, which enjoyed cheap foreign exchange rates for importing raw materials, while controlled prices in Bolivia resulted in the illegal export of industrial products.[5]

Before 1952 Bolivia was a semifeudal country. The great majority, the Indians, lived under conditions which closely resembled those of medieval Europe. The land was in the hands of a relatively small minority of the population, the whites and near-whites.

Before the coming of the European conquerors, the Indians of the Andean Highlands had a highly organized system of communal agriculture. Under the control of the Inca Empire, with its capital in Cuzco (now in Southern Peru), the Indians made the utmost possible use of the land and supported a considerably larger population than that which now lives in the area.

The population was divided into communities, each of which had control over a recognized portion of land. Supposedly these communities, the *ayllus*, were composed of people descended from a common ancestor, though this was probably not true in a literal sense. Before conquest by the Incas, some land was held privately, some of it belonged to the community. When the Incas took over a region, they made an agricultural survey of the area and sent in experts, seeds, and other things necessary to step up production. They began irrigation projects, which were sometimes as much as one hundred miles long, and had dams measuring as much as 1,200 yards across. The use of water from these projects was very closely regulated.

Part of the land was distributed to the people on the basis of the *tupu*, the amount deemed necessary to maintain a couple without children. There was annual redivision of the land among heads of families, including those who were incapacitated. Each head of a family got enough *tupus* of land to support the number of dependents for whom he was responsible. The land so distributed could not be sold, given away, or exchanged, and the peasant was entitled only to the product of his holding. Each family had a house and small lot which were virtually private property.

There was a strong tradition of cooperation among the

Indian peasants. In case of need, a member of the community could count upon the help of his neighbors. Also, certain lands set aside for the Inca and the sun-god were cultivated cooperatively by all members of the community. The proceeds were set aside for tribute to the Inca, for the purposes of the religious cult, and as a reserve for the community in the case of drought or other disaster.[6]

Since the Conquest, the Indians have clung doggedly to as much of this traditional pattern as they could maintain. They have sought to preserve the community and in some few cases have been able to do so. However, they have continually had to fight the encroachments of the conqueror and his descendants.

With the arrival of the Spaniards, the land was distributed among the conquerors on the encomienda system. The King or Viceroy granted to soldiers or others associated with the Conquest certain numbers of villages and by implication the land on which these villages were located. The encomendero who received this grant was supposed to defend, direct, educate, and Christianize the Indians, and pay his dues to the grantor of the encomienda. The Indians, or encomendados, had a duty to work the land under the direction of the Spanish titleholder. José Carlos Mariátegui, one of the severest modern critics of the Spanish regime, has thus described the encomendero: "Really, he was a feudal lord, master of lives and haciendas, and disposed of the Indians as if they were trees of the forest, and killed them or threw them out and took over their lands in one way or another." [7]

However, there is disagreement over the effects of the encomienda on the traditional way of living of the Indians. Baudin, author of the famous study of the Inca system, *El Imperio Socialista de los Incas*, maintains that the encomenderos did not fundamentally disrupt the Indian community, but merely took a large part of its production for themselves.[8] This would seem to have been the case in Bolivia.

The republican regimes which succeeded the Spaniards

did far more damage to the Indian community and way of life than had the conquerors. Motivated by economic liberalism, but politically unable to touch the lands belonging to the large landlords, the successive republican governments attacked the Indian community. The cooperative method of cultivation and the communal claim to ownership of the land implicit in the Indian community system made it anathema to the economic liberals. It had no place in a scheme of things based completely on private property.

The beginning of a concentrated attack on the Indian's land came in 1866 with a decree abolishing the communities and establishing each Indian as the owner of the land he then had in his possession. The aborigines, unaccustomed to the system of private property, easily fell victims to whites and mestizos, who set out to seize their land or bought it at a cheap price.

Although this legislation was repealed in 1871, and the sales made between 1866 and 1871 were annulled, the campaign against the Indian community continued. Although it was estimated that in 1877 about two thirds of the Highland Indians of Bolivia still lived in communities, by the early 1920's only about one twentieth of the land of the country was in the possession of communities. Along the main travel routes there were very few left, and the communities tended to survive principally in higher or more distant regions of the country.[9]

This struggle for the land continued virtually down to the National Revolution of 1952. The Peruvian writer, Ciro Alegría, in his famous novel, *Broad and Alien Is the World,* written about 1940, describes the process by which one Peruvian Indian community was slowly but surely deprived of its land and forced into servitude to the nearby landlords. The story might just as well have been written about Bolivia as about Peru.[10]

The Bolivian Indian was thus reduced to a sharecropping tenant on the landholding of a white or mestizo master. He was granted a small portion of land upon which to build a miserable adobe hut and on which to grow a small amount of wheat and maintain a few animals for the sustenance of his family. In return for this, the Indian tenant was supposed to work on the rest of the estate, cultivated for the account of his master. In some cases with which the writer is acquainted, the Indians were supposed to work as much as six days a week, although the average time in the couple of decades before the 1952 Revolution was undoubtedly less than this.

Not only was the Indian tenant bound to work on his master's land, he was also forced to render him personal service. Known in Bolivia as the *pongo,* this was a survival of the Spanish policy of drafting Indians for service in the mines or personal service for the conquerors themselves. It persisted in law until the administration of President Gualberto Villarroel 1943–1946, and in fact until the National Revolution of 1952.

All of the Indians, men and women, resident on the landlord's holding were bound to give service in turn. During the week when the peasant was serving his *pongaje,* he could be used for anything the landlord wished. One group of Indians whom the author visited after the land reform in 1954 complained bitterly that their former master had not only made them act on the estate as servants, taken them to the city to be servants in his house there, and rented them out to other landlords and even to businessmen in the nearby city, but had actually made them work in the kitchen, alongside the women. This humiliation of having to do "women's work" was apparently the addition of insult to injury.

During his period of service the Indian frequently had to provide his own sustenance. He was expected to bring along his food for a week, as well as blankets to cover him during the night, and any other accessories he might be expected to need.

Thus the latifundist hacienda of pre-revolutionary Bolivia was a feudal institution. It was a relic of the Spanish Conquest, and owed its existence to force and guile, not to honest work or capitalist business enterprise. The hacienda was uneconomic and could not meet the needs of the country's small urban population for food. It was cultivated gratis by the peasant and was resistant to modern technology and machinery. The landowner invested little or nothing in his holdings and lived off the labor and "feudal dues" he received from his peons. In a sense he was land-poor, since much of the "wealth" which he possessed consisted of these free goods and services, and without them his acres lost a large part of their value.

The peasant, except for the fact that he was not legally bound to the soil, was in much the same condition as the medieval serf in Europe. In return for the use of a small plot of land, he owed virtually unlimited service to his landlord. He seldom saw money income, except enough to purchase liquor for his fiestas and coca to chew to counteract the effects of an inadequate diet. He was often kept in perpetual debt by the landowner or the nearby mestizo shopkeeper.

Not only was the Indian landless, he was deprived of citizenship in the Republic. Suffrage was the monopoly of those who were literate, which excluded the great mass of the Indians. The peasants had little chance of qualifying for the right to vote, since they were given virtually no opportunity to obtain even the ability to read and write. The government paid but scant attention to building schools for the Indians.

Cultural activities were monopolized by the whites and near-whites of the cities. Although there were several universities, some publishing houses, and even a national symphony orchestra, the Indian had no part in these activities. The culture of the peasants was that which they had been able to preserve of what they had inherited from their ancestors. There was little contact between the two parts of the Bolivian nation.

Víctor Paz Estenssoro has summed up the split in the Bolivian people before the National Revolution thus: ". . .

ours was a nation whose economy, politics and culture developed within a small circle, disconnected from that which is the root of nationality, the source of energy and the solid and durable cement of all creative development which is truly Bolivian: the peasant class." [11]

The economic effect of this division of Bolivia into two nations has been described by the Keenleyside Mission *Report* thus:

Until tin mining began its spectacular growth at the beginning of the present century, Bolivia remained a country, by and large, outside the main currents of world economy. The majority of its people derived their sustenance from a primitive self-contained agriculture, and were practically unaffected by the impact of modern money economy. With the beginning of metal ore exports, however, it became possible to import goods from abroad on an increasing scale. The mining population, and the expanding urban population, which ultimately depended upon the income derived from mining, became dependent for their existence upon the exchange of their labor for food and other necessities, thus becoming part of an expanding market economy. But this new trading economy remained divorced to an extraordinary degree from that of the rest of the country. The agricultural section of the community continued to lead the same self-contained life as it had for centuries past, and Bolivia became a typical example of a split economy, part primitive and part trading. The dynamic impulses emanating from the new economy were absorbed by, but did not fundamentally affect, the old. Thus, when farmers received paper money for their scanty surplus products, they frequently buried it rather than demand goods in exchange.

This failure to create an integrated market economy . . . may be traced back to the conservatism of a primitive society, to a large extent lacking popular education and withdrawn from contact with a wider environment. It may also, perhaps, be explained in part by the racial cleavage running through Bolivian society. Here, however, it is enough to call attention to the fact that output of agriculture, per man or per acre, remained consistently low, or increased only exceptionally and in a small degree. Owing both to the economic policy of the Government and to the nature of existing institutions, agriculture lacked the incentive, and in many cases the ability to send substantial food surpluses to the mining or urban markets. . . .[12]

The effect on the Indian of this division in the nation is graphically described by Fernando Diez de Medina, President Hernán Siles's Minister of Education, when he says:

The Indian is a sphinx. He inhabits a hermetic world, inaccessible to the white and the mestizo. We don't understand his forms of life, nor his mental mechanism. The sociologist and the narrator don't succeed in molding the living material. . . . We speak of the Indian as a mass factor in the nation; in truth we are ignorant of his individual psyche and his collective drama. The Indian lives. The Indian acts and produces. The Indian does not allow himself to be understood, he doesn't desire communication. Retiring, silent, immutable, he inhabits a closed world. The Indian is an enigma.[13]

There are those who argue that the Indian was not exploited and overworked by the pre-revolutionary social and economic system, and that his miserable state was his own doing. They point out that although there were cases in which landlords were cruel and avaricious and drove their Indian retainers unmercifully, these were probably the exception, particularly in recent decades. Those who defend, or at least "explain," the system argue that in actual fact the Indian was forced to work only long enough to get the required job on his landlord's acres done, and that this usually was a great deal less than the time which he theoretically was bound to provide for his master.

Nevertheless, there is little doubt that the Indian peasant in Bolivia before 1952 was not his own master, nor can there be any doubt that this system was extremely inefficient. The landlord, getting his land tilled gratis by his tenants, and in addition being able to use the personal service of the Indians, had no incentive to modernize his methods of production, to use up-to-date agricultural implements and machinery. Why, if he made a good living—as most of them did—through the free labor of his tenants, should he bother to take part of the income which he could otherwise spend on personal pleasure and invest it in machinery which would make his tenants redundant?

For their part, the Indians learned through long experience all the methods of passive resistance. They learned the art of doing no more than was absolutely required of them. They had no great concern for the efficiency of their own labor or for the amount which they produced. Whatever enthusiasm for labor they had, they spent on their own small plots.

Those who argue in favor of the system destroyed in 1953 maintain that the Indians are by nature inefficient, slovenly, tradition-ridden, and resistant to change. They point out that even the Indian communities which survived were poor and miserable, and that when they apparently could do so, the Indians took no measures to improve their output or raise their standards of living.

The answer to this, of course, is that the Indians knew full well that if their communities appeared to be too prosperous, they would arouse the avidity of the nearest landlord, and they would be virtually certain to lose their land. Ciro Alegría describes very well the way in which this came about.

The Indian had little defense in the law. The local judges were either relatives or creatures of the landlord. The local government was subservient to the *latifundista*. The national government was a long way off, and it, too, during most administrations, was much more prone to listen to the story of the landlord than to that of the peasant.

Nor did the Indian have much hope of righting his wrongs by violence. The thing of which the white and near-white ruling class was most afraid was an "Indian uprising," and the slightest indication of violence by the Indians was likely to bring down upon the offenders the Carabineros or even the Army, and those who tried to resist would be killed, jailed, or drafted into the Army.

The Indians, therefore, appeared to be humble, perhaps stupid. They found their consolation in their animist religion, their periodic bacchanalian festivals, their haunting music in a minor key. To the white man, they always presented a poker face and an appearance of subservience. They were masters of nonchalance and of keeping their thoughts to themselves.

In this endeavor, the Indians had the advantage of their own language, or languages, since there are two great linquistic strains among the Bolivian Indians, the Quechua of the ancient Incas, and the Aymara of the even more ancient predecessors of the Incas. Relatively few white men took the trouble to learn these difficult and guttural tongues, and the Indians could think what they liked and say what they thought about their oppressors in their own language.

The Indians took out much of their energies in periodical fiestas. The Keenleyside *Report* describes this phenomenon thus:

The fiesta—typical of certain national and religious holidays—is also common in celebration of births, weddings, burials and other family occasions. These are characterized by dancing to a monotonous music of drums and flutes, and are followed by prolonged and intensive drinking often lasting for a week or more. Women and children take part and the ordinary routine of life is completely suspended. The deep orgiastic roots of this, only superficially Christianized, institution are obvious. The obligation to provide for fiestas is deeply ingrained in the Indian tradition.[14]

This mode of existence undoubtedly had a degenerating effect on the Bolivian Indian. He became stolid. Many of the arts which had flourished before the Conquest disappeared, and only the production of textiles of a marvelous brilliance and design remained. The Indian had little experience in government, and little incentive toward economic progress.

The constant chewing of coca may have dulled his nerves and his sensibilities.

However, there is little doubt that the Indian is capable of more than has been evident during the centuries since the Spanish Conquest. The way in which he organized during the first years after the Revolution, the enthusiasm with which he has endeavored to learn new methods of agriculture once convinced that the land would not be taken away from him, the avidity with which he sought education after 1952, are all evidences of this. There is no reason to believe that the Indians who produced the mighty and intricate Inca civilization are incapable of once again asserting themselves and building up a new civilization, which will borrow from the techniques of modern society, but add to it a great contribution from their own tradition and culture.

In the meantime, the average Bolivian has remained atrociously poor. The *Report* of the Keenleyside Mission commented on this as follows: "The conditions of life for the great majority of the Bolivian people, heirs of more than one brilliant civilization and inhabiting a country of vast potential resources, are harsh, static, and largely devoid of present satisfaction or future hope." [15]

Ambassador Víctor Andrade, in a speech given in New York City on November 15, 1952, elaborated on this in some detail:

In 1949 a survey of 500 workers' families in La Paz showed an average wage of 60¢ a day for the head of each family.

The average food consumption in terms of calories for each individual in the family was 1,612. The generally recommended allowance for an adult is around 3,000 calories. . . .

Among the Indians of the Bolivian Altiplano—the plateau area —infant deaths in mining communities average about 500 per thousand during the first year of life.

About one third of all children born in Bolivia die before they reach the age of five.

Life expectancy in Bolivia ranges somewhere between thirty and forty years. It is probably closer to thirty than forty.[16]

Poor nourishment is matched by poor housing. Of this, the Keenleyside *Report* said:

The typical housing unit both in cities and mining camps, and in the rural areas falls far short of even modest requirements of health and decency as accepted in the Western world. Except in the tropical and semi-tropical areas, it consists of a one or two-room adobe hut. It generally lacks windows, chimney, indoor heating facilities, running water or sanitary arrangements. The floor is often of packed mud, furnishings are sparse and elementary; although beds, chairs, tables and stoves are gradually coming into use. A surprising number of families possess a sewing machine.[17]

This poverty, the long-standing division of Bolivia into two nations, all but out of contact with one another, the four-centuries-old struggle over the land, and the lopsided and underdeveloped economy of Bolivia, all provided the fuel for nourishing the revolutionary flame ignited on April 9, 1952. However, a spark was needed to set this tinder alight. The spark was generated by the political, economic, and social events of the two decades before 1952, by the Chaco War and the forces which it set in motion.

2 . . .

The Chaco War and Its Aftermath

The Chaco War made the Revolution of 1952 inevitable. The four-year conflict with Paraguay from 1932 to 1936 disorganized the economy, discredited the Army, spread new ideas among the urban workers and miners, and sowed discontent among the intelligentsia. As a result, there began a process of social ferment which reached its high point on April 9, 1952.

The excuse for the Chaco War lies far back in history. During the period of Spanish colonialism, the Crown was frequently inexact in its delineation of the frontiers of various parts of the Empire. So long as all of Spanish America remained under Iberian control, this did not make a great deal of difference. However, once the Empire broke apart and independent countries were sliced out of its various fragments, the old question of boundaries achieved an importance which it had never before possessed. These boundaries now demarcated separate nations, jealous of their sovereignty, not provinces of a single empire.

The result was a series of border disputes which ranged the length and breadth of the hemisphere. Chile and Argentina, Peru and Ecuador, Colombia and Venezuela, virtually all the Central American countries, Mexico and Guatemala, have all had conflicts, which sometimes have erupted into wars, over the issue of their frontiers.

One of the most serious of these conflicts was that between Paraguay and Bolivia. The area in dispute was the Gran Chaco, a desolate waste area in the heart of South America which was of little immediate use to either nation. The issue had lain dormant for many decades, but in the late 1920's it became acute, and there were periodic skirmishes between garrisons of the two nations in the disputed region.

The reason for the conflict of 1932–1936, many people maintain, was the promise of oil in the Gran Chaco. The argument is frequently heard both in Bolivia and in Paraguay, that the interests involved in this dispute went far beyond the contested region, and indeed far beyond the two countries participating in the war. Many people in both countries, and in the neighboring nations as well, feel that the Chaco War was provoked by rival interests of American and British oil companies. The Standard Oil Company of New Jersey was well entrenched in regions bordering the Chaco on the Bolivia side of the frontier. British oil interests, and Argentines associated with them, were attracted by the possibilities of petroleum in the Chaco and supported Paraguay in the frontier dispute.

One can only guess at the importance of the part played by the international oil companies in encouraging the two nations to push their claims in the Chaco to the point of war. What is certain, however, is that Paraguay and Bolivia did not fight over known wealth in the area, but rather over wealth which both hoped to find there.

The Chaco War was calamitous for both sides. Insofar as Paraguay was concerned, she had not yet fully recovered from the blood-letting of the famous War of Paraguay, which she had waged against the united forces of Argentina, Uruguay, and Brazil in the 1870's, and which had resulted in the destruction of virtually the total adult male population of the country at that time. Today, she has not yet fully recovered from the effects of the Chaco War, which resulted in further destruction of her manpower, in a waste of her already scant wealth, and in a perturbation of her political life which still persists.

For Bolivia the conflict was even more disastrous. From the military point of view it was a fiasco. Bolivia's German-trained Army had a reputation before the conflict for being, within its sphere, a formidable fighting machine. However, in actual battle the leadership of the Army was shown to be inept and often cowardly, the tactics and strategy of its General Staff disastrous, and the corruption of the government administrative machinery colossal.

Víctor Paz Estenssoro has summed up the behavior of the Bolivian Army in the Chaco War: "The Chaco War demonstrated with tragic evidence the absolute ineptitude of the army created . . . as an instrument of defense of the national territory, in spite of the individual acts of heroism and the spirit of sacrifice of some officers and of the soldiers coming from the people." [1]

An example of the kind of incompetence demonstrated by the Bolivian Army was recounted to the author by President Víctor Paz in an interview on August 21, 1956. At one point the General Staff planned a general attack by the cream of the Bolivian Army, the cavalry. However, the whole attack was badly managed. It was foiled by the Paraguayans, who seized the only water hole in the area and then sat tight. Thousands of Bolivian troops died, largely of thirst, while the commander of the Bolivian forces occupied his time well behind the line in a bacchanal with some of his fellow officers and girls specially invited for the occasion.

The Chaco War had a disastrous effect insofar as the existing social and economic institutions of Bolivia were concerned. Edmundo Flores has well described the impact of the war:

Though a fiasco the war effort galvanized the country into action and broke, or at least cracked, the prevailing rigid caste system. Afterwards, it was impossible to restore the structure that had prevailed in the past. The stony immobility of the Indian could not be maintained once he left the lands that had been his only horizon. He began to be attracted to the city, where he became a "cholo" and climbed several steps up the social ladder, or to the mines where he lost his ties with the community and ceased psychologically to be an Indian, becoming rather a second-class citizen.

The "white man" could not preserve his previously unquestioned supremacy. Gradually a slow process of social capillarity began to take place. The traditional misery and abandonment of the Indian assumed a new character; it became a symptom of "social unrest" and was no longer considered as his inevitable condition.

The liberal ideas which were studied and discussed in the universities acquired more convincing tones and provided the ideological foundations for new and active political parties. The doctrines of the great social movements of the past gave a universal context to the doubts and aspirations born during the war. New parties formed by students emerged on the political scene and exerted great pressure in favor of change.[2]

Discontent was rife both in the Army and among the civilian populace as the war dragged to an end early in 1936. Even during the war the Army had become disgusted with President Daniel Salamanca's direction of the conflict and had deposed him, putting Vice President José Luis Tejada Sorzano in his place. As the war drew to a close, a group of young officers took the lead in establishing a new political party, known as the National Socialist Party and headed by Colonel David Toro, one of the commanders of Bolivia's troops in the field. Elections were scheduled for May 30, 1936, but the young officer group did not await their results. On May 17 they ousted President Tejada Sorzano and proclaimed Colonel Toro Provisional President of a Socialist Republic.[3]

The Toro government lasted for a little over a year. During this period it did a number of significant things. First of all, it created a Ministry of Labor for the first time, placing an old trade unionist, Waldo Alvarez, in this post. The Junta also issued a decree patterned on the Chilean Labor Code, which established a system of government-recognized trade unions, and provided for joint consultation between workers' and employers' unions for the regulation of working conditions in the country's various industries.[4]

The Toro government appealed to growing nationalist sentiment by decreeing the expropriation of the Standard Oil Company holdings in the Southern part of the country. This action presented the continent with a historic precedent, since it was the first time that the United States Government did not react violently against a nation which expropriated United States economic interests. President Roosevelt, in line with the Good Neighbor Policy, confined himself to demanding that Bolivia compensate United States investors for the properties which they had lost in Bolivia.

On July 13, 1937, Lt. Colonel Germán Busch, who had engineered the *coup* which put Colonel Toro in power, overthrew Toro. The Busch regime continued and intensified the general policies of the Toro administration. One of Busch's closest advisers was the extraordinary Gustavo Navarro, who had gained fame in the early 1920's, under the pseudonym of Tristán Maroff, as the founder of the country's first Socialist Party and as an early propagandist for social reform and particularly for the rights of the Indians.[5]

The Busch regime continued to foster the labor movement,

and issued the country's first full-fledged Labor Code. Even more important, it permitted and even encouraged the first serious attempts to form trade unions among the tin miners. Such attempts had previously been fought with great bitterness both by the tin-mining companies and by the government. By the end of the Busch administration, a Federation of Miners had been established.[6]

Under Colonel Busch, constitutional government was reestablished, and in May, 1939, elections were held under close government control. The Congress resulting from these elections contained for the first time a number of people representing the labor movement, and one of its most distinguished members was Tristán Maroff. The new Congress elected Busch Constitutional President of the Republic.

One of the most important moves of the Busch regime was to establish a Ministry of Mines and Petroleum, with Dionisio Foianini, the author of the oil expropriation decree of 1937, as the first Minister. On the occasion of a decree dissolving Parliament, issued on April 24, 1939, Colonel Busch noted that one of the purposes of his government would be to exercise strict control over the mining industry, so as to make the mine owners "comply with their duties to the country." [7]

Although the Busch regime was frequently labeled "totalitarian," and charges were often made that it was patterned after the Axis governments of Europe, there seems to be little truth to these claims. One outstanding fact would seem to controvert them: during Busch's administration several thousand German Jews were allowed to obtain refuge in the country. Although they were supposed to come in to be farmers, most of them settled in the cities of Cochabamba and La Paz, where they were of considerable importance in establishing new industries and businesses.

It has been frequently argued that Busch thus permitted Jewish immigration in return for the payment of large sums of money by the refugees. However, although bribes were sometimes paid to local consular officials who arranged for the entry of individual Jews into Bolivia, there is little evidence that Busch had any other than altruistic motives for opening his country's doors to those unfortunate victims of Hitler's terror.[8]

Germán Busch is widely hailed by the leaders of the National Revolution of 1952 as a forerunner of their regime. He is certainly a very controversial figure in recent history. By the people who have supported the government since 1952 he is regarded as a national hero; by the opponents of the revolutionary regime, he is regarded as a totalitarian and a demagogue.

The Busch regime came to a sudden end with the mysterious death of the President. The official story, published in *The New York Times* on August 24, 1939, the day after his death, was that he committed suicide. However, many of his supporters felt that he was in fact murdered, probably because of his campaign against the tin-mining companies.

With the death of Busch there died also the revolution upon which he had hesitantly embarked. During the three and a half years which followed, the country returned to its customary "constitutional" regime, presided over by two generals in succession—first, General Quintanilla, then General Enrique Peñaranda—and no further steps were taken in the direction of taxation of the tin companies, or in other ways disturbing the *status quo*. These regimes had the international reputation of being "democratic," and, after some hesitation, the Peñaranda government came out in support of the Allies in World War II.

During this period three important political parties were established, which were destined to play leading roles in the 1940's and 1950's. A fourth party had been established during the Toro administration which also was to become in later years a major element in the country's political life.

The first of these parties to gain importance was the Partido de la Izquierda Revolucionaria (P.I.R.). The P.I.R. was established in 1940 as the result of a congress which brought together a number of small left-wing political groups of general Marxist orientation. It proclaimed itself to be an "independent Marxist" party, and never became a fullfledged Communist group. However, it contained within it those who more than a decade later were to establish the official Communist Party of Bolivia.

The P.I.R. was led by a distinguished group of intellectuals, the most outstanding of whom was José Antonio Arze, the country's leading sociologist. Others included the writers Fernando Sinani and Ricardo Anaya and the country's principal novelist, Jesús Lara. It also quickly gained considerable support in Bolivia's infant labor movement. By 1943 it had full control of the nation's principal central labor organization, the Confederación Sindical de Trabajadores Bolivianos. Its particular bulwark was the Railroad Workers Confederation.

In 1940, soon after its establishment, the P.I.R. named José Antonio Arze as its candidate for the presidency. He was the only nominee against the official government candidate, General Peñaranda, and to everyone's surprise—including that of the leaders of the P.I.R.—Arze got a majority of the votes in several of the principal cities, and did very well almost everywhere, though losing out to General Peñaranda. This election performance established the P.I.R. as a real force in the country's political life.[9]

The second party to be established during the 1939–1943 period was the Partido Obrero Revolucionario (P.O.R.). This organization had its roots in an exiles' group in Argentina during the Chaco War, the Grupo Tupac Amaru. The leader of these exiles was Tristán Maroff, and when he returned to the country early in the Busch administration, a number of the members of the group joined him in forming the Partido Socialista Obrero Boliviano. However, the P.S.O.B. was too much a vehicle for Maroff to suit many of the old Tupac Amaru people, and in 1940 they formed the P.O.R. The leaders of the P.O.R. had been ardent students of Leon

Trotsky, and soon after its foundation, the P.O.R. affiliated with the Fourth International.[10] The party remained a minor element in the political picture until after the Revolution of 1943.

The third party of importance founded in this period was the Movimiento Nacionalista Revolucionario (M.N.R.). This was formed in 1941 by a group of young intellectuals, outstanding among them being Víctor Paz Estenssoro, a brilliant economist, Hernán Siles, son of a former President, and Luis Peñaloza, an economist and one-time member of Tristán Maroff's Grupo Tupac Amaru.

The M.N.R. was not of as defined an ideology as either the P.I.R. or the P.O.R. Its leaders were first and foremost nationalists, and as such were very critical of the Big Three mining companies—Patiño, Aramayo, and Hochschild—which had their headquarters outside of Bolivia, and drew most of their capital from foreign sources. The M.N.R. leaders were also socially minded, had supported the social programs of the Toro and Busch regimes, and were sympathetic to the labor movement, particularly among the miners.

The Movimiento Nacionalista Revolucionario was frequently criticized as being fascist, or at least pro-Nazi. There perhaps seemed to be some justification for this claim in the first program of the M.N.R., which denounced as anti-national

. . . all possible relations between international political parties and the maneuvers of Judaism, between the liberal-democratic system and secret organizations and also the invocation of "socialism" as an argument for aiding the introduction of foreign influences in our internal and international politics. . . . We demand the formation of a register of all employees of foreign firms with notation of their origins, salaries, wages, under the control of the General Staff of the Army. We demand the absolute prohibition of immigration, Jewish and of any other sort which is unproductive.

In spite of this verbal anti-Semitism, fundamental divergence from the Nazi racist pattern was noticeable in the third article of the program, which said: ". . . we affirm our faith in the power of the Indo-mestizo race; in the solidarity of the Bolivians to defend the collective interest and the common good of the individual. . . ." [11]

Víctor Paz Estenssoro answered the charge that the M.N.R was fascist in a speech in the Constituent Assembly on September 12, 1944:

The principal objective of my speech is to demonstrate that the Movimiento Nacionalista Revolucionario is not Nazi, could not be Nazi; and that its position on international affairs has been and will be based on the fundamental interests of the Bolivian Nation. . . .

We are the Revolutionary Nationalist Party. . . . We have seen that a country with a semicolonial structure like Bolivia, in a revolutionary period, and within the present realities, must insofar as possible achieve a socialist regime which will permit the realization of social conquests appropriate to any nationalist policy, the grand objectives of which will be economic liberation and reform of the agrarian system. It is not possible to apply to Bolivia, as was suggested a moment ago, principles applicable or already applied to other people in other countries. Here social phenomena are of a different nature. . . .

. . . We profess a nationalism not of European extraction, even less one dependent on German nationalism . . . the political phenomenon of Nazi-fascism [is] a phenomenon characteristic of some supercapitalized countries. . . . These countries, which do not have colonies or countries dependent upon their interests, see themselves constrained for industrial reasons to seek political-economic expansion by means of programs such as those of Nazi-fascism, which lead fatally to a policy of aggression and conquest.[12]

Paz went on to argue that all parties represented social classes, quoting Bukharin to this effect. Fascist parties represented "the oppressing classes," which in Bolivia meant the great mining companies. No one, he added, could accuse the M.N.R. of speaking for these firms.

Insofar as the M.N.R.'s international policies were concerned, Víctor Paz Estenssoro noted that:

The deputies of the M.N.R. have indicated in many speeches that the character of this war is imperialist; that democratic ideals and incitations to struggle for liberty on the one hand, and the policy of expansion and conquest on the other, mask its true purpose: struggle for raw materials and markets for the manufactured produce of the great capitalist powers. . . .

What we have never sought is to use the international situation to improve our political position, and thus with energy and directness we have won the support of the people without appealing for the acquiescence of the Department of State; which would imply in any case the permitting of the intervention of foreign powers in the national life, and subordination of the sovereignty of Bolivia.

He went on to define his party's position with regard to Bolivia's role in the second World War, then in progress: "With the United States joining one side of the present war, we, a country economically dependent, producing raw materials and needing manufactured goods, in our own interest could not and cannot be against the United States."

To prove that he did not take this position merely because it had become obvious that the Allies were going to win, Paz cited a speech which he had made in a secret session of Congress in 1941, with regard to a discussion about sending Bolivian products to the Axis. He had spoken as follows:

It would be absurd to think that anyone wishes to make a revolution in Bolivia in order to send tin to Germany. . . . A puppet government, Mr. President, would not last twenty-four hours in Bolivia; because America, whether it likes it or not, must be democratic, like the United States. Furthermore, the sending of our raw materials to Germany, such as the government discusses, is ridiculous; how would we send them? By air? By submarines from Lake Titicaca?

Paz summed up his position thus:

Bolivia must, then, necessarily align itself with the United Nations, and cooperate with them in the development of their war program. This is not to say . . . that we renounce the right to discuss the conditions of our cooperation in the interests of national defense, an absolutely necessary guide to those who conduct international relations, particularly when these deal with the economic life of the country.

Years later, in an interview with the author on August 21, 1956, Víctor Paz Estenssoro described the M.N.R. in its early years as a nationalist party, with socialist leanings, which attempted to be a faithful reflection of the situation of Bolivia, without any doctrinal rigidity. It was, Paz summed up, a national revolutionary party.

During the early part of the Peñaranda regime the M.N.R. had three members of the Chamber of Deputies who, however, had been elected individually, not as members of any party. They had been deputies during the Busch regime, and stayed in Parliament during the administration of his successor. Then, in the first elections of the Peñaranda regime, Hernán Siles and one other were elected as M.N.R. members, thus bringing the party's delegation up to five.

A massacre in the mining camp of Catavi, not far from the city of Oruro, in December, 1942, gave the M.N.R. its first chance to bid for major influence in the country's politics. Víctor Paz led the handful of M.N.R. deputies in Congress in interrogating the government of General Peñaranda concerning the causes for its troops' shooting at an unarmed group of men, women, and children in the mining camp.

In the debate on the Catavi massacre, the M.N.R. deputies had an advantage over the representatives of the P.I.R. who had first tried to take up the case. The Secretary General of

the Miners Union of Catavi, who had escaped death in the
massacre as well as capture by the police, had made his way
to La Paz, and had come to Víctor Paz's house late one night.
He had given Paz the workers' version of what had happened
in Catavi. As a result, Paz and the other M.N.R. deputies
were able to blast the position of the government, and defend
the point of view of the workers. The influence of the M.N.R.
among the miners dates from this incident.[13]

One other party is worthy of note. It is the Falange Socialista Boliviana, which was established somewhat earlier than
the other three, in 1937, among a group of exiles in Chile. It
was frankly patterned after Franco's Falange in Spain, and
took its name from that organization.[14] During this period it
did not assume major importance, though it was to do so
later, after the Revolution of 1952.

In December, 1943, almost exactly a year after the Catavi
massacre, the government of General Peñaranda was overthrown by a military *coup d'état* headed by Major Gualberto
Villarroel, who was proclaimed Provisional President. This
regime represented a coalition between an Army lodge known
as the Radepa (Razón de Patria), and the M.N.R. party. The
Radepa people, whose representative Major Villarroel was,
were a somewhat heterogeneous group, but on the balance
were probably sympathetic to the Axis in the world war
then raging.

The revolt occurred while a presidential election campaign
was under way. On the night of the uprising, the revolutionaries went to the house of each of the candidates, telling him
that there was a revolution going on, that it was in support
of him, and then when they had him in the car, announcing
that he was a prisoner, and that the revolution was of a quite
different nature.

Apparently the P.I.R., which at this time was very strongly
in favor of the Allies, did not believe that the Villarroel government was pro-Axis. José Antonio Arze, who had been in
the United States, rushed home soon after the *coup d'état*,

and immediately proposed that a quadripartite government be established, consisting of representatives of the Radepa, the M.N.R., the P.I.R., and the P.I.R.-controlled Confederación Sindical de Trabajadores Bolivianos. Only when this proposal was rejected, did the P.I.R. pass over into the opposition to the new regime.[15]

The Villarroel government lasted for a little more than two and a half years. During much of this time the M.N.R. was represented in the Cabinet, and Víctor Paz Estenssoro served as Minister of Finance. The regime accomplished a number of things which were of importance in the light of future developments.

Perhaps the most important single action of the Villarroel regime was its sponsorship of the establishment of a strong trade union movement in the mining areas. The M.N.R. had built up considerable support among the miners even before the Villarroel regime came to power, and it capitalized upon this support to organize unions in all the important mines, and to establish securely the Federación Sindical de Trabajadores Mineros as the central organization of all the mining unions.

From the ranks of the Miners Federation there emerged a new figure who was to be of outstanding importance in the years to come. This was Juan Lechín. Son of an Arab father and a Bolivian mother, he was a man of more than usual height and weight for a Bolivian, and was a champion football player. It is believed that he was originally hired as an office worker by the Patiño Mines so that he could be a member of that company's football team.

Early in the Villarroel regime, he was appointed prefect (perhaps sheriff is the best translation) of the Siglo XX mine area. The story goes that when he was approached by the mine authorities with an offer to supplement his skimpy government salary, an offer made in a routine fashion to all prefects in the mining areas, he indignantly turned down the offer and threw the company representative out of his office. This won him immediate acclaim from the miners, and made him a virtual hero among them. In 1945, when the Federación Sindical de Trabajadores Mineros held its first Congress, Juan Lechín emerged as Executive Secretary of the organization, a job he has held ever since.

Juan Lechín was a man of little political education. As a result of this, he relied heavily on a group of members of the P.O.R. who were active in the Miners Federation. Although these Trotskyites did not have very wide support among the rank and file, they used their influence with Lechín to push through the 1945 Congress of the Miners Federation the famous Thesis of Pulacayo, a document in extreme Trotskyite Marxist terminology which has been used ever since as "proof" of the Marxism and dangerous attitude of Juan Lechín.

Another important move of the Villarroel government was to make overtures to the Indian peasants. A National Indian Congress was called, which was attended by President Villarroel and a number of his ministers, and at which there was frank discussion of the Indians' grievances. This was the first time in many decades that any government of Bolivia had shown an active interest in the situation of the Indian masses.

The Villarroel government also officially abolished the compulsory personal service (*pongaje*) which Indian tenants had traditionally owed to their masters. This measure, however, never became effective until the Revolution of 1952, nor did a proposal of the Villarroel regime to give the franchise to members of Indian communities.[16]

The Villarroel government met with very strong opposition, both from inside and outside of the country. The United States waited six months before recognizing it, claiming that the inspiration for the December, 1943, *coup* in Bolivia had come from Argentina, where six months before a pro-Axis military group had seized power, paving the way for the Perón Era.

Within Bolivia, the opposition consisted not only of the old parties, such as the so-called Republican Socialist and Socialist groups, and the Liberals, but the P.I.R. as well. José Antonio Arze ran against Villarroel for President in elections held in 1944, but in the middle of the campaign was shot during an election rally, and had to go to the United States for medical treatment. There he occupied his time, in part, by teaching at the Communist Party's Jefferson School in New York City.

The opposition was roughly treated by the Villarroel regime. Dr. Alberto Ostria Gutierrez, in his book, *A People Crucified—The Tragedy of Bolivia* (pp. 40–57), presents a graphic description of the most outrageous incident of oppression of the opposition which occurred during the Villarroel regime. This involved the murder of former minister Ruben Terrazas, General Demetrio Ramos, Senator Luis Calvo, La Paz university professor Carlos Salinas Aramayo, and other opponents of the regime by a group of Army officers in November, 1944.

The M.N.R. was frequently blamed for these murders and other violations of the rights of the opposition which took place during the Villarroel administration. However, it is only fair to note that even Dr. Ostria Gutierrez does not present any direct evidence to link the M.N.R. with the murder of Terrazas, Ramos, Calvo, and the others. Years later, Víctor Paz Estenssoro, in an interview with the author on August 21, 1956, denied that the M.N.R. was in the government of Villarroel at the time the murders took place, and insisted that it would have opposed them, had it had any say in the matter.

The Villarroel government was finally overthrown on July 21, 1946, by a mob which seized control of the city of La Paz. While the Army remained in its barracks, the mob seized President Villarroel and several of his aides, and strung them up to lampposts in front of the presidential palace on the Plazo Murillo.*

From July 21, 1946, until April 9, 1952, the Movimiento Nacionalista Revolucionario was in the opposition. Its leaders were severely persecuted. Víctor Paz and other M.N.R. chiefs, who had been dismissed from Villarroel's Cabinet a few days before his death, were able to take refuge in foreign embassies and thus find their way abroad, where many of them remained during all of this period.

Virtually all the top leaders of the M.N.R. spent these six years in exile. Many of them were in Perón's Argentina, which gave rise to the assertion that the M.N.R. exiles were on the payroll of the Perón regime. According to Víctor Paz Estenssoro, however, the attitude of Perón toward the M.N.R. leaders varied a great deal depending on the circumstances. Immediately after their arrival in Buenos Aires, a number of M.N.R. people were given jobs by the Argentine Government. Subsequently, relations between Perón and the Bolivian exiles cooled, and for a year Víctor Paz was forced to change his place of residence to Montevideo, Uruguay. Only after Paz won the election of 1951 did Perón once again court him and his followers.

The M.N.R. was severely persecuted in Bolivia by the regimes in power between 1946 and 1952. Paz Estenssoro spent four months in the Paraguayan Embassy before the new government would give him a safe-conduct. At one time there were some five thousand exiles belonging to the M.N.R. and its allies in Argentina alone, and there were thousands who were jailed in Bolivia, though many of them were released after short periods. The M.N.R. was not permitted to maintain its own press. Although the party presented candidates in every election, and did surprisingly well, its leaders

* After the 1952 Revolution the lamppost on which Villarroel was hung was converted into a shrine, a plaque being put in front of it commemorating the martyrdom of Major Villarroel, and a constant watch being mounted by members of the presidential palace guard.

who were elected to public office were, as a rule, got rid of in one way or another, usually being exiled.[17]

Dr. Ostria Gutierrez, a strong opponent of the M.N.R. and a supporter of the regimes in power from 1946 to 1952, admits that the governments of that period were "provoked . . . into taking harsh and not always strictly legitimate measures of self-defense, which had the effect of generating sympathy for the trouble-makers" of the M.N.R.[18] He credits these actions by the regimes of the "six years" with helping to pave the way for M.N.R. victories in the elections of 1949 and 1951.

The six years in which the M.N.R. was out of power were turbulent, particularly for the labor movement. In 1947 the Patiño Mines discharged all their employees and only rehired those whom they considered "loyal." However, the miners re-formed their unions, and in 1949 they declared a general strike. In the process of this walkout, two foreign engineers were killed, and the Miners Federation was virtually destroyed, to be re-established only a few months before the 1952 Revolution.

Juan Lechín, who was elected Senator in the 1947 elections and was head of the Miners' Bloc in Congress, was deported several times during this period, but each time he returned to Bolivia. The same fate befell most other important miners union leaders, and in 1951 two leaders of the Catavi Miners Union were sentenced to execution, though the sentence was not carried out.[19]

In August, 1949, the M.N.R. led a serious revolutionary attempt which Harold Osborne has described as "a revolution planned on the idea of civil war, the people of the country against the army, the country against the capital." [20] The rebels held the Department of Santa Cruz and part of Cochabamba for some days, but were in the end defeated.

In October, 1949, President Enrique Hertzog, who had been elected in 1947, retired due to bad health, and was succeeded by Vice President Mamerto Urriolagoitia. The new chief executive had to face a general strike in 1950, which was crushed.

The P.I.R. cooperated with the government during most of this period. The candidate whom it supported in the 1947 elections was defeated by President Enrique Hertzog. However, members of the P.I.R. served for a considerable period in Hertzog's Cabinet, and José Antonio Arze was President of the Chamber of Deputies in 1947. In general, the line of the P.I.R. was one of support of the government, and violent opposition to the M.N.R.

On the other hand, the Trotskyite P.O.R. was allied with the M.N.R. during this period. It succeeded in electing one senator and several deputies on a general "miners" ticket in the 1947 elections, and they cooperated with Juan Lechín and the M.N.R. people in and out of Parliament.

The Falange Socialista Boliviana was also in the opposition during this six-year span, although it did not cooperate with the M.N.R. This record of opposition to the governments of Presidents Hertzog, Urriolagoitia, and Ballivían from 1947 to 1952 was to be a major factor in the growth of the party after the 1952 Revolution.

The term of President Urriolagoitia was drawing to an end in 1951 when presidential elections were called. There were several candidates in this poll. The government's choice was Gabriel Gosálves, who had been the regime's Ambassador in Buenos Aires, and who many years before had been President Busch's Minister of the Interior. He was backed by the Partido Unión Republicana Socialista, the principal party supporting the governments of the "six years," and the small Partido Social Democrático. The Falange named General Bernardino Bilbao Rioja; a third nominee was Guillermo Gutiérrez Vea-Murguia, editor of the newspaper *La Razón* (which was owned by the tin magnate Carlos Aramayo), and candidate of Acción Cívica Boliviana. Tomás Manuel de Elio was the nominee of the Liberal Party.[21] Finally, the P.I.R. put forward the name of José Antonio Arze.[22]

There was considerable discussion within the ranks of the M.N.R. as to whether it should put up its own nominee or back someone who was not in the party, though friendly to it. Víctor Paz maintained that if the M.N.R. felt that it was mature enough to undertake the government of the country, it should name its own candidate; if not, it should not back anyone. His point of view finally won out, and Víctor Paz himself was named as candidate for the presidency and Hernán Siles as nominee for Vice President.[23] They received the backing of the Trotskyite P.O.R. and the newly formed Partido Comunista de Bolivia.[24]

When the votes were counted, it appeared that Víctor Paz had won. The government maintained that he had not received the constitutional 51 per cent required for election and that the matter must therefore be thrown into the hands of Congress to decide between the two leading candidates— Paz and Gosálves. Subsequently, the M.N.R. claimed that it had discovered proof in government files that Paz had in fact received 79 per cent of the total vote.[25]

Whether Paz won or not became academic soon after the poll. Dr. Ostria Gutierrez has described what occurred:

Two or three days after the elections Urriolagoitia summoned his Ministers, the Commander-in-Chief of the Army and the Chief of the General Staff and informed them that he had decided, his message of May 7 notwithstanding, to hand the reins of government over to the Army rather than let the MNR-Communist alliance take power. The two Army officers at first protested, insisting that Congress should decide the election in accordance with the Constitution. Under pressure from the Ministers, however, the Commander-in-Chief finally agreed to consult the other leaders of the armed forces. He then called together the Chief of the General Staff, the Inspector-General of the Army, the Chief of the Air Force, the commandants of the seven military regions of the country and several regimental commanders. As the result of a vote taken by these officers it was decided that the M.N.R. candidate should not be allowed to take office.[26]

The result was that the government was turned over to a Military Junta by President Urriolagoitia, who soon afterwards left for Chile. Dr. Ostria Gutierrez has summed up the record of the Military Junta government in the following terms:

The Military Junta tried to govern with wisdom and justice, but it was composed of soldiers rather than statesmen. It suffered from the classic delusion that governing a country was no different from commanding a regiment. Soon it began making mistakes, acting over-hastily, making shortsighted decisions. It alienated the workers, for example, by an anti-strike decree and prohibited "public demonstrations of any kind" which "might be considered acts of sabotage or attempts against the security of the nation." It also interfered with the free expression of ideas in a misguided attempt to restrain the excesses of the press. Finally, it did not fulfill its pledge to remain in power only as long as might be necessary to conduct new elections. It let days and months go by, enjoying its power, lowering its own prestige and arousing discontent within the ranks of the Army itself, which wanted to relinquish its political role as quickly as possible.

On the credit side, it obtained technical assistance from the United Nations, signed important agreements with neighboring countries, tried to secure a good price for tin through skillful negotiations in Washington, increased imports of foodstuffs to ease shortages and decreed a generous political amnesty under which all exiles were granted permission to return to Bolivia.[27]

The regimes from 1946 to 1952 are generally regarded in Bolivia as governments controlled by what is colloquially referred to as "the Rosca," an indefinable term, meaning the landlord aristocracy and the mining companies, among other elements. However, it is worthy of note that during the administration of President Urriolagoitia the government presented to the mining companies a sizable bill for back taxes, which some people, at least, interpreted as a threat to nationalize the industry. This tax problem had not been resolved when the junta was overthrown.

There is little doubt that the regimes of the "six years" dealt severe blows to the labor movement, which was the principal mass organization presenting some challenge to the Rosca. This occurred in large part because of the influence of the M.N.R. in the labor organizations and the desire of the government to stamp out this influence. Nonetheless, the fact is that by April 9, 1952, the trade union movement was in probably the weakest position it had held since the end of the Chaco War. Most of the more important labor groups were disorganized, many of their leaders were in jail or in exile, and the organizations themselves were having a very difficult time functioning.

One further note should be made concerning the activity of the governments of this period. The Ballivián government, late in 1951, took a very important step in inviting the United Nations to send a large mission to Bolivia to advise the government on, and play an active part in, a program of economic development. In the previous year a United Nations mission headed by Hugh L. Keenleyside, a Canadian, had made a study of the needs of the Bolivian economy, and the sending of the second mission was a direct result of the Keenleyside *Report*. The mission arrived a few weeks before the outbreak of the National Revolution.

The whole period between the Chaco War and the National Revolution was thus one of constant turbulence and instability in government. The Keenleyside *Report* summed this up well:

Prospective or possible sources of investment capital will not fail to note that no legally elected Bolivian President has served out his term in the last quarter century; that there have been seven Presidents and eight revolutions in the last ten years; that there have been eighteen Ministers of Labor in four years; that the Corporación de Fomento Boliviano has had five complete changes in its Directorate in the six years of its existence; that there have been eight Ministers of Finance within eighteen months.

These governmental changes have been paralleled and accompanied by a similar variability in policy and legislation, particularly in the fields of taxation, labor and fiscal administration, including the management of rates of exchange.[28]

On April 9, 1952, there began the armed insurrection against the government of the Military Junta. The uprising was the result of a conspiracy between General Antonio Seleme, Chief of the Carabineros (the national military police) and the M.N.R. It was led in La Paz by Hernán Siles and Juan Lechín. The police were supported in the revolt by workers loyal to the M.N.R., who were supplied with arms.

For two days the issue hung in the balance, and on the second day it appeared as if the revolt were going to be suppressed. General Seleme took refuge in the Chilean Embassy, and when he left the Embassy again on the following day, things having taken a turn for the better from his point of view, he was told that he was no longer in charge, and that the revolution was now completely in the hands of the M.N.R.

Pro-government troops fought their way from the military school down below the center of La Paz almost to the heart of the city. Besides the police and armed workers, they were opposed by the Indian market women of La Paz, reported to have played an important role during the fighting by going up to the simple Indian soldiers who made up the regiments garrisoning the capital, and seizing their guns from their hands. The Army troops were finally turned back, and the victory of the revolt was sealed when batteries mounted on the rim of the plateau above La Paz were dismantled by cadet volunteers of the Police Academy and when armed miners arrived from the camps near Oruro.

Thus, an armed rising gave power once more to the M.N.R. Due to his lack of faith in victory, General Antonio Seleme, who might otherwise have become President, turned over full control of the movement to the civilians of the

M.N.R. As a result, the M.N.R. was able to carry through without major opposition in the years that followed its program of fundamental changes in the economic, social, and political life of the country.

3 . . .

The M.N.R. in Power

What would the leaders of the Movimiento Nacionalista Revolucionario do with the power which they had seized with such difficulty? It soon became clear that this was not a traditional Latin American upset in which the ins and outs exchange positions and little else of significance occurs. The new regime was the government of a political party which knew what it wanted to do with power, and it set out rapidly to do it.

That the new administration was to be a party and not a personalist regime soon became clear when the leaders of the revolt, Hernán Siles and Juan Lechín, summoned Víctor Paz Estenssoro back from exile in Buenos Aires to become Constitutional President of the Republic. The M.N.R. insisted that it had won the presidential election of 1951, and that Paz was merely assuming the post of which he had been unfairly deprived at that time. Hernán Siles became Vice President, the post to which he, too, had been elected in May, 1951.

Once the M.N.R. regime was fully organized, it began to take measures to carry out the policy to which it was pledged when it led the Revolution. The first move was to dissolve the Army which had been defeated in the bitter fighting of April 9–11. At the same time the Carabineros were reduced to a relatively small force, and the new regime set about systematically to arm its followers among the workers in the mining camps and in the factories of the cities.

The new government indicated its intention to come to grips with the single most serious problem facing the nation: the incorporation of the Indian into the life of the community. A Ministry of Indian and Peasant Affairs was established, which was given the task of defending the peasants and the additional job of planning the fundamental reforms in their economic, social, and political position which were promised by the M.N.R. Within a month of the Revolution, President Paz and his government endowed the Indians for the first time with the right to vote by establishing universal adult suffrage.

Under the direction of the Ministry of Peasant Affairs, peasant unions were established throughout the country, for the first time giving the Indians organizations which could defend their interests. In the beginning of 1953 the government took the step of appointing a commission to study the problem of giving the Indians the land, a project which was finally launched with the Agrarian Reform Law of August 2, 1953.

Meanwhile, the M.N.R. government had fulfilled another of its major promises, the nationalization of the Big Three tin-mining companies. A month after the Revolution, President Paz appointed a commission to study this problem. Within three months it presented its report, and on October 31, 1952 the properties of the Big Three mining companies were taken over by the Bolivian Government, and the Corporación Minera de Bolivia was established to take charge of and operate them.

In still another field the revolutionary government sought to reorganize the nation's life. In 1953 a Commission for Educational Reorganization was established. Upon the basis of its report, a few months later, the work of revising the educational system in accordance with a new philosophy was begun. Instead of education being designed merely to train a small intellectual elite, mass education was to be provided for the rank and file of the populace as well. In the meantime, the Ministry of Peasant Affairs had already undertaken a program of extending educational facilities as rapidly as possible to the rural areas.

However, the work of the M.N.R. regime was not confined to destroying old institutions. It sought, through a program of economic development which was extensive for the resources of the country and the government, to lay the basis for economic expansion. Road building, amplification of the country's electric power resources, colonization of the rich lands in Eastern Bolivia, building of plants to refine locally grown sugar, process locally produced milk, and fabricate cement were among the different aspects of this program of economic diversification. At the same time, with the help of Point Four and United Nations aid, serious attempts were made to improve the quality of the country's agriculture, through teaching the peasants better methods of production and providing them with better seeds and other necessities of modern farming.

Thus, the government of the Movimiento Nacionalista Revolucionario has carried out a program which has had as its objectives destruction of the semifeudal economic and social system of pre-revolutionary Bolivia, and laying the foundation for building a diversified and stable economy. In doing all this, it has provided Bolivia with the most stable government which it has enjoyed in more than a generation.

By its fifth anniversary in power on April 9, 1957, the M.N.R. government had outlasted any previous regime since 1930. It had not had to face any serious attempt to oust it by the classical *coup d'état* method. It had successfully transferred power from one president to another after holding the first election in the country's history in which all adults of the nation were eligible to participate, when Hernán Siles was elected to succeed Víctor Paz Estenssoro and the full membership of Congress was elected. Thus, it had begun the process of establishing a tradition of peaceful and democratic transference of power.

There is little doubt that the M.N.R. regime has had the support of the overwhelming majority of the people from the day on which it seized power. However, it has been faced with stubborn opposition, both from the Left and from the Right. On the Left have been the Stalinist parties (Partido Comunista de Bolivia and Partido de la Izquierda Revolucionario) and the Trotskyite Partido Obrero Revolucionario. Their opposition might have been more effective, had not both these groups been deserted by the overwhelming majority of their trade union leaders early in the M.N.R. administration. On the Right the opposition unified under the banner of the Falange Socialista Boliviana, a party which antedates the M.N.R. by four years, but which was never important until after the April 9, 1952, Revolution. It was the only opposition group which was able to elect members of Congress in the 1956 election.

The M.N.R. government's attitude toward these opposition groups varied from time to time. Although the revolutionary regime began with a very mild attitude toward the opposition, it claimed that its opponents' unwillingness to give up the traditional *coup d'état* method of overthrowing Bolivian governments forced it to adopt more stringent measures against the Falange. The M.N.R. regime's attitude toward the left-wing opposition has been more moderate.

During the administration of President Paz Estenssoro the

government's approach to the opposition was a tough one. Under President Siles, the administration's attitude has modified; the President has invited all exiles to return, and he has held no political prisoners.

In carrying out its program the M.N.R. government has had to face difficulties which might have proven insuperable for a regime with less unity, determination, and popular support. During the first year it had serious diplomatic problems with the United States because of the expropriation of the tin-mining companies, which resulted in considerable trouble in selling the country's principal mineral exports. However, once these difficulties were resolved, the Paz and Siles governments enjoyed extensive support, both moral and economic, from the United States.

From the beginning of the Revolution, the M.N.R. regime faced a drop in the price of tin and some of the other mineral products of Bolivia, which seriously reduced the resources of the government for its social reform and economic expansion programs. This difficulty was compounded by the steady decline in the nation's mineral output.

The most serious economic headache of the revolutionary regime, however, has been a rapid inflation. The government's own policies inadvertently contributed to this inflationary spiral, which had been under way for two decades before the advent of the M.N.R. to power. The revolutionary government made two important attempts to halt the inflation, the first by the Paz administration in 1953, and the second an all-out attempt by the government of Hernán Siles in 1956–1957. The first Stabilization Program was only moderately and temporarily successful, though the more serious attempt of Siles promised to have more profound and lasting results.

Some of the gravest problems of the regime have originated within the M.N.R. itself. One of these has been corruption. Previous regimes had made corruption a tradition in Bolivian government, and this is one tradition which the M.N.R. has not broken. Although corruption is a very difficult thing to prove, particularly about a regime still in power, there seems to be little doubt that many of the political and trade union leaders of the M.N.R. government have succumbed to the temptation to take advantage of their positions to enrich themselves.

Probably the most important source of corruption has been foreign exchange dealings. Some of those who, before the 1956 Stabilization Program, were granted the privilege of buying goods abroad at the favorable rate of 190 *bolivianos* per dollar, have been widely accused of diverting some of these funds to bank accounts abroad or to the importation of unauthorized commodities for resale. Others who were supposed to turn over goods imported under the favorable exchange rate to their unions or peasant cooperatives are widely believed to have sold part of them for their own account.

Rumors have also been widespread that government funds have been siphoned off to private pocketbooks. Government workers' wages are so low as to make this almost inevitable. Finally, there is widespread belief that corruption has existed in the administration of the Agrarian Reform Program, and in particular that minor agrarian reform officials have been subject to graft by one or another party in the cases which have been brought before them.

Although graft and corruption have been present in the M.N.R. regime, they have not been serious enough to undermine the faith of trade unionists, peasants, and rank-and-file M.N.R. members in their leaders. Such corruption is probably inevitable in a revolutionary development of the sort that has occurred in Bolivia since 1952. The same phenomenon has been an unfortunate corollary of the Mexican Revolution. It owes its origin to the rapid change in economic and social institutions, as well as to the low pay of most public officials and the galloping inflation which has plagued Bolivia since the Revolution began.

The Stabilization Program of 1956 put an end to some of the worst forms of corruption in the M.N.R. regime. In any case, the problem has not been so acute as to imperil the National Revolution or seriously to compromise the moral and political standing of its leaders.

Also a source of difficulties for the revolutionary regime has been internal factional fighting. In spite of the fact that the M.N.R. government stuck to the promises it made upon taking power, two factions developed within its ranks at a very early date. Much of the difficulty lay in the role which organized labor played in the regime. From the beginning it was made clear by Paz Estenssoro and others that the government was based jointly on the M.N.R. and the labor movement, unified soon after the Revolution in the Central Obrera Boliviana.

What soon came to be called the "Left Wing" of the M.N.R. was made up largely of the trade union leaders in the party. They established an organization, the Vanguardia Obrera Movimientista (V.O.M.), which functioned as an organized faction within the M.N.R. ranks. Juan Lechín, Nuflo Chávez, Germán Butrón, and other trade unionists were the principal leaders of the V.O.M. and of the Left Wing.

The "Right Wing" of the M.N.R. consisted largely of professional men and intellectuals, including some of the original founders of the Movimiento. It was opposed to the preponderant influence which it felt that the labor movement was assuming in the M.N.R. government, and urged caution in carrying out the program of the government. The Right Wing also established a pressure group within the Movimiento, known as the Acción de Defensa del M.N.R. Among the leaders of the Right Wing were Walter Guevara Arze, Foreign Minister of the Paz government, Luis Peñaloza, one of the founders of the M.N.R. Jorge Ríos Gamarra, Mayor of La Paz; and Hernán Siles, who was generally thought of as leader of the faction.

Víctor Paz Estenssoro was not generally considered to

belong to either faction. It was his job to keep the various wings of the party in line behind his administration and the program which it was carrying out. In any case, he was the undisputed leader of the party and was generally given the support of both groups so long as he remained in office.

The first clash between the two factions came on January 6, 1953. A group of Right Wing M.N.R. leaders, including Luis Peñaloza, Ríos Gamarra, and others, plotted with some retired military men to bring about by force changes in the administration of Víctor Paz. Nuflo Chávez was arrested, and other Left Wing leaders were sought. Walter Guevara Arze was generally credited with acting as mediator in this dispute and preventing it from actually coming to a showdown. The Right Wing leaders involved in the plot were all ousted from government positions.[1]

Some months later, when the agrarian reform became a matter of immediate urgency, there was a fresh divergence between the two groups in the party. Generally, the Left Wing won out, however, and it was decided to expropriate virtually all landholdings, exempting only those cultivated by modern methods.

A further showdown between the Right and Left Wings came at the time of the Sixth Congress of the party, held late in 1955. Although supposedly Right Wing Hernán Siles was nominated for the presidency, his running mate was Nuflo Chávez, one of the most outspoken of the Left Wing leaders. The Left Wing won out when it came to writing the party's program. Two drafts for the document were presented, and that supported by the labor elements won acceptance by the Congress. At the same time, the Left forced the retirement of Walter Guevara Arze, by that time the principal spokesman of the Right, from the National Executive Committee of the M.N.R. The new executive was manned largely by the Left Wing, including Juan Lechín, Nuflo Chávez, Alvaro Pérez del Castillo (who took Chávez's place as Minister of Peasant Affairs), and others.

The Left also scored a considerable victory in the selection of M.N.R. candidates for Congress. The trade union members of the new Congress elected in 1956 included a majority of the Chamber of Deputies, and a sizable number of senators. Miners' leader Juan Lechín was elected President of the Senate, and thus second in line to succession as President of the Republic.

The Left received a serious setback as a result of the general strike threat of July 1, 1957. During this struggle the Left split, a large part of the labor movement backing President Hernán Siles, who also enjoyed the backing of the entire Right Wing of the party. As a result of the conflict those Right Wingers who had defied Víctor Paz's leadership in January, 1953, were restored to grace, and Luis Peñaloza was named President of the Central Bank, and Jorge Ríos Gamarra was restored to the post of Mayor of La Paz.

Probably the most violent Left Wing denunciation of the Siles group at this time came from Vice President Nuflo Chávez. From his retreat in the Department of Santa Cruz, the Vice President sent a wire to the newspapers *El Diario* and *Ultima Hora* and radio stations Amauta and Altiplano in La Paz, which started as follows:

Before opinion of party and citizens in general, condemn dictatorial attitudes President Siles, transformed into unconstitutional dictator by means of special powers obtained under pressure from National Congress, taking advantage my absence as chief of legislative branch, doesn't want any control now even of own party. . . .[2]

This attack, followed by another in a similar vein a few days later, brought sharp responses from the Siles side. The railroad workers' newspaper, *El Ferroviario*, for instance, published the Vice President's statements under the headline: "Infantile Accusations by Vice President."

The Left Wing was reduced largely to the Miners Federation and some other trade unionists allied with it, led principally by ex-members of the Trotskyite Partido Obrero Revolucionario. For the time being it was ousted from all participation in the executive branch of the government or the leadership of the M.N.R., with the reorganization of the party's executive committee by President Hernán Siles, who replaced Lechín and other Leftists with trade unionists, peasant leaders, and middle-class M.N.R. leaders loyal to him. At the same time, Vice President Nuflo Chávez's "irrevocable" resignation was accepted by the Congress, now safely under the leadership of President Siles. A successor to Juan Lechín, Senator Alvarez Plata, friendly to Siles, was elected to the presidency of the Upper House.

Ex-President Víctor Paz Estenssoro took relatively little part in this crisis. Although he was urged to do so by the Lechín group, he did not return from his post as Ambassador in London. He confined himself to sending a cable to Vice President Chávez, urging him to retire his resignation before it had been considered by Congress.

Subsequent to the Stabilization crisis, the antagonism between the Right and Left Wing factions of the M.N.R. continued. In Congress, representatives of the two groups were bitterly opposed to one another over the issues of the terms on which certain small mining concessions were to be granted and the continuation of Special Powers to deal with the economic situation—powers under which the original Stabilization Program of 1956 had been enacted by President Siles.

These differences within the M.N.R. were due to a number of factors. Personalities undoubtedly played an important role. So did ancient rivalries between elements of the P.I.R. and the P.O.R. who entered the government party after the 1952 Revolution.

However, it is also undoubtedly true that there have been fundamental ideological differences between certain Left Wing elements and such leaders as Siles on the Right. Many of the Left Wingers, particularly those recruited from the Trotskyite P.O.R., felt that the Bolivian National Revolution should be "permanent," should not stop with the agrarian reform, tin-mining nationalization, universal suffrage, and other achievements of the first five years of the M.N.R. regime. Their objective was a "Socialist" revolution, and they were therefore dissatisfied with the program of stabilization of the Revolution carried out by Siles.

Factionalism within the M.N.R. had not by 1958 proven to be a serious handicap to the National Revolution. Although making still more complicated the always delicate job of being President of Bolivia, it had perhaps served to bring out the essential unity of the workers and peasants of Bolivia behind the government which they felt represented them, and which they felt was carrying out policies which would make their country healthier and themselves better off.

Revolutions of the profundity of the one which has been in progress in Bolivia since 1952 always result in the disaffection of some of those who participate in them. They are always buffeted by controversies over how fast and in what direction revolutionary changes should be made. The Bolivian National Revolution has not been different from others in this respect.

The administrations of Víctor Paz Estenssoro and Hernán Siles have only started the process of transforming Bolivia from an underdeveloped, semifeudal, semicolonial society into a modern nation-state. As in the Mexican Revolution, the process will go on when many of those who began it have passed from the scene. However, the Paz and Siles governments brought about transformations which have forever altered the nature of Bolivian politics, economics, and society, and it is these changes which we shall examine in more detail in the pages that follow.

4

The Indian Gets the Land

The National Revolution gave the land back to the Indians. It reversed a three and a half century process of spoliation of the aborigines by the Spanish conquerors and their descendants, and thereby fulfilled a long-term promise of the Movimiento Nacionalista Revolucionario.

Agrarian reform is the cornerstone of the National Revolution. Social justice demanded it. Economic development was impossible without it. Advance toward a democratic society was inconceivable until it had been accomplished. Bolivia would not truly be a modern nation until agrarian reform had been achieved.

As has been said, the pre-revolutionary system of landholding served to keep the Indian masses, the great majority of the people, in virtual servitude to a small minority of

white and near-white masters. Over a period of centuries
the land had been stolen from the Indians by force and by
guile. The extent to which the concentration of land ownership had gone before the 1952 Revolution was indicated by
the Census of 1950, which showed that approximately 4.5 per
cent of the rural landholders of Bolivia owned 70 per cent
of the country's private agricultural property, in holdings of
from 1,000 to 10,000 hectares (approximately 2,500 to 25,000
acres). Only a small percentage of the land was cultivated by
modern methods, as is shown in the following table:

Methods of Land Cultivation (in percentages)

Semifeudal cultivation	90.54
Properties worked by their owners	1.5
Properties worked with aid of wage-earners, etc.	2.44
Rented properties	2.66
Properties of Indian communities	2.86 [1]

The semifeudal landholding system kept the great majority of the people out of the market for all but the simplest
of goods. It has been estimated that of the 3,500,000 people
in Bolivia only 500,000 to 600,000 were "in the market" before the Agrarian Reform Program. It was impossible to
undertake an expansion of the country's manufacturing industries or agricultural output until the land had been redistributed and more modern methods had been adopted to
cultivate it.

Until the Indians were given a degree of economic independence, they would be unable to become responsible
citizens in a democratic society. The large landholding system made democracy in Bolivia before the Revolution a
sham at best, because the landlords did not want their tenants to participate in affairs of state, and because only
literates were permitted to vote. Thus, in the election of
1951, the last held before the National Revolution, less than
200,000 of Bolivia's 3,500,000 citizens voted.

So long as the landowning patterns of colonial times continued to exist, Bolivia remained divided into two separate nations. On the one hand there were the landholders, who spent a large part of their time away from their haciendas, and the residents of the cities. These spoke Spanish, dressed in European clothes, and had a culture of European origin. On the other hand there were the Indians, largely country folk, with their own language, their own dress, and a culture and religion of their own.

In the Program and Principles of Action of the M.N.R., first approved in 1942 and ratified again in 1946, the party said the following concerning the position of the Indian peasants:

We demand a law regulating the work of the peasant, in accordance with the peculiarities of each region without modifying the customs imposed by geographical conditions, but guaranteeing the health and the satisfaction of the needs of the Bolivian worker. We demand that every work of colonization show recognition of the need to make every Bolivian, man or woman, a landholder. . . .

We demand the identification of all Bolivians with the aspirations and necessities of the peasant, and we proclaim that social justice is inseparable from the redemption of the Indian for the economic liberation and sovereignty of the Bolivian people. . . .

We demand the study of a scientific basis of the Indian agrarian problem so as to incorporate in the national life the millions of peasants now outside of it, and to obtain an adequate organization of the agricultural economy so as to obtain the maximum output.[2]

During the Villarroel regime from 1943 to 1946 the M.N.R. members of Congress brought in a number of suggestions for commencing an agrarian reform. One of these was introduced by Víctor Paz Estenssoro and Walter Guevara Arze, another by Hernán Siles and Carlos Morales Avila. Neither these nor other proposals made during this period were passed. Abraham Maldonado sums up the fate of these bills when he says ". . . nothing could be done in the face of the resistance of some and the indifference of others, and everything remained the same as before." [3]

Víctor Paz Estenssoro himself stated the objective of the M.N.R.'s policy during these years when, in a speech in Congress in 1944, he said, "The problem . . . is not that of returning the land to its [original] owners, but simply putting it in the hands of those who work it; this is the significance of agrarian reform in general, which could be the agrarian reform in Bolivia." [4]

Eight months passed after the April 9, 1952, Revolution before the first legal steps were taken toward carrying out the M.N.R.'s promise of an agrarian reform. However, this time was put to good use by the Movimiento. The Paz government immediately established a new Ministry of Indian and Peasant Affairs, with Nuflo Chávez in charge, to prepare the way for the land reform. This Ministry had a variety of jobs to do. It sought to establish or re-establish Indian communities and encourage those still remaining in existence. It launched a program of extending education to the Indians.

One of the most important tasks of the Ministry of Indian and Peasant Affairs was to organize a network of peasant unions. Indian miners, who could speak the native languages, were sent to the villages, telling the Indians of the promise of agrarian reform, establishing peasant unions on every hacienda in the Highlands of Bolivia. At the same time, the new peasant union members were brought into the Movimiento Nacionalista Revolucionario. [5]

Antezana tells of the activities of these new peasant organizations: "In the first year, the peasant unions met daily to attend to most immediate social needs. As time passed, the meetings became less frequent. These meetings raised the social level of the affiliates and the sense of work, and community and private initiative developed." [6]

The Ministry established a system of rural inspectors,

whose job it was to oversee the new peasant unions and supervise their negotiations with their employers. These negotiations were for the purpose of establishing contracts for more equitable distribution of the returns of the soil than had been prevalent theretofore, pending the launching of the agrarian reform.

For the first time, the Indians had a protector of their interests. The miners who were the organizers of the peasant unions and principal agents of the Ministry were able to speak the language of the Indians, both literally and figuratively. Thus the Ministry soon gained the confidence of the Indians, and they streamed into La Paz to present their complaints and their problems to the officials of the Ministry of Indian and Peasant Affairs, in spite of the fact that virtually all the officials of the Ministry were white men of the upper classes.

In some cases, the peasants did not wait for the passage of an agrarian reform law before they took the land. Particularly in the Department of Cochabamba, the leaders of the new peasant unions drove the landlords from their haciendas, seized control of the land, and began to cultivate it as their own. Some of these unions were under the control of the Partido Obrero Revolucionario, the Trotskyite party, and for a time this party controlled the Federation of Workers of Cochabamba, in which the peasant organizations played a leading role. Early in 1953 the government arrested a number of the P.O.R. organizers and leaders in the Cochabamba area, and the M.N.R. recaptured control of the Cochabamba Federation of Workers. According to Minister of Peasant Affairs Nuflo Chávez, interviewed by the author on July 11, 1953, there were only four or five peasant unions at that time under the control of the Partido Obrero Revolucionario. The Communists controlled none. The overwhelming majority were under control of the Movimiento Nacionalista Revolucionario.

On January 20, 1953, President Víctor Paz Estenssoro appointed an Agrarian Reform Commission and gave it ninety days to bring in a projected land reform law. The Commission was headed by Vice President Hernán Siles as its President, and included among others Eduardo Arze Loureiro, a former associate of Tristán Maroff, Hugo López Avila, a former member of the P.O.R., Arturo Urquidi Morales, ex-leader of the P.I.R., and Hugo López Avila, representing the Central Obrera Boliviana.[7]

The Commission presented its report on schedule, and then there began a period of debate concerning the details of the new statute soon to be enacted. The Cabinet discussed the report of the Agrarian Reform Commission at great length and made certain changes in the proposed law. All the political parties, as well as the press, made their suggestions as to the form the agrarian reform should take. Some skeptics on the Left suggested that there never really would be an agrarian reform.

The Central Obrera Boliviana devoted considerable time to discussing this issue. The author attended one of these meetings. Each of the three parties which had members in the C.O.B.—the Partido Comunista de Bolivia, the Trotskyite P.O.R., the Movimiento Nacionalista Revolucionario—presented a version of what it thought the Agrarian Reform Law should be like.

The C.O.B.'s representative on the Agrarian Reform Commission, Dr. Hugo López Avila, an M.N.R. member, outlined the government's proposal for an agrarian reform law. It provided for taking over all land defined as belonging to latifundists. It called for compensation in the form of 25-year government bonds.

When López Avila had finished, Nuflo Chávez, Minister of Peasant Affairs, presented another document, similar to that of López Avila, which called for nationalization of the land, compensation of the landowners, provision of agricultural credit, and technical assistance. It said that the agrarian reform problem broke down into four parts—the human beings, the land, credit, and technical assistance—and the project of agrarian reform should take all these into account.

The project presented to the C.O.B. in the name of the Communists by Communist Party Secretary General Sergio Almarás, called for outright confiscation of the land and its distribution among the peasants. It said that the heart of the agrarian reform process was to define the class groups existing in the countryside, which were the latifundists, the rich peasants, the middle peasants, the poor peasants, and the agricultural laborers. The object, Almarás said, was to confiscate the lands of the latifundists, "neutralize" the rich peasants, make an alliance of the government with the middle peasants, and give the land to the poor peasants and the agricultural laborers. He stressed the dangers of a "right deviation," whereby some latifundists would not have their land confiscated because they were taken for rich peasants, or a "left deviation," whereby the lands of some of the rich peasants would be taken on the presumption that they were latifundists. The document also called for a Patriotic Front of Anti-Imperialist and Anti-Feudal National Liberation, including the peasants and the workers, but under the hegemony of the urban workers, arguing that no land reform could be really a land reform unless it was carried out under the leadership of the proletariat.

The draft presented by Edwin Moller in the name of the P.O.R. group urged the nationalization of the land and its confiscation without compensation. It proposed that the peasants should occupy the land and divide it themselves, and that the property of small peasants should be respected. Moller also urged that land reform should be not just one step in the long process of evolution, but a long step toward "a higher form of economic organization."

These four reports were then subject to discussion from the floor. Speaking for the Communists, José Pereira read a long criticism of the reports of Nuflo Chávez and Edwin Moller, interspersed with appropriate quotations from Lenin and Stalin. He read the text of a proposed agrarian reform law as urged by the Communists, which Nuflo Chávez later said was patterned almost word for word after the Chinese agrarian reform law of 1950.

Chávez answered Pereira, and did so as a schoolteacher might talk to a child who had not learned his lessons well. He cited Marxian dialectic against Pereira's position, and was at pains to spell out the reasons why he thought the land should be nationalized. Finally, the C.O.B. endorsed the government's Agrarian Reform Program.

On August 2, 1953, President Víctor Paz finally issued the Agrarian Reform Law. He chose to make the announcement at the village of Ucureña, near the city of Cochabamba, where the peasants had already seized control of the land and driven off the landlords.

The Agrarian Reform Law started out with a short outline of the history of the land problem in Bolivia from the time of the Incas to the date of the agrarian reform. It also described the division of land at the time of the 1950 Census, and noted that as a result of this inequitable division of the land, the country's agrarian economy was unable to supply the food needs of the people. Finally, before the operative article of the decree, the objectives of the agrarian reform were listed:

a. To distribute the arable land to the peasants who do not have enough, on condition that they work it, expropriating for this purpose the lands of the latifundists who have them in excess or receive an income without any personal work in the fields;

b. To restore to the Indian communities the lands which were taken from them and cooperate in the modernization of cultivation; respecting, and where possible making use of, collectivist traditions;

c. To free the agricultural workers from their condition of serfdom, proscribing gratuitous personal obligations and services;

d. To stimulate increased productivity and commercialization of agriculture and grazing, aiding the investment of new capital, respecting the small and medium cultivators, encouraging agrarian cooperatives, lending technical assistance, and opening up the possibilities of credit;

e. To conserve the natural resources of the country, adopting indispensable scientific and technical methods;

f. To promote currents of internal migration of the rural population, now excessively concentrated in the Inter-Andean region, with the objective of obtaining a more rational distribution of the population, strengthening national unity, and connecting the Eastern and Western parts of Bolivian territory.[8]

Once the agrarian reform had been decreed, it was necessary to set up the machinery to carry it out. This meant the selection of large numbers of people to run the land-distribution apparatus, from the local agrarian boards to the Servicio Nacional de Reforma Agraria.

President Paz Estenssoro took an active part in selecting such personnel, even down to the local level. He demonstrated his extensive acquaintance with people in all parts of the country, during a meeting which was attended by Minister of Peasant Affairs Nuflo Chávez, the head of the new Servicio Nacional de Reforma Agraria, Eduardo Arze Loureiro, and the Mexican adviser to the Servicio, Edmundo Flores. There was some discussion of filling the post of president of an agrarian reform board in a remote part of Santa Cruz. A name was suggested, but President Paz answered, "No, he wouldn't live very long in that job. He's not very fast with a gun. Let's choose this one, he is fast on the draw." [9]

President Paz Estenssoro, in his report to Congress before turning over his post to his successor in 1956, summed up the immediate effect of the Agrarian Reform Law:

The Decree of Agrarian Reform made the peasants proprietors of the land, which they had cultivated under servile conditions, from the day of its promulgation, and even before the National Agrar-

ian Reform Service gave them additional land as provided in
the same Decree, so as to make them small proprietors as specified
in the law. Half a million peasants, heads of families who before
the 2nd of August, 1953, worked with their wives and children
gratis for their employers, became proprietors on this day and
commenced to earn an income.

This latter fact resulted in an immediate improvement of the
living conditions of the peasant, who now had money to acquire
what before was denied to him and could sell for his own benefit
the fruits of his labor.[10]

Thus the little plots of land which the landlords had
granted the Indians for their own use became immediately
the property of the peasants. In addition, the peasants were
promised a portion of the holdings of the landlords which
they had formerly cultivated for the benefit of their masters.

Carter Goodrich thus describes what has happened to
those parts of the landowners' estates which have not yet
been subjected to division:

But what of the hacienda lands, the areas formerly worked for
the owners' account? . . . Here the answer is a mixed and confused one. In some cases the patrón or his representatives (*mayor-
domos* or overseers) abandoned the estate in fear or disgust or
were driven off by violence. Where the estate was abandoned, the
Indians usually took over the hacienda land and were encouraged by the government to cultivate it in advance of final disposition. In other cases, the patrón remained on the estate and continued to operate it with the labor of his campesinos. Under the
decree, he was required to pay them a minimum wage of two
hundred bolivianos per day. Where he lacked ready cash, like
our Southern planters after emancipation of the slaves, he was
permitted to enter into sharecropping arrangements with the
workers or into schemes of payment which combined cash with a
share in the crops.* Apparently abandonment and seizure more
often took place where previous relationships between the owner

* The author was informed in 1957 that most such sharecropping contracts
had been eliminated by the government, because the authorities feared that
sharecropping might pave the way for a return to pre-1952 conditions.

or his mayordomo and the Indians had been harsh, and cooperative relationships were more likely to continue where relations
had been more patriarchal. In a few of the latter cases, a pattern
beginning to form—which was partly foreshadowed in the language of the decree—is the transformation of the old latifundio
into a medium-sized property with the possibility of the continuation of work on the old hacienda land under arrangement between
the proprietor and the new owners.[11]

The reaction of the enemies of the M.N.R. to agrarian reform was violently hostile. A typical example of this is the
following statement from page 6 of Demetrio Canelas's
pamphlet, *Bolivia After Three Years of Revolutionary Dictatorship:*

The purpose of this revolution is neither economic nor social,
but political: to supplant an energetic and cultured citizenry of
European extraction with an illiterate Indian electorate. In order
to gain the Indians' support, they have been handed the land
seized from its rightful owners, and at the same time have been
given arms to defend the Government.

The racial intolerance stirred up by the M.N.R. has directly
harmed the landed proprietors who, in addition to being devoted
to the principle of providing the people with their daily sustenance, are creative and embody the nation's virtues and traditions.
It has also damaged the Indian peasants themselves, most of
whom realize that nothing good can be expected from these irre-
sponsible and criminal practices.

In order to make these tactics seem reasonable to world public
opinion, official propaganda is distorting the characteristics of the
Bolivian problem. The efforts exerted to civilize the native masses
have undoubtedly been modest up to now in Bolivia, as is also
the case in every country where this problem exists. The mission
of civilizing native peoples belongs to the civilized minorities who
live in contact with them. The idea should never be accepted that
in order to civilize the Indian, the white man must be expelled.

It soon became clear that this process of dividing up the
estates of the landlords would be a time-consuming task. The

first titles to haciendas which had been divided were actually presented to their new owners by President Paz Estenssoro on August 2, 1954, the first anniversary of the proclamation of the agrarian reform.

The first haciendas to be parceled out were "typical" *fincas* purposely selected in various parts of the country. The Technical Division of the Servicio Nacional de Reforma Agraria gathered all possible information on these *fincas,* concerning their soil, crops, the number of people on them and the age and sex distribution of these people, the income of the *fincas* and how it was distributed. On the basis of all this information, the Servicio then carried through the division of the land in question.[12]

President Paz Estenssoro himself pointed out some of the causes for the slowness of the process of giving titles to the Indians, in his report to Congress in July, 1956:

Two principal factors have retarded the application of the Agrarian Reform, the limited number of topographers available and the scarcity of personnel capable of serving as rural magistrates to handle the process of land distribution. These two factors made it necessary in many instances to annul the decisions of lower rural authorities on appeal . . . with the consequent loss of time.[13]

According to the President, the National Agrarian Reform Service started work with only some three hundred topographers to do the job of surveying and dividing the properties to be distributed. Intensive courses were given to Carabineros and rural schoolteachers in the Military School and Military Geographic Institute, so that by June 30, 1956, there were 642 topographers working on the agrarian reform, a number which was still insufficient.

Mobile agrarian reform boards were established, to go from one place to another in parts of the Departments of La Paz and Cochabamba, where the land problem was most acute, and get the first stages of the reform under way. This stepped up somewhat the work of getting the redistribution process started in those areas.[14] However, by 1958 it was still moving with excruciating slowness.

One of the principal causes for the slowness of the execution of the agrarian reform decree was the fact that there were four stages at which the landowner could appeal the decision to expropriate his holding. He could object to the work of the topographer. He could protest the decree of the local agrarian board, which decided in the first instance how much of his land should be divided and in what way. He could then appeal from the decision of a member of the Council of the National Agrarian Reform Service whose job it was to pass on the decisions of the local agrarian board, and could take the matter to the full membership of the Council. He could then appeal the Council's final decision to the President of the Republic.

Most landholders took full advantage of this right to appeal. The result has been that many cases have lingered on for years. In July, 1957, the author was shown by a member of the National Agrarian Reform Council a case which had just come to his desk. This case had been started in November, 1953. It would take him several weeks to pass upon the case, and it was certain to be appealed to the full membership of the Council, which would mean that it could not possibly be settled until the end of 1957, more than four years after the case had been started.[15]

By the end of June, 1956, only 109 haciendas had definitely been divided by decree of the President of the Republic—the last step in the land distribution process. These decrees granted 7,621 titles to 6,271 heads of families, and covered 67,904 hectares, of which 39,881 hectares were given to individuals as private property and 28,023 were granted to communities or cooperatives. At that time the National Agrarian Reform Council had some 833 other cases pending, and the subordinate agrarian reform authorities had 9,923 cases in process. Since the Census of 1950 showed that there were 17,755 landholdings which could possibly be affected by the agrarian reform, this meant that the process of bringing about a division of land had been started on approximately 60 per cent of those *fincas* subject to the reform.[16]

The Agrarian Reform Law laid down in detail what land could be expropriated and under what circumstances. Article 1 of the law provided that "the soil, the subsoil and the waters of the territory of the Republic belong originally to the Bolivian Nation," and Article 2 went on to codify this as follows:

The State recognizes and guarantees private property when this fulfills a useful function for the nation; it plans, regulates, and rationalizes the use of the land and supports the equitable distribution of the land, to assure the freedom and the economic and cultural welfare of the Bolivian population.[17]

The Agrarian Reform Law took into account five different types of landholdings in Bolivia: small holdings, medium holdings, *latifundia,* agricultural enterprises, and agricultural cooperatives or communities. Each of these was treated differently under the law.

Small holdings were defined in various ways by the law, depending on the part of the country in which they were located and the conditions under which they were cultivated. Thus, they ranged from three hectares of vineyard land in the valley areas, to eighty hectares of crop land in the subtropical Chaco area. Small holdings in general were not supposed to be divided under any circumstances.

Medium holdings were also defined in accordance with their region and type of cultivation. They ranged from six hectares for vineyards in the valleys to six hundred hectares in the Chaco region. There was a further qualification for medium holdings, that "they be exploited through the use of wage workers or with the use of improved techniques in such a manner that most of their production is destined for the market." This provision has been criticized on the basis that a holding should not cease to be considered of medium size, merely because most of its output goes to serve the needs of its owner and his family, rather than being sold in the market. Legally defined medium holdings are not subject to redistribution under the law.

The Agrarian Reform Law was aimed principally at what it defines as "latifundio." Thus Article 12 of the decree says:

The State does not recognize latifundio, which is rural property of size varying with the geographical situation, which remains unexploited or insufficiently exploited by an extensive system, with antiquated methods and implements, which give rise to the waste of human effort; . . . characterized, further, in the Inter Andean zone by the concession of parcels and other equivalent units, in such a way that the return depends fundamentally on the surplus value which the peasants produce in their condition as serfs and which is appropriated by the landlord in the form of labor service, thus establishing a regime of feudal oppression, which brings with it agricultural backwardness and a low standard of living and of cultivation for the peasant population.[18]

Article 35 of the law goes further in its definition of latifundio:

Property will not be considered latifundio . . . on which the proprietor has invested capital in machinery and modern methods of cultivation, and which is cultivated permanently by him or members of his immediate family. In those regions in which the topography of the cultivable land impedes the employment of machinery, only the personal work of the proprietor and his immediate family will be taken into consideration.[19]

Latifundio is the most severely dealt with of any type of landholding. It is to be totally redistributed among the resident peasants, or if there is more land than is needed by them, grants can be made to peasants from other regions.[20]

Holdings which might otherwise be considered latifundio

are classified as "agricultural enterprises," if, according to
Maldonado, "exploitation is carried out by modern systems
and methods using science and technology, employing machinery, modern implements, fertilizers, methods for the
conservation of the soil, if possible specialized production,
etc., with the product destined for the national or international market. . . ." [21] Such "agricultural enterprises" may
be subject to redistribution of up to 33 per cent of their
acreage if these holdings exceed certain limits; otherwise,
they are not to be touched.

Finally, there are the cooperatives or communities. These
are encouraged by the agrarian reform decree, which says
that they can be formed out of the following types of land:

Land conceded to the agriculturalists who associate as a cooperative to obtain the land. . . .
Lands of small and medium proprietors brought together to
constitute the capital of the cooperative.
Lands of peasants favored by the division of latifundio and
who organize a cooperative society to cultivate it.
Lands belonging to agricultural cooperative societies which
have been formed in any other way.[22]

The Paz Estenssoro administration sought to encourage
the formation of cooperatives. Its vehicle for this was the
General Directorate of Cooperatives and Agrarian Communities, which was established as part of the Ministry of
Indian and Peasant Affairs.

The Indians belonging to existing communities, and those
whom the General Directorate was seeking to get to form
cooperatives, were hostile at first to the approaches of agents
of the Ministry. The General Directorate then hit upon the
idea of using the *cupo* system as a means of attracting the
Indians. The government of President Paz made available to
the Ministry a number of permits (*cupos*) for the importation of foodstuffs and other articles from abroad at a rate
of 190 *bolivianos* to the dollar. These foodstuffs were then

sold at low prices in cooperative stores, and the agricultural cooperatives were built around these stores.

Once the Indians had been attracted to the cooperatives, the Dirección General sought to get them to adopt new methods of cultivation. The peasants were encouraged to cultivate collectively the land which they had formerly worked for the benefit of the landowner, and in doing so to use the new techniques suggested by the Ministry. The government agents introduced new seeds, fertilizers, and methods in this cooperatively cultivated land. When the Indians saw the contrast between the results there and those on their own fields, they were frequently more willing to adopt the innovations on their own individual plots.

All products of the cooperatively farmed fields were sold in the market, upon the insistence of the Ministry. As a result, the Indians in some cooperatives were able to earn three to five times as much as the going rate for agricultural workers' wages from these fields. From the profits of the cooperatively cultivated areas, approximately 20 per cent was put back into the land for capital improvements.

In July, 1957, the Dirección General de Cooperativas y Comunidades Indígenas had about two hundred cooperatives under its supervision. However, it recognized that only about fifty of these were operating satisfactorily. The struggle to teach the Indians to make better use of their soil on cooperative lines was a difficult one.[23]

Luis Antezana has described the way in which the peasants of the Department of Cochabamba, in which the agrarian reform was first generalized, put the land which they received—or took—to work. He notes that there were three systems found in the Department, which he describes thus:

The first may be called accidental mutual aid.

Each peasant has his individual parcel and works it with his family. But for some work he counts on the aid of other peasants, who help out in harvesting and other seasonal work. In such a case the individual peasant is owner of all of the means of production and only requires aid occasionally.

The second form is superior and the division of labor demands more specialization. There is permanent cooperation in almost all steps of production in which many peasants work together in cultivating their individual plots and those of the community, increasing the productivity of labor, avoiding the isolation of the individual, and creating a more ample concept of aid and cooperation in work. In this case, the land and other instruments of production are the property of the owner of the parcel. However, the majority of the working tools belong to the group.

Labor in this system is on the basis of permanent aid and specialization of activities. Almost all work on the land is carried out in a cooperative fashion, especially the most difficult and important jobs, such as ploughing, sowing, harvesting, transport to the market, etc.

An important part of the production remains in the hands of the owner of the land, who uses it for his family's consumption and sells it in the market. The rest serves for the common use of the people of the district.

These two forms are the best known and most common in the countryside, and are tending to develop into superior forms with a more beneficial sense of cooperation. . . . Occasional and permanent cooperation have not encountered any resistance among the peasants, due to the conditions of life, the customs, and the low degree of mechanization of agriculture. Thus they are following a line of development toward real cooperatives. . . .

In these cooperatives the peasants making them up have their own parcels and work them with their families. But the members of the cooperative possess in collective form considerable amounts of land which they work cooperatively. The production of the parcels almost entirely feeds the peasant's family. . . .[24]

Although encouraging the formation of cooperatives, the M.N.R. government did not assume a doctrinaire attitude concerning the form which agriculture should take after the agrarian reform. From the beginning, it was felt that the decision on whether land should be cultivated individually by the peasant families, or jointly in some form of cooperative was one which the peasants themselves had to make. There were peasants whose traditions tended to make them look more favorably on some kind of communal farming; there were others who were more prone to individual cultivation. The latter group was considerably in the majority.[25]

This non-doctrinaire attitude of the M.N.R. agrarian reformers differed profoundly from the position assumed by Communist governments, which have undertaken agrarian reforms merely for the purpose of gaining peasant support temporarily, and with the full intention of forcing the peasants to merge their holdings in collective farms as soon as that became politically feasible.

The M.N.R. government's attitude has also been in striking contrast to the agrarian policies followed in the Mexican Revolution. The Bolivians learned from the Mexicans the disadvantages of trying to set out in advance in what way the peasants should cultivate their newly acquired land. There has been no attempt in Bolivia comparable to that of the Mexican *agraristas* to establish a semicommunal arrangement such as the *ejido* as the universal pattern of Bolivian peasant agriculture.

The agrarian reform has had a profound effect upon the peasant. This began to be felt even before the task of dividing the haciendas of the landlords among the peasants had begun. Antezana notes this change, then he says:

A profound psychological transformation was produced in the peasants when the announcement of the reform was made; they began to walk on their own land and to feel free, as if they were standing on the top of a mountain. They learned to speak in a loud voice, with pride and without fear.[26]

One interesting aspect of this psychological change was an alteration of the popular vocabulary. Antezana explains this in the following words:

From that moment the word "Indian" disappeared and was wiped from the language to become a relic in the dictionary. Now there existed the "peasant." The worker of the countryside had been dignified by being given land and liberty in all of its aspects. "Indian," a feudal concept, was the serf of an epoch which had disappeared. Today the peasant is the equal of anyone. . . . The peasant is a human being capable of receiving instruction, of reaching the University, of being owner of the land he works and making it produce, since the land belongs to him who works it.[27] *

This change in the psychology of the Indian was noted by the officials of the Ministry of Peasant Affairs, which was more closely in touch with him than any other branch of the government. Although the peasants who came to present their problems and their requests to the Ministry continued to show respect for the authorities, they tended to become increasingly insistent in demanding a solution for their difficulties, whatever they might be. They no longer were coming hat in hand to ask favors, but were coming to demand what they now had come to consider their rights.[28]

The agrarian reform authorities were very conscious of the fact that a mere redistribution of the land was not sufficient to achieve all the objectives of the agrarian reform. Without credit and technical instruction the Indian peasants would be unable to expand production.

In fact, it is probable that many of the Indians who received land actually reduced output from what it had been before the agrarian reform. Master of the plot which he had formerly been given by the landlords to cultivate for his own use, but not sure of the fate of the rest of the landlord's hacienda, the peasant often saw no reason why he should cultivate land which was not yet his and might never become so.

The government was severely hampered in its desire to provide credit and technical instruction to the new Indian proprietors of the soil. The shortage of foreign exchange

---

* In spite of this alteration in the Spanish vocabulary in Bolivia, the author has used the word "Indian" interchangeably with "peasant" in this book, since for the North American reader this is more logical and understandable.

which plagued the country from the beginning of the National Revolution made it very difficult to obtain the agricultural implements needed for the program. By the middle of 1957 the Banco Agrícola's supply of imported implements for the peasants was reduced almost to zero.

The principal instrumentality for imparting modern agricultural techniques to the Indian peasants was the Servicio Agrícola Interamericano, part of the Point Four program in Bolivia. It is discussed elsewhere in this book.*

The principal means of providing credit to the new landowners was the Supervised Credit Section of the Banco Agrícola, which was set up in conjunction with the Servicio Agrícola Interamericano and headed by a North American, Ernest J. Sanchez. The program of the Supervised Credit Section was started in January, 1955, when President Paz Estenssoro launched it with a ceremony at which the first loans were granted. By the middle of 1957 the Section had some 4,300,000,000 *bolivianos* to work with, and had made loans to some 2,163 borrowers, of whom 528 had already paid back their loans. Grants averaged about 1,000,000 *bolivianos* apiece, though there had been some small ones for as little as 50,000 *bolivianos*, and the largest was for 70,000,000. Generally, the loans were given for eighteen months, though they ranged from three to thirty months in duration.

In deciding whether to grant a loan, the Section took into account not only the farm production for sale, but also the home situation, that is, whether the farmer had a cow to provide milk and butter; whether he had chickens to provide eggs and meat, whether he had a garden to provide his vegetables. The Section sought to encourage the farmers to supply these products for themselves.

Before granting a loan, the Section also took into consideration the resources of the farmer himself. Special attention was paid to the cattle who were to remain after the year's sales, and the cash which the farmer had on hand.

* See Chapter 14, on the United States program of aid to Bolivia.

This investigation was designed to avoid giving the farmer more credit than he really needed.

The Section sought to finance the costs of making the crop and getting it to market, rather than to provide funds for capital improvements. The funds of the Section were not sufficient for capital loans, and as has been noted, implements and other capital goods were very difficult to obtain, because of foreign exchange shortages. Therefore, in addition to financing the farmer's acquisition of seed, his preparation of his crop, and so on, the Sections's loans went toward the renting of agricultural equipment which the Servicio Agrícola Interamericano had available.

The loans made to farmers were not given in cash. Rather, a checking account was opened in the Banco Agrícola or its nearest branch. The loan recipient was able to draw checks on this account, but these had to be countersigned by the agronomist of the Supervised Credit Section in charge of his loan. Thus, the agronomist had a check on whether or not the credit was being used for the purposes for which it was intended.[29]

The lack of sufficient credit and technical facilities is only one of the weaknesses of the Agrarian Reform Program. Serious, too, has been the fact that there have been violations of the law itself by the peasants, and perhaps by the government authorities entrusted with carrying out the program. It is impossible to know how widespread such violations of the law have been. However, on various visits to Bolivia the author has heard sufficient complaints from those who have suffered from them or know others who have, to believe that they are worthy of attention. There have been instances in which landless peasants have seized small and medium-sized landholdings, which are not legally subject to expropriation. In other instances, large-scale holdings which have been cultivated by modern methods, and therefore are not subject to expropriation under the law, have in fact been divided up among the peasants.

Probably the most serious difficulty with the agrarian reform is the slowness with which it has been carried out. A member of the National Agrarian Reform Council told the author in 1957 that at the rate at which the land was being divided, it would take twenty-five years to complete the job of redistributing the land subject to expropriation.

The success or failure of the whole National Revolution depends upon the Agrarian Reform Program. So long as the M.N.R. government retains the loyalty of the armed peasantry, it is politically secure. Even if the incumbent president were to be overthrown, the peasants would be in a position to reinstate the revolutionary regime in power. However, it is also true that the continuing loyalty of the peasantry to the M.N.R. regime depends in large part on the rapidity of the fulfillment of the agrarian reform. If the peasants were to become convinced that they were being defrauded in their hopes to acquire the land, they could become as much of a menace to the M.N.R. regime as they have hitherto been a support.

The future of the agrarian reform, in turn, depends on the continuance of the revolutionary regime in power. The organized right-wing opposition does not favor the agrarian reform, and when the author was in Bolivia in 1957, even elements which were not particularly friendly to the M.N.R. government expressed fear that its overthrow would mean an attempt to re-enslave the peasantry and to return to the *status quo ante* 1952.

As for the left-wing opposition of the Stalinists and Trotskyites, they favor the agrarian reform only as a means of gaining potential support among the peasants. There is no doubt that if they were to achieve power, they would institute the type of State-dominated collectivized agriculture which is prevalent in other countries controlled by the Communists. The peasants would have no more chance of being their own masters under Communist control than they had under the pre-revolutionary feudal regime.

5 . . .

The Indian Becomes a Citizen

The Bolivian National Revolution has not only given the Indian the land, it has made him a citizen. This has not been an easy job. It has involved not only giving the aborigines the rights of citizens, but making them capable of exercising these rights.

One of the very first acts of President Víctor Paz Estenssoro was to issue a decree on July 21, 1952, establishing the principle of universal adult suffrage. With this decree the right to vote was extended to the country's illiterates, which is to say, to the great majority of the Indians. President Paz, in his Message to Congress of July, 1956 (p. 140), commented on the significance of this decree:

With this measure, one of the most important among the many which during the last four years have changed forever our national physiognomy, the old system was overcome by which a qualified vote limited the citizenry to a little more than one hundred thousand persons in a country of three and a half million.

Democracy, in its profoundest sense, signifies government of the majority for the majority. That is to say, government of the people and for the people, government originating in the votes of the majority, which consequently represents the ideals and serves the interests of the majority.

Universal suffrage, extending the right of citizenship to women, workers, peasants, soldiers, and priests, has established the only means capable of guaranteeing the functioning of a true democracy.

The universal suffrage decree explained in its preliminary passages the government's official reasons for its issuance:

Considering that it is a fundamental essential of democracy that sovereignty reside in the people and be exercised through a system of representation, and that this principle, universally approved, has not had practical application in Bolivia until the present time because of the system of qualified vote established for the benefit of the privileged minority. . . .

Considering that this unjust limitation of suffrage had its origin in the contradiction between the ideological principles which inspired the Revolution of Independence, and the economic interests of the class which directed that historical process, and which thereafter was in political control and organized our first institutions;

Considering that that restriction was maintained throughout our life as a republic, because the economic interests which originated it continued without alteration, insofar as their control over the land was concerned and were strengthened by the exploitation of the mines;

Considering that the feudal mentality, characteristic of the organizers of the political regime, could not allow the important participation in politics of the Bolivian people which was demonstrated in the valiant struggle of the last six years against the oligarchy;

Considering that the dominant oligarchy excluded from the

right to vote the members of the armed forces, members of the regular clergy, and policemen, for the purpose of keeping those institutions or persons as unconditional defenders of their privileges;

Considering that the National Revolution would not fulfill its high and noble ends if a radical and definitive change were not made in a political regime which contradicts in practice the democratic ideals of those who founded it. . . .[1]

Article 1 of the decree provided that "all Bolivians, men and women over twenty-one years of age, if they are unmarried, or eighteen years if married, regardless of their level of instruction, occupation, or income," were to be able to vote. Article 2 provided for certain exceptions, including deaf-mutes unable to write, those legally declared vagrants, traitors, false witnesses, violators of electoral laws, and defrauders of the government, if condemned by the courts. Other minor exceptions concerned those guilty of certain crimes.[2]

On a partisan political level, the Movimiento Nacionalista Revolucionario set out to arouse the interest of the peasants in political affairs. Large numbers of Indians were brought into the M.N.R., and branches of the party were organized simultaneously with the establishment of local agrarian trade unions.

The first chance which the Indians had to exercise their newly won franchise came in the presidential and congressional elections of 1956. Approximately 85 per cent of the total number of registered voters cast their ballots, and in the rural areas of the country support of the M.N.R. was overwhelming. It should be noted that opponents of the M.N.R. claimed that they had little chance of presenting their case to the peasants. However, even if they had had the fullest freedom to appeal to the Indians, it is doubtful whether the aborigines would have voted in large numbers for the groups opposed to the M.N.R. government, which had given them the land. Subsequent to the election, leaders of the Falange began active attempts to penetrate the Indian masses, and in the middle of 1956 held their party's first Indian congress.[3]

It took a long time before political leaders began to emerge from the Indian masses. In the years before the 1952 Revolution, the M.N.R. had succeeded in recruiting some full-blooded Indians, particularly among the miners, and these became the spokesmen for their people at a national level. By the time of the 1956 elections a few Indian leaders were of sufficient distinction to justify their becoming M.N.R. candidates for Congress. A handful of people were elected to the Chamber of Deputies who spoke only their Indian language and knew no Spanish.

By the end of 1957 the Indians were still playing a minor role, insofar as the leadership of the National Revolution was concerned. Although a truly peasant leadership was developing at the local level, it would be some time before there would be Indians qualified to become important figures on a national scale. Certainly the prospect of an Indian President of the Republic, who had arisen from the peasant masses, was some distance in the future. However, the important fact, even in 1957, was that the Indian masses had now begun to stir politically, and their weight, even if principally a passive one, was being felt more and more in the spheres of government.

Before the Indians could become really effective citizens, they must be provided with education. The Indians had had little opportunity to receive education before the National Revolution. According to the Census of 1950 approximately 70 per cent of the population was illiterate. Of the 650,480 children of school age (between five and fourteen years of age), only some 200,840 were actually in school.[4]

The illiterates were concentrated among the Indian population. Antezana emphasizes this fact when he says:

Only 15.9% of the peasants are literate, 84.1% of the population between the ages of five and eighty-five being unable to read and write.

The Aymara Indians have 81.3% who are illiterate.

The Quechua race has 83.1% who must learn to read and write.

Some 82.1% of the peasants of the Eastern zone await teachers and schools.

More than 15,000 schools are needed in the whole country, and some 30,000 more rural teachers. Some 768,000 children between the ages of five and nineteen are not attending school. . . .[5]

Most of the schools which did exist were in the urban areas, where the population was largely white and mestizo. Víctor Paz Estenssoro's explanation for the relatively few Indians in school before the National Revolution is the following:

The peasants were systematically excluded from the benefits of education because in a regime in which political power was in the hands of minority groups whose economic power rested precisely on the exploitation of the great majority, there could be no sincere desire to extend education. The peasant was better exploited as an ignorant worker than as one who knew his rights.[6]

In order to extend education to the Indians, the government of President Paz Estenssoro launched a program of completely reorganizing the Bolivian educational system, and of establishing so-called "basic education" institutions in the rural areas under the direction of the Ministry of Peasant Affairs.

The government leaders felt that there was need for a reorientation of the country's education system to make it more compatible with the changes which were under way in other aspects of Bolivian life. They felt that education hitherto had been directed toward training an elite, and that this should be changed. Primary and secondary schools must be adapted to the needs of all classes, and the development of an elite must be confined to the universities.

They also felt that Bolivian education, which had been copied from the French model, put too much emphasis on the humanities, neglecting the need for vocational and technical training. President Paz Estenssoro summed this up by saying that what the country needed was to train skilled workers.[7]

On June 30, 1953, the President appointed a Commission to Study the Integral Reform of Public Education, consisting of one representative of the President, two representatives of the Ministry of Education, two representatives of the Ministry of Peasant Affairs, three representatives of the Teachers Confederation, one representative each of the Central Obrera Boliviana, the University Councils, the Bolivian University Confederation (students), and the private secondary schools.[8] Several of these had formerly been members of the Partido de la Izquierda Revolucionaria, and José Pereira, the representative of the Central Obrera Boliviana, was one of the leaders of the Partido Comunista de Bolivia.

The Commission was the scene of some very hot arguments. One of the subjects of greatest discussion was the language of instruction in the new school system, particularly in the rural schools. Certain members of the Commission sought to have instruction only in Quechua and Aymara, the two principal Indian languages in Bolivia. However, the majority felt that this would result in keeping the Bolivian Indian separated from the main cultural currents of the Western world, and the Commission agreed that teaching should be in both Spanish and the Indian language spoken by the student.[9]

There was also a good deal of controversy over the weight which should be given to humanities as opposed to technical subjects in the secondary schools. Some members of the Commission sought to make secondary education purely technical. However, Fernando Diez de Medina, the Chairman of the Commission, and others opposed this, and in the end it was decided that the secondary schools should have both technical training divisions and cultural divisions.[10]

There were also conflicts between the M.N.R. majority on the Commission and Communist and pro-Communist elements in the membership. President Paz had been aware of the possible dangers of having Communists on this body, and the M.N.R. members were particularly alert to prevent the party line of the Stalinists from seriously influencing the future course of Bolivian education.[11]

The report of this Commission was submitted to the Cabinet. There it was subjected to various changes, and then on January 20, 1956, President Víctor Paz issued the decree on educational reform. President Paz described the purposes of this decree in his Message to Congress in 1956:

The Educational Reform is in harmony with what we are and what we propose to be. It conforms to the needs of an economically underdeveloped country, with a population which is not only illiterate in its great majority, but also divided by different languages and with human groups in distinct stages of civilization.

The government is now in the hands of workers, peasants, and people of the middle class. The educational system created by the Reform responds to the interests of those classes which are the immense majority of our people.

It is the proposition of the Reform to extend education, taking its benefits to the great masses, liquidating illiteracy and giving equal opportunities of learning to all the inhabitants, so that education will no longer be the privilege of the few.

With fundamental education, which is also covered in the Decree, and operates not only on the student but also on his family and the community, there has been created an effective instrument to improve the life of the peasant.

For the development and the diversification of the economy, we need men who know how to put into use under the best conditions the immense potential resources of this country. So we have given to education a predominantly technical criterion, without ignoring spiritual values.[12]

The decree of January 20, 1956 promulgated an Education Code. Thus educational matters received a standing in Bolivian jurisprudence equal to matters treated in the Commercial Code, the Criminal Code, and the Labor Code. The purpose of establishing such a code was to raise the status of education and give it a new dignity.[13]

The Bolivian Education Code is a complicated document, covering all phases of education except the University. The various chapters of the Code indicate its scope:

Chapter I	Bases and Purposes of Education
Chapter II	General Rules
Chapter III	Concerning the Structure of the Education System
Chapter IV	Concerning Pre-School Education
Chapter V	Concerning Primary Education
Chapter VI	Concerning Secondary Education
Chapter VII	Concerning Vocational, Technical, and Professional Education
Chapter VIII	Concerning Educational and Vocational Orientation
Chapter IX	Concerning Teachers' Education and Improvement of Teaching Staff
Chapter X	Concerning Literacy Campaign
Chapter XI	Concerning Fundamental Peasant Education
Chapter XII	Concerning Labor Education and Popular Universities
Chapter XIII	Concerning Special Education for Rehabilitation
Chapter XIV	Concerning Esthetic and Artistic Education
Chapter XV	Concerning Physical Education and School Hygiene
Chapter XVI	Concerning Private Education
Chapter XVII	Concerning Extra-Mural Education and Cultural Extension
Chapter XVIII	Concerning the Relations of the University and Pre-University Training
Chapter XIX	Concerning the Government and Administration of the Educational System

Several parts of the Code are particularly worthy of note. One of these establishes for the first time a system of tenure for teachers and provides for promotion on the basis of seniority and merit, instead of political influence. Furthermore, promotions to principal are to be made on the basis of open competitions among those teachers who have enough seniority to qualify. Minister of Education Fernando Diez de Medina, in an interview with the author on July 19, 1957, noted that this was in contrast to the previous system, whereby a Minister could merely select a teacher for a principal's post on the basis of personal friendship or political preference. He added that this provision of the Código had come back to haunt him upon occasion when teachers reminded him that he presided over the Commission that wrote the Código, and that he therefore must abide by it, even when he didn't particularly want to do so.

Another important part of the Code is the separation of rural education, which is placed under the control of the Ministry of Peasant Affairs, from urban education, which remains under the Ministry of Education. This is done because virtually all matters concerning the peasants are assigned to the former Ministry. However, even officials of the education service of the Ministry of Peasant Affairs regard this separation as a temporary measure, until the agrarian reform has been generally carried out, and there is no further need of maintaining the Ministry of Peasant Affairs as a separate political unit.[15]

Specific permission is given to teachers to unionize. Article 255 of the Code states, "The right of the teachers to form unions in the defense of their professional interests, improving the dignity of the teaching profession, and the improvement of education."

In addition to reorganizing the whole educational system, the revolutionary government has considerably extended the scope of that system. President Víctor Paz presented a report on what his administration had done in his Message to Congress of July, 1956. He pointed out that the percentage of the budget devoted to education had risen from 16 per cent to 28 per cent between 1951 and 1956. He added, "The economic and social conditions of the teachers have been improved insofar as possible, given the general financial situation," and noted that in the 1956 budget there was provision for spending $128,168 for the acquisition of furniture, laboratories, maps, pictures, and models used for education. In addition, $107,454 was spent for sports materials, and $434,341 was spent for equipment for industrial education.

In the urban areas, the number of schools increased between April, 1952, and July, 1956, from 735 to 847. The number of urban school buildings owned by the government increased during this period from 282 to 330. The number of teachers increased from 7,663 to 9,377, and the number of students rose from 137,503 to 214,778 in the cities.[16]

Special attention has been given by the revolutionary regime to urban technical education. Previous to April 9, 1952, there had existed a vocational school, Pedro Domingo Murillo, but it had been housed in a rickety old building and had had barely twenty-five students.[17] With the aid of the Inter American Education Service, the Paz government undertook the construction of a beautiful new building in the capital, with greatly expanded facilities, adequately equipped machine shops, and residences for some of the students. It was built to take care of one thousand students.[18]

Much more important, however, than expansion of education in the cities has been the effort to develop an educational system in the countryside. This effort, under the direction of the Ministry of Peasant Affairs, has encountered a number of difficulties. One of the most pressing problems has been the lack of adequately trained teachers. The Ministry has been forced to employ considerable numbers of teachers without any formal training, and in some cases, people who are only slightly educated themselves.

Another difficulty has been lack of sufficient funds. The rural school establishment has been frequently plagued with strikes of teachers, provoked by the failure of the Ministry to pay their salaries. Lack of funds is complicated by the long distance from some of the rural schools to the centers upon which they are dependent, making very difficult the delivery of salary payments with any regularity. This same problem of distance has made it exceedingly difficult for those supervising the school system to maintain control over the more remote schools and keep track of how they were functioning.[19]

The Indians were very enthusiastic about obtaining education. There were frequent occasions on which they built a schoolhouse and then came to the Ministry of Peasant Affairs seeking a teacher. In other cases, the Indians turned the home of the ousted landlord on an estate, or some other building on the hacienda, into a school building. They sought education not only for their children, but for themselves as well.[20]

The enthusiasm of the Indians for education was described thus by Antezana:

> The teacher is the principal element in the peasant community, and he is essential for the education of the children. The peasants request a teacher before articles of prime necessity, and in their requests "a teacher" heads the list. In some districts the teacher is employed and paid privately by the community, and only later do they take the necessary steps to have him paid from the education budget of the government.[21]

President Paz Estenssoro reported to Congress on the government's rural education efforts in his Message of July, 1956. He noted that between 1952 and 1956 the State established 1,327 rural schools, and the number of students increased from 61,230 to 132,167. The number of teachers engaged in rural schools rose from 2,811 in 1951 to 4,495 on June 30, 1956.[22] During the following year the rural educational work of the Ministry of Peasant Affairs continued to increase.

The basic element of the rural school system is the *núcleo escolar*, established in a village center in the rural area. This, ideally, has six classes, and in addition to the director and his assistant and a teacher for each of the six grades, has a teacher of home economics, one of hygiene, and one of shop crafts. On each of these *núcleos escolares* there depend a number of outlying rural schools, some of which have to be reached by mule and are days away from their *núcleo*.[23]

The effect of the opening up of educational facilities to the peasants is dramatically described by Luis Antezana:

Social liberation has brought as a consequence new horizons to the peasants, and they can fulfill their desire for knowledge which had previously been available only to the minority of latifundists and small privileged castes. The peasants, once their horizons were opened, saw their mental world grow in all fields from mathematics to literature. The world of numbers for the peasants had not gone beyond the fingers of their hands. Those who had been able to count to 100 were few, and to speak in thousands was to confound them in abstractions. For them the infinite began beyond 100. However, those limits were now overcome, and they were learning operations superior to those of the simple arithmetic table.

The desire to learn of the peasants is notable, and their interest in learning brought them to the cities to buy magazines, pamphlets, periodicals, notebooks, etc. Whatever pamphlet was given them became a valuable means of instruction. . . .[24]

Education is only one of the things needed to make the Indian peasant into a citizen. He also needs improved medical facilities, so that he can have the health which will permit him not only to do his work, but to participate in the life of the community as well. The government of the National Revolution has sought to provide these facilities. Antezana describes this problem in the Department of Cochabamba:

The peasants also wished to have hospitals and medical posts in their districts, and they immediately began to construct buildings for this purpose. The Ministry of Health provided medical instruments and sometimes professional services when they were not contracted for by the peasants. According to official figures more than ten rural hospitals have been constructed during the last year in the valley of Cochabamba and its environs.[25]

According to President Víctor Paz Estenssoro's Message to Congress in July, 1956:

The Ministry of Health established a program of rural health centers which has begun in the departments of Tarija and Oruro, installing dispensaries in Bella Vista, Polla, Concepción, Padcaya, Canasmoro, San Lorenzo, Entre Ríos, in the former department, and Toledo, Poopó, Challacolla, Pária, and Machacamarca in that of Oruro. In addition, mobile rural units were established in Montero (Santa Cruz) and Pillapi (La Paz).[26]

In addition to these general health centers, special dispensaries for maternal and child care were established. Forty-two such centers were established during the Paz Estenssoro administration. Some 50,400 births were handled in these institutions, and 82,000 children under three years of age were taken care of in them.[27]

Thus, the program of the revolutionary government for incorporating the Indian into the general life of the nation went considerably beyond merely giving him the land. Although the possession of the land was designed to give him a solid economic base, education and the improvement of health facilities will in time make him worthy of the use of the political power which the National Revolution has given the Indian.

6 . . .

Nationalization of the Mines

Perhaps the most controversial aspect of the Bolivian National Revolution is the nationalization of the Big Three tin-mining companies. This has brought down upon the M.N.R. government a widespread and violent propaganda campaign in foreign countries on the part of the expropriated companies. The nationalization has been pictured as a "Communist" move; many millions of words have been used to describe the "disaster" which nationalization has brought upon the Bolivian mining industry; the decline in production since nationalization has been stressed. The alleged inability of the Bolivians to run their mining industry has been emphasized over and over again.

However, what most of this propaganda overlooks is the fact that the nationalization of the tin mines was only a small part of the National Revolution. It was certainly not the most important accomplishment of the government which came to power on April 9, 1952, and pales into relative insignificance when compared with the Revolution's efforts to incorporate the Indians into the life of the country, to overcome centuries of oppression, obstinate tradition, and the chasm-like division of the Bolivian nation into two separate peoples.

Furthermore, the nationalization of the tin mines was prompted by peculiar conditions which had arisen in Bolivia during the preceding half-century, and was not the result of any "foreign" ideology possessed by the leaders of the M.N.R. Finally, nationalization has not been the abysmal failure which it has been pictured as being by the enemies of the National Revolution.

The nationalization of Patiño, Aramayo, and Hochschild was an absolute political necessity. The companies were waist-deep in politics, and had long been hostile to the M.N.R. To carry out the Movimiento Nacionalista Revolucionario's program of economic nationalism its leaders were anxious to get into the hands of Bolivians the source of wealth which produced 80 per cent of the country's foreign exchange. Finally, the nationalization of the tin mines was a test of the good faith of the M.N.R. government. If it had failed to take this step, its worker and middle-class supporters would have doubted its willingness or ability to carry out the other parts of its program.

Conditions were admittedly very bad in the mining companies' camps, though this was not entirely the fault of the Big Three. Carter Goodrich has summed up these conditions:

The more serious causes for concern over the conditions of life of the Bolivian miners lie not in their wages, but in what appears to be a lack of active or natural social life in the cheerless encampments to which they have been transplanted and in the dangers and hardships of the work itself. Mining is carried on at high altitudes, mostly between fourteen and seventeen thousand feet. Yet in a number of mines, the heat of the working face is so great that men work almost naked and in short spells of labor alternating with periods of rest. Throughout the industry, and most of all in the smaller mines, the dangers of accident are very great. In 1949, for example, 475 fatal accidents were reported from a working force of about 49,000. Silicosis is common, though authorities differ on its extent and seriousness, and few men have a long working life in the industry. In a visit to the principal mining centers early in 1952, it was found that the average length of service was from seven to eleven years and that almost 90 percent of the miners were under forty-five years of age. A number of the miners, though now a decreasing proportion, are seasonal workers, spending part of the year in their native villages. Others return permanently to the land when they are no longer fit for work in the mines. Ironically, some men pensioned off by the larger mines because of disease go on to work in the unregulated smaller mines under still greater risks to life and health.[1]

There is little doubt that Patiño, Aramayo, and Hochschild companies had long been active in politics. They had subsidized candidates for office, they had financed revolution, they had made a regular policy of "tipping" the local government officials in the mining areas. They had contributed heavily to the funds of candidates opposed to the M.N.R. ticket in the 1951 election.[2] *

For its part, the M.N.R. had been in the vanguard of the fight against the Big Three mining interests since its foundation. In 1939, even before the M.N.R. was established, Víctor Paz Estenssoro proposed to President Germán Busch a decree forcing the mining companies to sell all foreign

*Ambassador Víctor Andrade, in a speech delivered at Pennsylvania State University on February 23, 1957, asserted:

"The M.N.R. party held power once before in the 1943–46 period. During that time the tin barons paid for and directed a propaganda campaign against us. As a result of that campaign of slander, the M.N.R.'s reputation in your country was destroyed. Some persons in the United States thought us Fascist, some Communist, but the consensus was that we were no good."

exchange they earned to the Banco Central. This decree was adopted by Busch, but he died two weeks thereafter, and it was never put into execution.

Movimientista deputies took the lead in denouncing the companies and the complicity of the Peñaranda government with them at the time of the Catavi "massacre" of December, 1942. Subsequently, in the administration of President Villar-roel, Víctor Paz as Minister of Finance revived a somewhat modified version of the Busch decree on foreign exchange, and it went into operation.[3] At the same time, the M.N.R. was taking the lead in establishing trade unions in the mines, and bringing them together in the Federación Sindical de Trabajadores Mineros. Finally, during the 1951 presidential election campaign, the M.N.R. promised that if its candidates won, they would undertake the nationalization of the Big Three mines.[4]

The M.N.R. was undoubtedly motivated in its opposition to the Big Three tin-mining companies by its belief that they had become a State within a State. Controlled from abroad, and with little or no say by Bolivians in the determination of their policies, these companies had a life-and-death grip on the country's economy, and particularly upon its foreign trade.

President Víctor Paz, in his final speech to Congress before giving up the post of chief executive in 1956, summed up the attitude of the Movimiento Nacionalista Revolucionario toward this problem:

From colonial times until our own day mining has constituted the principal economic activity of the country, which gives it a peculiar character. From the beginning of this century, and the beginning of the exploitation of tin, mining has increased, has been modernized, has become the only capitalist economic activity of importance, and has become part of an international financial consortium. It is the principal source of foreign exchange with which we cover our needs for foreign money, and it provides the principal source of funds for our modest government budget. These factors, to which should be added the concentration of the industry in the hands of three firms, converted it into a growing power which would soon be unchallengeable and whose rule weighed upon the whole life of the nation.

The process of development of mining, typically semicolonial, consumed irreplaceable human capital. The Bolivian was considered an Indian whose labor was cheap and whose life was worthless. He was miserably paid; the diseases and accidents resulting from his work were not considered worthy of compensation until almost the middle of this century. And, when this exploitation created a spirit of class consciousness among the workers and they made their first demands for better living conditions, these demands were unmercifully smothered in blood.

The wealth of the mines was exported, without return for the country, to build vast fortunes abroad. Some governments, faced with budgetary necessities, attempted to keep back a small part of this wealth by taxes on exports. The firms responded to this by becoming international, so as to get the help and protection of the Great Powers, and making rebellion the habitual method of maintaining their servants in the Presidential Palace.

The economic and political preponderance of Patiño, Hochschild, and Aramayo, kept Bolivia in a long and painful state of agony. . . . Without eliminating the omnipresent power of Patiño, Hochschild, and Aramayo, it was impossible to carry out the other fundamental objectives of the Revolution.[5]

There is no doubt about the dependence of the Bolivian economy on the tin-mining industry, and particularly on tin for its foreign exchange. This is made clear by the report on the Bolivian economy of the Economic Commission for Latin America (Vol. I, p. 73), which says:

During the last quarter of a century, minerals have never represented less than 90 per cent of the value of exports, and the tendency has been for this percentage to increase. Although the relative importance of tin—which contributed about three fourths of the exports during the five years before the World Depression —has tended to decline, the export of other minerals (principally tungsten) has increased sufficiently to more than counteract that tendency. However, tin still represents more than 55 per cent of the value of exports, and the increase in sale of tungsten has had the artificial stimulation of special contracts which guarantee prices double those prevalent in world markets today. With the expiration of those contracts in 1957 there will be an adverse effect on the production of tungsten and tin will return to its former relative position among mineral exports.

The E.C.L.A. report gives the following table showing the relative importance of various minerals over a period of more than three decades (Vol. I, p. 74):

Composition of Exports (in percentages)

	1925–1929	1930–1940	1941–1945	1946–1949	1950–1952	1953–1955	1956
All Minerals	93.3	94.8	95.3	95.6	96.8	96.6	93.2
Tin	74.2	74.8	72.9	71.5	63.5	61.5	55.6
Tungsten	0.3	3.0	8.9	2.6	6.8	14.1	13.5
Lead	4.8	2.6	2.2	5.9	8.5	6.1	7.1
Zinc	1.3	2.5	2.5	2.7	7.7	5.2	4.7
Silver	6.0	7.4	3.7	5.2	4.5	4.7	6.4
Other Minerals	6.7	4.5	5.1	7.7	5.8	5.0	5.9
Petroleum	—	—	0.1	0.2	0.2	1.0	2.7
Agricultural & Other Products	6.7	5.2	4.6	4.2	3.0	2.4	4.1

Not only is the economy of Bolivia highly dependent on tin exports, but the government finances have for many years been even more dependent upon them. The Keenleyside *Report* of the United Nations Technical Assistance Mission of 1950 made this clear when it said: "Export and other taxes levied on minerals account for almost half of the ordinary government revenues; the outcome of the budget is critically dependent upon the fluctuations in the world demand for tin." [6]

The Economic Commission for Latin America survey, speaking of the period after 1930, notes that:

. . . it is necessary . . . to distinguish between the large mining companies and the medium and small ones. The former include

Patiño, Aramayo and Hochschild. Together they accounted for between 75–80 per cent of the exports of tin and a considerable proportion of the exports of other minerals. The Patiño group alone produced 60–65 per cent of the total exports of tin immediately before and after the beginning of the Great Depression, which indicates the degree of concentration of production of tin existing in Bolivia. But this percentage has tended to decline since then. . . . In consequence, the proportion of the Patiño group declined by half during the decade of the 1930's and diminished further—to a figure between 40 and 45 per cent—since the end of the last year.[7]

Upon the victory of the M.N.R. in the April 9, 1952, Revolution, the new government proceeded to implement its promise that one of the first things it would do would be to expropriate the Big Three tin companies. On May 13, 1952, President Paz Estenssoro established a commission composed of economists, lawyers, and engineers to study the problems involved in nationalization of the mines.

After careful study, the commission presented its report, which was studied by the government, as well as by the Central Obrera Boliviana. In the latter organization the discussion provoked a serious crisis when a casual majority in the C.O.B., controlled by the Trotskyites, urged the government to confiscate the mines without compensation and to turn them over to the miners, neither of which moves figured in the government's plans. The following week, the C.O.B. reversed itself, when the M.N.R. took control of the organization once again.

The nationalization decree, issued on October 31, 1952, in the mining camp of María Berzola at Catavi, started with a long preamble, setting forth the reasons for its issuance. The preamble indicted the Big Three mining firms, in the following terms:

. . . as a consequence of the high commercial value which tin acquired since the end of the last century, and of the possession of the best mines by Simón I. Patiño, the Aramayo Company, and Mauricio Hochschild, there was produced a concentration of wealth in the hands of these firms, disproportionate to the general level of the economy of the country;

. . . the economic power derived from this concentration of wealth also produced a concentration of political power, resulting in a hegemony which deformed to its benefit all of the life of the nation.[8]

This indictment continued with a bill of particulars, which included the following:

. . . in contrast with the rapid enrichment of the tin companies, the Bolivian State was impoverished gradually and this resulted in budgetary deficits which each day became larger, because mining, the principal source of national wealth, was practically exempt from taxes, behind the incontestable control which it exercised over public officials.

. . . the foreign debt, originating in the fiscal penury brought about by the privileged tax system maintained by the political influence of the large mining firms, could not be met, because the fiscal resources and the foreign exchange available scarcely covered the most pressing needs of the country, while the tin barons continued accumulating enormous fortunes abroad.

. . . those firms, on being organized abroad with capital taken from Bolivia, and not by bringing new capital to the country, not only sought the support and protection of the Great Powers, but also attempted to legalize the flight of wealth practiced for twenty-five years and continued without interruption down to the present day. . . .[9]

The decree accused the Big Three of converting "The Bolivian State into a typical instrument of semicolonial oppression, which served to guarantee the easy and continued exploitation of the natural resources of the country and their free transport abroad." It attacked the labor policies of the Big Three as "so inhuman and oppressive that the average life span of the workers employed in the interior of the mines is only twenty-seven years . . ." and that all attempts to organize the workers and obtain better conditions "were systematically repressed by persecution, mass dismissals, closing of light and water services, work under armed guard, blacklists, and finally, periodic indiscriminate massacres of men, women, and children, meticulously prepared by the firms and executed by the government at their service." [10]

The preamble of the nationalization decree was followed by the substance of the law, which declared the properties of the three firms to be national property, and set a tentative amount to be paid in recompense to the companies involved. In practice, these amounts were not accepted by the firms, and negotiations continued for more than four years thereafter.

There is little doubt that the popular reaction to nationalization of the tin mines was favorable. On December 15, 1952, *Time* magazine reported:

> Bolivians are united behind this action as they have not been in years. They are generally convinced that 1) the companies were bigger than the state, 2) the companies were draining away resources without investing the profits in Bolivia, and 3) the tin barons themselves, particularly the heirs of Patiño were living lives of luxury in the outer world while scorning their own country.

The expropriation of the mines even had the support of certain elements opposed to the M.N.R. regime. Former President Enrique Peñaranda was quoted by *La Nación* of Buenos Aires as denouncing the former tin mine owners as "a super-state within the State" and as approving of expropriation. Waldo Belmonte Pool, a leader of the regime overthrown by the M.N.R., commented, "I do not believe there is a person with a contrary opinion on this subject." [11]

That this measure did not represent any general policy of the M.N.R. government in favor of socializing the Bolivian economy was made clear by the Bolivian Ambassador to the United States in a speech which he gave at Rutgers University on December 19, 1952. He said:

In previous statements and speeches in the United States, I have tried to summarize the policy of my government on questions which the revolution last April and the nationalization of the tin mines have created. With your permission, I will again try to summarize these today:

1. My government subscribes wholeheartedly to the principles of democracy.

2. The nationalization of the properties of the Patiño, Aramayo, and Hochschild groups represented a special case. Nationalization of private property is not the policy of Bolivia.

3. Nationalization of the tin mines did not mean confiscation of the property. We intend to pay the former owners of the properties every cent that is due them.

4. The Government of Bolivia realizes the part which private capital can contribute towards the development of its resources and hopes to attract that private capital.

One may say that nationalization of the tin mines is not the way to attract that capital and that the precedent set in Bolivia is alarming to the United States investors. It need not be. The tin barons forced nationalization and have only themselves to blame. Only the properties belonging to the Patiño, Aramayo, and Hochschild groups were taken over. Hundreds of mines remain and will continue to remain, in the hands of their owners. We know that some United States citizens bought stock in the Patiño mines and did so in good faith. Obviously, if we did not intend to deal fairly and sympathetically with these stockholders, it would be useless to try to establish satisfactory relationships with your great country.

The former holdings of the three tin companies were placed in the hands of the Corporación Minera de Bolivia, a government-owned corporation. Two of the seven directors of the COMIBOL were allotted to the workers, to be selected by the Federación Sindical de Trabajadores Mineros. The turnover of these representatives has been fairly rapid, since they have tended quickly to lose the confidence of the workers. After the first few years, they confined themselves largely to dealing with social and labor problems.

The organizational structure of the COMIBOL also called for the institution of the *control obrero* on a local level in each mine. The purpose of these officials originally was to supervise all expenditures of the company, for materials, wages, and other such things. However, most of them interpreted their position as being that of a kind of super trade union leader. Over and above all other trade union officials in a given mine was the *control obrero*. Only a minority of the miners occupying such positions devoted their attention to the job they were originally supposed to do.

Labor problems have constituted one of the most serious difficulties faced by the COMIBOL. The workers have felt themselves masters in the mines, and they have tended frequently to abuse their position. Often, stoppages have been called because of alleged "abuses" by management personnel. In a number of cases the miners have forced dismissal of engineers and managers. Not infrequently, management personnel has been threatened with physical violence.

There is little doubt that discipline tended to break down and that the productivity per worker declined in the mines after expropriation. This was partly due to the fact that the mines had a considerable surplus labor force after they were nationalized. All miners who had been dismissed for political reasons between 1946 and 1952 were reinstated in their jobs after the April 9 Revolution, while no workers then employed were dismissed.

Thus, particularly in the operations above ground, there tended to be an excess of personnel. Few miners could be induced to abandon the mines so long as they enjoyed the benefits of low prices in the mine commissaries, where they could buy goods at 1 per cent or less of current market prices. This situation continued until the initiation of the Stabilization Program of December, 1956.[12]

The payroll of the COMIBOL increased from 26,000 workers in 1952 to 37,000 at the end of 1954. Carter Goodrich notes that "production per man, already lower than in other countries of Latin America, decreased still further." [13]

Political unrest tended to increase the labor difficulties in the mining areas. Thus, there was good evidence in the early months of 1957 that the miners were purposely slowing down production as a protest against the Stabilization Program and as a reflection of the political struggle of Juan Lechín and other mine union leaders with President Hernán Siles.

The report on Bolivia's economy of the Economic Commission for Latin America summed up the difficult labor situation in the mines after nationalization thus (Vol. I, p. 130): "This situation has brought about a certain lack of discipline, greater absenteeism, the employment of unnecessary personnel, which in turn has contributed to the diminution by about 15 per cent of the average productivity per worker in the nationalized mines. . . ."

Indirect labor costs were also increased after nationalization by a liberal social welfare program for the miners. Large sums were spent on improving the living conditions of the mine workers. For example, in the Huanuni mining camp, which the author visited in July, 1957, the COMIBOL since nationalization had built several hundred new houses, had doubled the size (though not notably improved the quality) of the hospital, had constructed a new school, and was building a new theater.

Another serious problem facing COMIBOL was its lack of capital. The three private companies had withdrawn all funds, and the government enterprise was left without operating capital. The government, therefore, had to create such capital by printing paper money. This, of course, contributed considerably to inflationary pressure. The COMIBOL's foreign currency needs had to be obtained from sales of its products abroad. However, since mining provided virtually the only source of foreign exchange, and the government had to use this foreign exchange for all of the country's important needs, it was able to spare only a small amount for re-equipment and other expenditures of the mining industry.

The need of the COMIBOL to obtain foreign exchange, for its current operations as well as for renewing the mines' equipment and expanding the country's mining operations, was complicated by the fact that five years after the National Revolution, no decision had as yet been made concerning compensation of the expropriated companies. For several months after expropriation, there was no agreement of any kind on this subject. However, in the latter half of 1953 an accord was reached which did not set any final figure for compensation but did provide a procedure by which COMIBOL was to pay certain sums "on account," pending a final agreement as to how much it owed the old owners. President Paz Estenssoro, in his Message to Congress in July, 1956, described this accord as follows:

On June 10, 1953, it was agreed with the affected firms to pay them on account by means of discounts on the exports of tin, a percentage to vary in accordance with the price of the metal; and with regard to wolfram, with 50 per cent of the difference between the price of the world market and that fixed in the contracts the companies had had with the buying agency of the Government of the United States, which was considerably higher. To this end, the firms agreed to maintain these contracts in effect.

President Víctor Paz also noted that some $9,611,657.77 had been paid to the companies by the time he went out of office. According to Paz, the Patiño Group received $3,080,-286.50, the Aramayo Group received $1,783,751.18, and the Hochschild Group, $4,748,196.22. He added, "The Government has permanently maintained the proposal to reach a definitive accord concerning the amount which was to be paid, which has not so far been possible because of the excessive pretensions of some of the firms." [14]

By July, 1957, the COMIBOL, according to Señor Goosen

Broersma, General Manager of COMIBOL, who was interviewed by the author on July 18, 1957, had paid the ex-owners of the mines over $12,000,000. This, Señor Broersma maintained, was more than they probably would have earned had the mines remained in the hands of Patiño, Aramayo, and Hochschild.

By the middle of 1958 a final agreement was still being negotiated between COMIBOL and the ex-owners of the mines. Until this agreement was reached it would be impossible for the COMIBOL to obtain loans abroad which would permit it to expand and modernize its operations. The General Manager of the Corporación had sought loans abroad, but had not been able to obtain them on conditions which he felt he could accept. No respectable banking institution, private or public, was willing to make loans to COMIBOL until it was clear how much the Corporación owed and under what terms it had agreed to pay.

There is considerable doubt in the minds of the COMIBOL officials, doubt shared by the author, that the old mining companies have been anxious to reach an agreement on terms of compensation. Officially, they have been ready and willing to do so. Thus, the Thirty-third Annual Report of Patiño Mines & Enterprises Consolidated (Incorporated), issued on February 28, 1957, and signed by Antenor Patiño R., President, put the official position of the Patiño interests as follows:

For over four years we have been endeavoring to arrive at a final agreement. Our representatives filed with the Government representatives a number of proposals, but through no fault of ours, nothing was accomplished. As a new President has been elected in Bolivia and as Congress is again functioning in that Country after a five-year vacuum, we can only hope that this time the Government representatives will not fail to realize that a prompt, just and fair settlement is in the interest of the good credit of the Country.

However, there is some indication that the old tin companies still hoped that they might be able to regain control of their former properties. They continued to carry on a violent campaign against the M.N.R. government. A sample of this campaign is the statement in this same Patiño Thirty-third Annual Report, cited above, to the effect that:

A propaganda campaign with political aims, built on a deliberate misrepresentation against the mining industry, the mainstay of the Bolivian economy, led to the seizure on October 31st, 1952 of all the assets of the three largest mining groups. The appalling results of this wild undertaking are reviewed in the report to the Bolivian Government of Ford, Bacon & Davis, Inc., the New York firm whose services were engaged under a contract financed by the U.S. Government to make a study of all phases of the Bolivian mining industry.

No development work has been continued since the seizure, working capital has been consumed, machinery has deteriorated for lack of proper care, management has been destroyed, political patronage flourishes and productivity keeps on the down trend.

The author became personally aware of the campaign of the tin companies when a letter of his, expressing general support of the program of the Bolivian Government, was published in *The New York Times* in October, 1956. Thereafter he was deluged with anti-M.N.R. propaganda virtually every day for more than a year; it came in envelopes without return addresses, but postmarked New York, where the Patiño Mines has its headquarters. The Thirty-third Annual Report of the Patiño Mines was one of the items forwarded.

Another very serious problem facing the COMIBOL was the scarcity of engineers and technicians. Carter Goodrich has described this problem:

A greater problem, of course, was that of operating and technical management, in which almost all of the major responsibilities had been held by foreigners. The government made strenuous efforts to keep these men, offering them security and the continuation of their contracts. In this, despite the earlier hostility between miners and managers, the Corporación was seconded by the Miners' Union. But the managers and engineers, either because of distrust of the new conditions or because of the terms of their contracts with the companies for the most part refused these offers. More than two hundred left the country—North Americans, British, Dutch, German, and others; and these included almost every man who had been manager or chief engineer at a major operation.[15]

As a result, Bolivians who had always held secondary positions in the mines were promoted to top positions, and many of them were not really qualified for these jobs. Many lacked sufficient educational background for the posts which they were now asked to fill.

The mining schools of Bolivia have attempted to make up for the lack of trained managerial personnel by giving special courses to those already in managerial posts in the mines. The principal difficulty has been a lack of sufficient elementary training in mathematics, physics, and chemistry. It will take considerable time before the mines will again have an adequate staff of engineers and other technicians.

Even more serious for the COMIBOL has been the growing impoverishment of the mines belonging to the Corporación. The Keenleyside *Report,* of the United Nations Technical Mission to Bolivia in 1950 indicated that this was not a problem which began with the National Revolution. It commented:

No important new tin mines have been developed in Bolivia during the last 20 years, and the gradual exhaustion of the known high grade tin ore reserves can only result in increased costs of production and a steadily declining output in the near future. The average essays of ores mined have already decreased 40 per cent within the last 5 years. Consequently, if Bolivia is to maintain its position as a large producer of tin, it will, on the basis of existing knowledge, be necessary to mine and treat the present known reserves of low grade tin ore, and this can only be done by the additional investment of large sums of new capital. Even if such capital can be obtained, steps should be taken at the same time to bring about diversification of the industry, by developing the known deposits of non-tin minerals.[16]

The Economic Commission for Latin America's report on the Bolivian economy adds further details concerning the depletion of the mines:

Many of the oldest and most important mines of Bolivia have to face difficulties which are principally of natural origin: for instance, the declining percentage of metal in the ore, the complexity of the ore, the narrowing of the veins, the larger proportion of rock in the ore, and the excessive extension of underground tunnels. Thus, for instance, it has been estimated that during the last five years the proportion of metal in the tin ore exploited by the Corporación Minera has declined 31 per cent. . . .[17]

A bit further on, the report says:

The majority of the installations and equipment which are used for treating and concentrating the minerals taken from the mines are worn out and antiquated. In spite of this, since the percentage of metal is declining, it is necessary, in order to get the same amount of metal concentrate, to treat increasingly large amounts of ore, with the result that there has been an alarming decline in the efficiency of recovery of ore. So grave is the situation, that many concentration plants are treating the waste thrown out in previous years and which had already been treated by the same equipment. . . . However . . . the metallurgical problems can be resolved by means of new investment to modernize and renovate the equipment. . . .

The problem of re-equipping the mines has given rise to a great deal of controversy within government circles. The Miners Federation suggested soon after the nationalization of the mines that a certain percentage of the foreign exchange acquired through sale of mineral products should be set aside each year for the purpose of recapitalizing the mines of the COMIBOL. However, this approach to the problem was not accepted either by the Paz Estenssoro or the Siles government, and although small amounts were spent for the importation of absolute essentials for the maintenance of the mines, no regular allotment was made for this purpose.[18] In 1958, re-equipment of the mines depended upon settlement of the question of compensation to the old companies, and the consequent negotiation of a sizable foreign loan for the purpose of recapitalization.

Closely allied to the problem of re-equipping the mines was that of exploring for new sources of mineral. Virtually everyone seems agreed that there is a great deal more tin and other minerals to be exploited if they can only be discovered.

In discussing the problem of exploring for new mines, the Economic Commission for Latin America had this to say (Vol. I, pp. 142–143):

In the mines now being exploited and in many of the known reserves, the deposits are found at distances below the surface which present difficult mineralogical characteristics. These characteristics demand a higher degree of mechanization to recover the same quantity of metal from low-grade ores. But it is worth investigating in more detail the possible reserves. According to the experts of the Ford-Bacon firm, the possibilities from a geological point of view of discovering new mines are very good, and the mineral is easy to identify in the case of tin. Explorations could be carried on from the air.

Relatively little exploration work had been done by the Big Three mining companies in the years preceding the 1952 Revolution, and only Patiño maintained a geological division for this purpose. There seems to be considerable difference of opinion among those who should be in a position to know, as to how much such work was undertaken after the mines were nationalized. However, COMIBOL General Manager Goosen Broersma told the author on July 18, 1957, that the

Corporación Minera was carrying on prospecting activities in the areas between its present mines, and was also prospecting in an area in the southern part of the country which had not hitherto been opened for exploitation. He maintained that the COMIBOL was doing more prospecting than its predecessors had done for many years, but was severely handicapped by lack of equipment and lack of funds for such activities.

A continuing problem for COMIBOL and the whole economy of Bolivia has been that of selling the country's mineral products, the chief source of its foreign exchange income. Almost immediately after nationalization of the mines, the international price of tin began to fall, for reasons having little or nothing to do with the Bolivian Government's action. Thus, though the price of tin was $1.21 per pound on April 9, 1952, it fell rapidly until reaching the low level of seventy-three cents and then recovered to ninety-five cents, around which price it continued to fluctuate for several years. As President Paz Estenssoro pointed out in his Message to Congress in July, 1956 (p. 18), "Each cent drop in price represented from $600,000 to $700,000 drop in the annual income of Bolivia."

Bolivian sales of tin were principally to the United States and to Great Britain. Although in February, 1953, the Williams Harvey firm in the latter country signed a contract for high-grade mineral concentrate which was to run until 1960, more difficulty was found in placing the product in the United States market. The United States Government, the principal purchaser, was hesitant to enter into a contract with the COMIBOL until some kind of settlement was made with the expropriated companies. Only very small amounts were contracted for, and much of the output of the COMIBOL mines was piling up on the docks at Arica, Chile, awaiting a purchaser.

It was not until after an agreement was reached, on June 10, 1953, for the partial compensation of the old companies (though without setting a total for such compensation), that the United States again began contracting for Bolivian tin to supply the United States Government refinery in Texas. Such contracts remained in force until the closing down of this refinery on January 31, 1957.

Similar difficulties were encountered in selling other products of the Bolivian mines, notably tungsten. The old companies had contracts with agencies of the United States Government for the sale of tungsten, which were kept in effect after the agreement of June 10, 1953. However, by the end of 1957, all these agreements had expired, and the United States Government refused to renew them.[19]

Much controversy has centered on the question of the financial situation of the nationalized mines. Opponents of the M.N.R. regime have insisted that they were being run at considerable loss, due to the COMIBOL's labor policies and general inefficiency in management. The Economic Commission for Latin America, in its report, says the following concerning this (Vol. I, p. 131):

Even though it is true that the net return in foreign exchange was maintained at between $41 and $44 millions, the net costs in bolivianos was doubled between 1953 and 1955. But, if credits and direct income from the sale of foreign exchange is included, the net result of the transactions with the Banco Central have meant that the COMIBOL has been able to obtain the amount of national currency necessary to cover its increasing costs. As a matter of fact, the accounts indicate a profit in national currency of from three to five billion bolivianos a year. These results cannot be considered government subsidies in the true sense of the word, since the rate of exchange granted COMIBOL has been lower each year. . . . It can be said that the Corporación has been paying subsidies to the government (on foreign exchange transactions). . . . Taking into account the net transactions with the Banco Central, the income arising from other operations and from those of previous years, it is clear that in two of these three years there was a net profit in dollars, which in 1955 was considerable.

However, it must be pointed out that this profit was due to the fact that the Corporación did not spend much foreign exchange for the importation of materials and equipment and that in two of these three years it did not put aside anything for depreciation. The essential fact, from the point of view of the general value of its transactions, is that COMIBOL contributed to the Bolivian economy from $40,000,000 to $44,000,000 a year and that it could count on the foreign exchange and national currency necessary to meet its annual current obligations. . . .

General Manager Goosen Broersma of the COMIBOL insisted to the author on July 18, 1957, that the claim that the company was generally losing money was not correct. He said that some of the mines were losing money, but the company was making a profit on most of them. He added that before Stabilization it was very difficult to tell just what the true situation was, since the company was buying dollars at seven or eight different rates and had to keep two different sets of books, one in dollars and one in *bolivianos*. The situation was much simplified by the Stabilization decree.

Recognizing its limited resources, the revolutionary government sought to overcome those problems of COMIBOL which were within its control. In July, 1956, President Víctor Paz Estenssoro reported to Congress on the measures which had been taken:

In the face of this situation, and in spite of the lack of capital and scarcity of technicians, the Government has taken all possible steps to remedy those causes of declining production which were not outside its control.

To counteract the declining percentage of metal in the ore, an expert in treatment and recuperation of ores was hired, and in accordance with his studies and suggestions a new "Jiggs" plant was constructed at Catavi, which is now in operation, although not fully so because of lack of electric power. In San José a "sink and float" plant was constructed which will be finished at the end of the year. The flotation section of Huanuni and the mills at Tasna and Santa Ana have been enlarged; likewise, a new mill for the processing of wolfram has been established in Sagrario in the Quechisla area.

To overcome the acute scarcity of electricity, diesel motors were acquired as an intermediate measure, for Tasna, Huanuni, Colquiri, and Corocoro; as a more fundamental solution, the Corporación Minera signed a contract with The Bolivian Power Co., for the construction of two hydroelectric plants at the cost of $1,800,200 and with a capacity of 7,800 kw. for the mines of Catavi, Huanuni, Japo, San José, Morococala, and Colquiri.

To overcome the administrative and technical deficiencies of the Corporación Minera, the Government contracted, with funds drawn from American aid, on October 3, 1955, with the Ford, Bacon & Davis firm, specialized in the reorganization of industrial enterprises. It is undertaking a complete study of Bolivian mining and particularly the functioning of the state firm, advising the Executive on the means of improving its operations. In accord with one of its first reports, we have proceeded to issue the Decree of July 18, 1956, reorganizing the administrative system of the Corporación. People with long experience in the mining industry have been named to the Board of Directors of the Corporación.[20]

The Ford, Bacon & Davis report on the Bolivian mining situation was presented to the government early in 1957, in nine fat volumes. It was a detailed study of all aspects of the industry, and although it was not made public by the Bolivian Government for several months, the services of Ford, Bacon & Davis were retained to aid in the implementation of the suggestions given therein.

In the beginning of August, 1957, President Siles summoned a "round table" conference in the Presidential Palace, for the purpose of discussing further ways and means of improving mining output. Representatives were present from the Ministry of Mines, the Corporación Minera, the private mining firms, and the Federación Sindical de Trabajadores Mineros. Felipe Barrau, Minister of Foreign Affairs, presided. Some shadow was cast on the meeting by the political conflict then taking place between the Miners Federation and the President.

In spite of the difficulties faced by the nationalized mines, the COMIBOL has done what on the balance is a remarkable job of maintaining production. Carter Goodrich has summed up the performance of the nationalized tin-mining industry:

Total production of the industry . . . has been well maintained since nationalization. The output of tin from all the mines, including those of the Corporación, was slightly greater in 1953 than in 1952. In the nationalized sector of the industry, though not in the private, the level of output was again maintained in 1954. Nor has this been, as some experts feared it might be, obtained by a policy of short-run robbing of the higher-grade ores. The Bolivian engineers, previously held down to minor posts within the industry, appear to have risen rather remarkably to their new responsibilities, with the aid of the minority of foreigners who remained and a few more who have been recruited. There remains a shortage of skilled mining and managerial personnel, and of competent mine foremen, but the results of nationalization have not borne out the widely held expectation that the industry would suffer physical deterioration or collapse.[21]

According to figures published by the *American Metal Market* on March 21, 1957, tin exports had dropped from 35,394 metric tons in 1953 to 29,186 metric tons in 1954. By 1955 exports had fallen to 28,470 metric tons, and in 1956 they amounted to only 27,272 metric tons.

The nationalization decree of October 31, 1952, affected only the mines and other properties belonging to the Big Three mining companies, Patiño, Aramayo, and Hochschild. Hundreds of smaller mining enterprises continued to operate under private ownership. However, they suffered considerable difficulty after the April 9, 1952, Revolution. The Paz Estenssoro government was hostile toward the smaller mining firms.

First of all, the Paz Estenssoro government decreed that all foreign exchange earned by the small mining companies had to be sold to the government-owned Banco Minero, which in turn had to turn these funds over to the Banco Central. In return, the Banco Minero was instructed to acquire for the small mining companies the equipment and other materials needed for their operations and was supposed to receive funds from the Banco Central for this purpose. The effect of putting the small mines under the control of the Banco Minero was discussed by the Economic Commission for Latin America in its study of the Bolivian economy (Vol. I, p. 105):

Although, according to information available at this time, this did not result in 1953 in a significant increase in these companies' share of the total value of exports sold to the Banco Central, it is notable that in 1954 and 1955 the proportion increased to 67 and 78 per cent respectively. As might be expected, this high proportion of return had a disastrous effect on the small and medium mines, many of which were forced to contract their operations or suspend production altogether. The problems of these mines were aggravated even more by the bureaucratic inefficiency in the provision of necessary materials. . . . As a consequence, in 1954 the Banco Minero had in its hands less than 15 per cent of the exports of tin and only around 20 per cent of the sales of all kinds of minerals, in contrast to 30 and 36 per cent respectively for the medium and small mines in 1952.

Politics also intervened, and a sharp conflict developed between the Banco Minero and the Banco Central. After the adoption of the Stabilization Program in December, 1956, it became apparent, according to officials of the Banco Minero, that the Banco Central had not in fact made foreign currency available in the quantities it was supposed to for the purpose of supplying equipment and materials for the small and medium mines. As a result, many of the small and medium firms found themselves virtually defrauded by being forcibly obliged to sell their foreign earnings to the government, while receiving nothing in return for this foreign currency. The Stabilization Program had disastrous results for the privately owned mines, and 20 per cent of them had to close down by the first half of 1957.[22]

The fate of many of the other privately owned mines was sealed by the refusal of the United States Government to continue to purchase tungsten at prices above those on the general world market. However, during 1957 there were indications of a coming improvement in the output of at least some of the privately owned mines. The International Mining Company, a subsidiary of W. R. Grace and Company, received permission in July to open up a new placer tin mine, which promised to be very rich.[23] At about the same time a new placer gold mine was opened in the jungle area east of La Paz, which also promised to be very successful.

The situation of the Bolivian mining industry was summed up in the conclusions of the Ford, Bacon & Davis survey completed during 1956.

1. The mining industry of Bolivia, directly and indirectly, contributes more than 50% of the total gross national income of the country; consequently the expected decline in mineral production will have a very serious effect on the economy of the country.
2. The general economic situation of the mining industry of Bolivia, the principal basis of its economy, has declined seriously in the last three years, as the following indicates:

    a. A very significant decline in the income from tin, lead, silver, antimony and copper, with only a moderate increase in tungsten, which enjoys a high subsidy;
    b. A general condition of deterioration of equipment and installations, as well as a diminution of capital.
    c. A high percentage (25%) of the industry at present in an unprofitable situation, with important producers operating near this limit (on the basis of comparison with Western Hemisphere mines) and other mines are on the way to becoming unprofitable.

  d. Low efficiency and serious deficiencies of administrative and technical personnel, general lack of discipline and demoralization among the workers, are characteristic of the majority of present operations.

  e. Decline in the number of mines since more than 1660 closed during the 1953–54 period, in spite of the fact that high prices for metals predominated.

3. In spite of certain preferential treatment for the very small mines, private industry has suffered its greatest decline during the last three years, due to the protection by the Government of the nationalized mines and the general disorganization of private capital.

4. Unless the Government separates politics from the administration of the nationalized mines, the mining industry as a whole will continue suffering the consequences.

5. During the next three to five years the disappearance of many important Bolivian mines will increase, due to the exhaustion of economic mineral reserves and, unless these mines can be replaced by new discoveries, the mining industry of Bolivia will be faced with a serious decline.

6. The mines which are decidedly losing money are maintained in operation, thus wasting foreign exchange and energy.

7. Many of the important mines of Bolivia have gotten into a situation in which they need a considerable investment a) to develop additional mines or prepare them for future operations; b) to put their equipment and installations in good operating condition; and c) to carry out necessary improvements and extensions. Unless these expenditures are made (in bolivianos and foreign exchange), mineral production will decline and costs will increase.

  . . . .

10. The principal factors which contribute to the cost of mining operations are largely the result of social and political conditions. Labor, the Government and what remains of the administration have not been able to resolve these urgent social problems in order to improve the industry. As the result of this, the majority of the mines present a lack of administration and of technical and administrative personnel, which are essential to resolve the future problems of the industry.

Furthermore the general low efficiency throughout the organization, and the lack of discipline are problems which have their roots in the disequilibrium of authority and responsibility. . . .[24]

Thus, five years after the beginning of the National Revolution, mining was still the key to the economic relations of Bolivia with the outside world. Its future seemed to depend in large part on the reaching of an agreement with the expropriated companies for the settlement of their claims against the Corporación Minera de Bolivia, which would permit COMIBOL to obtain loans essential for the modernization of old mines and the discovery of new ones. It depended, too, on an improvement of labor relations in both privately and publicly owned mines, which presented perhaps the most difficult problem of all to the mining industry. Finally, it depended on the international prices for the minerals which Bolivia had to sell; since Bolivia continued to depend so heavily on minerals for its foreign exchange, good prices represented prosperity and progress for the country, poor prices meant crisis and possible disaster.

7 . . .

Organized Labor's Role in the National Revolution

Organized labor has had a dominant position in the Bolivian National Revolution. The government of the Movimiento Nacionalista Revolucionario has depended for its political support on the labor movement, and the union leaders have been well aware of this. Since the beginning of the Revolution the labor leaders have been, after Víctor Paz Estenssoro and Hernán Siles, the country's most important politicians. They have sat in the Cabinet since April 9, 1952; they have had a majority in the Chamber of Deputies since 1956; they have consistently made up a large part of the National Executive Committee of the M.N.R.

The economic role of the unions has also been very great. They not only have had the customary job of negotiating with the employers—in which negotiations they have generally had the upper hand—but they have played an important part in the management of the nationalized industries. They were, under Víctor Paz, a key factor in the distribution of foodstuffs and other consumer goods to their members, though this role was taken from them by the Stabilization Program initiated by President Siles in December, 1956.

In the midst of all this, the union leaders have shown a maturity which is surprising for a labor movement as young as that of Bolivia. Although the workers have been buffeted by various ideological currents, they have generally stayed loyal to the government of the National Revolution, have refused to be beguiled by demagogic promises, and have become increasingly aware of the responsibility which goes along with the power which they have enjoyed since April 9, 1952.

The labor movement was largely disorganized during the 1946–1952 period. As the result of attempted revolutionary movements and political general strikes, and the close association of the unions with the M.N.R. and other political groups opposed to the governments of that period, the trade unions were weak at the time of the 1952 Revolution.

However, after April 9 the trade union movement came back strongly. One of the first national union groups to be fully revived was the Federación Sindical de Trabajadores Mineros. Its principal leader, Juan Lechín, had been Hernán Siles's lieutenant in the April 9 uprising in La Paz, and the miners claimed much of the credit for the success of the Revolution. They had quickly seized control of the mining camps and the cities near them, and important units of armed miners had helped to clinch the victory in the capital city.

The local miners' unions were quickly reorganized. Even before the Revolution the mine unions had been rebuilt in the more important camps, and in the wake of the April 9 uprising, unionization became universal in the mining industry. The headquarters of the Federación Sindical de Trabajadores Mineros was established in the building of the new Ministry of Mines and Petroleum, headed by Lechín.

Other important unions were re-established on a strong basis. These included the Confederación Sindical de Trabajadores Ferroviarios y Ramos Anexos (railroad and electric power workers), the Confederación Sindical de Empleados de Comercio (commercial employees), the Federación Sindical de Trabajadores Petroleros (oil workers), and the Federación Sindical de Trabajadores Gráficos (printing trades workers). Other groups which had not formerly had national organizations quickly established them. These included the Confederación Sindical de Trabajadores Constructores (building trades workers), the Confederación Sindical de Trabajadores Transportadores (chauffeurs), the Confederación Sindical de Trabajadores Harineros (millers), and the Confederación Sindical de Trabajadores Fabriles (factory workers).

All these organizations were under the control of the M.N.R. and its allies. Trade union groups under other leadership attempted to rally their former members, but were not notably successful. Thus, although the Confederación Sindical de Trabajadores de Bolivia and its La Paz affiliate, the Federación Obrera Sindical de La Paz, which were still under the influence of the P.I.R., issued a May Day, 1952, manifesto, this was virtually the last evidence of these organizations' activity. Most of the regional groups of the C.S.T.B. either disappeared entirely or transferred their allegiance to the new Central Obrera Boliviana.

The Federación Obrera Local, the oldest central labor organization in Bolivia, of anarchosyndicalist orientation, also failed to make any headway after 1952. Its strongholds had been among the artisans of the city of La Paz and the peasants in the Altiplano area near the capital. In the beginning the Federación Agraria Local, the peasant affiliate of the F.O.L., was given representation in the Central Obrera Boliviana,[1] but it later refused to have anything to do with this "government-controlled" organization, and its unions were largely absorbed by M.N.R.-dominated peasant groups. Most of the rest of the F.O.L. disappeared, the only part remaining being the Federación Feminina Local, consisting of the market women of the capital, which became affiliated with the C.O.B.'s Confederación de Trabajadores Profesionales.[2]

While organizations were being established in various industries and trades a move was also made to set up a new central labor organization. Representatives of virtually all the country's trade union groups met at the end of April, 1952, to establish the Central Obrera Boliviana. Pending the calling of a national congress of the new organization, it was agreed that a national council would be set up, consisting of representatives of the national trade unions and regional trade union groups established in each of the nation's departments (states).

There was a peculiar method of representation in the council, and later in the congresses of the C.O.B., which ultimately was to cause trouble to the organization. Since meetings of the council were held frequently, and it was impossible for distant organizations—particularly the regional labor federations, set up as local central labor bodies dependent on the C.O.B.—to send direct representatives to every meeting, these organizations adopted the policy of deputizing people in La Paz to represent them permanently in meetings of the council. Frequently, these permanent representatives were government officials or employees.

The Central Obrera Boliviana was of key importance in the National Revolution. The revolutionary government was officially based from its early days jointly on the Movimiento Nacionalista Revolucionario and the C.O.B. All major decisions of the government, such as the nationalization of the mines, the agrarian reform decree, and the reorganization of education, were considered by the Central Obrera Boliviana before being promulgated by the government.

An important aspect of the partnership of the M.N.R. and the C.O.B. in the direction of the revolutionary government was the fact that there were labor ministers in the cabinet. From the beginning, four ministerial posts were given to the trade union movement, those of Mines and Petroleum, Peasant Affairs, Labor, and Transportation. Occasionally one or two other positions were also filled by labor men. Upon the resignation of a labor minister, the procedure was for the union in whose province that ministry was considered to be to send to the Central Obrera Boliviana a list of three choices for the vacancy. The C.O.B. then passed this list on to the President, and he selected whichever of the three he preferred. It became a tradition that the Minister of Mines and Petroleum was selected by the Miners Federation, the Minister of Peasant Affairs by the peasant unions, the Minister of Labor by the factory workers' organizations, and the Minister of Transport by the Confederación Sindical de Trabajadores Ferroviarios.

However, the dependence of the revolutionary government on the labor movement went further than the mere nomination of ministers by the unions. In a real sense the revolutionary regime has depended for its security and tenure in office on the workers' organizations. The workers, and in particular the mine workers, factory workers, and peasants, have been armed, and the government has had occasion to call upon them for physical support of the regime. The workers' militia has thus been the very backbone of the governments of Víctor Paz Estenssoro and Hernán Siles.

From the beginning there was considerable political rivalry among representatives of various political parties represented in the C.O.B. national council. Although the M.N.R. was considerably stronger in the council than either the Communists or the Trotskyites, the leaders of the M.N.R. were busy with so many other affairs that, for awhile, they did not have much time to devote to the work of the Central Obrera Boliviana. Juan Lechín, the Executive Secretary of the new C.O.B., was Minister of Mines and Petroleum, and was one of the principal political leaders of the government. Nuflo Chávez, another noted figure in the C.O.B., held the newly created job of Minister of Peasant Affairs, and was kept busy establishing a network of peasant unions throughout the country and laying plans for the government's promised agrarian reform. Germán Butrón, most important leader of the factory workers' unions, was Minister of Labor, which kept him much occupied.

Major posts in the C.O.B. were therefore given to Trotskyites or ex-Trotskyites. Principal among these was the post of editor of *Rebelión*, the Central Obrera Boliviana's newspaper, which appeared for the first time on May 1, 1952. José Zegada, who had resigned from the Partido Obrero Revolucionario only a few months before the 1952 Revolution, was given this assignment.[3] As a result of Zegada's editorship, the C.O.B. newspaper had a decidedly Trotskyite slant. For instance, the first issue carried a eulogistic article about P.O.R. leader Guillermo Lora. A lead editorial proclaimed that "only democratic centralism and armed workers will impede the reaction from raising its head and strangling popular aspirations." An article demanded a "free market for tin," meaning that the contracts providing for sale of the country's output to the United States should be canceled. An article signed by Zegada himself talked of the "petty bourgeois" nature of the M.N.R. and warned it that it better fulfill its promises or the workers would turn against it. Finally, it is worth noting that this first issue of *Rebelión* carried one curious Peronista article, signed by Isaías Santín, at that time Administrative Secretary of Perón's General Confederation of Labor, attacking Serafino Romualdi of the A.F. of L. and accusing him of "selling American trade unionism in the dollar exchange."

Although there were minor clashes during the first months

of the C.O.B.'s existence between the M.N.R. representatives and members of the council belonging to the Communist Party and the P.O.R., the first serious one occurred in October, 1952. The C.O.B. periodical, *Rebelión*, published early in that month a document entitled "The Ideological Position of the Bolivian Working Class," the core of which was the following paragraph:

> The Bolivian revolution must have the character of a combined revolution—bourgeois-democratic in its immediate objectives and socialist in its uninterrupted results. It is quite impossible to separate the two phases of the revolution: that means that the workers in power must not halt at bourgeois-democratic limits but must strike ever more deeply at the rights of private property, going over to socialist methods and in this way giving the revolution a permanent character.

This apparently Trotskyite statement caused a crisis in the relations of the M.N.R. leadership with those leading the C.O.B. Juan Lechín announced that this was not an official statement of the C.O.B., and that such an official statement could only be issued by the First Congress of the organization.[4]

Shortly afterward, the C.O.B. leadership issued an Open Letter to Víctor Paz Estenssoro, calling for nationalization of the tin mines without compensation and also demanding that the nationalized mines be put under the control of the mine workers. This brought a further crisis between the M.N.R. and those who up until that moment had run the C.O.B. What happened then is told in *Labor Action*, the organ of a dissident Trotskyite group in the United States, in its issue of November 3, 1952:

> A session of the Central was thereupon organized with a strong turnout by the Nationalists (who ordinarily do not participate in the sessions); and at this meeting they revoked and condemned the position on nationalization, which had just been published by

"La Nación," the official government organ. They then formed a new commission to draw up a new Open Letter to the president, with a Nationalist majority on it. . . .

When the C.O.B. was first established, it was planned to call the First Congress of the organization at the end of 1952. However, two years more passed before this congress actually met. The First Workers Congress was opened by Juan Lechín, and President Víctor Paz Estenssoro attended its first session. There were some 310 delegates present, including the following:

Miners Federation, 60 delegates
Confederation of Factory Workers, 30 delegates
Railway Workers Confederation, 26 delegates
Construction Workers Confederation, 15 delegates
Chauffeurs Confederation, 15 delegates
Petroleum Workers Federation, 10 delegates
Flour Mill Workers Federation, 7 delegates
Federation of Printers, 7 delegates
Federation of Rubber Workers, 7 delegates
Federation of School Teachers, 15 delegates
Confederation of White-Collar Workers, 10 delegates
Confederation of Public Employees, 10 delegates
Bank Employees Federation, 10 delegates
Telecommunications Workers Confederation, 5 delegates
Federation of Health Service Workers, 3 delegates
Hotel and Restaurant Workers Federation, 3 delegates
Confederation of Self-Employed Workers, 3 delegates

In addition to these, there were fifty representatives of agricultural workers' unions and thirteen delegates representing writers', artists', and university professors' groups. The twelve members of the Executive Committee of the C.O.B. and two of the trade union ministers in the government were also seated with voting rights.

The two principal speeches of the congress were delivered by President Víctor Paz and C.O.B. Executive Secretary

Juan Lechín. Paz Estenssoro outlined his government's program, laying particular stress on tin nationalization and the agrarian reform. He also stressed the government's economic development efforts, and outlined the social security legislation which it had passed. He stressed the fact that the M.N.R. government was based on a partnership with the trade unions.

Juan Lechín praised the gains which the workers had made under the M.N.R. government. He emphasized that the regime was "composed of representatives of the three classes most seriously concerned with national liberation: the workers, the farmers, and the middle class."

According to the International Labor Organization's periodical *Industry and Labor* of May 15, 1955, "The congress approved a statement of principles and statutes of the organization, based on democratic trade unionism and independence from political parties." It also adopted a program supporting educational reform, liquidation of monopolies which hindered the economic development of the nation, the establishment of consumers' and producers' cooperatives, the maintenance and construction of highways, the agrarian reform, and other measures of the National Revolution.

A dissident Trotskyite reporter of the First Workers Congress interpreted its political significance thus:

. . . the congress, kept well in hand by Lechín, confirmed and approved the Nationalist policies, even the concessions to the U.S. which are so unpopular among the Bolivian masses. Víctor Paz Estenssoro, the president of Bolivia, was hailed as the "economic liberator" and Lechín was re-elected secretary of the C.O.B.

In spite of attacks by the C.P. and the P.O.R., the congress was so organized and prepared by the Lechín caucus that opposition was absolutely eliminated, and the M.N.R. controlled the discussion and all resolutions. Thus the congress demonstrated the Nationalists' stability in control of the state power, and their control of the workers' movement.[5]

One of the principal decisions of the First Congress concerned the Bolivian labor movement's international affiliations. The decision adopted when the C.O.B. was first established, to keep it independent of any international group, but to maintain friendly relations with all international labor organizations, was continued in force.

Throughout the first six years of the National Revolution, the C.O.B. maintained this policy of international independence. However, delegates were sent to various international labor meetings as fraternal representatives. José Zegada attended the 1953 Congress of the World Federation of Trade Unions, the Communist-controlled international group. Mario Torres, second-in-command of the Miners Federation, headed a local committee of the Peronista Comité de Unidad Sindical Latinoamericano in 1952.[6] Bolivian fraternal delegates also attended the Rio de Janeiro meeting of the Organización Regional Interamericana de Trabajadores, the American regional organization of the anti-Communist, anti-Peronista International Confederation of Free Trade Unions; and a group of labor members of the Bolivian Chamber of Deputies visited the headquarters of the O.R.I.T. in Mexico City in June, 1957, on their way home from a visit to the United States. It is significant that they did not visit the Communist-controlled continental labor group, the Confederación de Trabajadores de America Latina (C.T.A.L.), which has its headquarters in the same city.[7]

The attitude of the C.O.B. on international labor matters was influenced by several factors. First of all, there was considerable Communist and Trotskyite influence in the C.O.B., which favored affiliation with the W.F.T.U. In the second place, Mario Torres and others had had friendly relations with the Peronista trade unions during their period of exile between 1946 and 1952. In the third place, the M.N.R.-controlled unions had a justified grievance against the O.R.I.T., based on the latter's attempt to work with the Bolivian Government in 1950 and 1951 to set up an anti-M.N.R. trade union movement in Bolivia, an attempt which failed but which left a hostility toward the O.R.I.T. in the minds of the M.N.R. trade unionists. It took several years to overcome this hostility.

Before and after the First Workers Congress, the unions of the C.O.B. were active in pushing for increases in wages and improvement in working conditions for their members. The struggle was a difficult one, because the inflationary spiral was becoming increasingly severe. Many groups of workers were seriously affected by the discrepancy between prices and wages.

Under Bolivian labor law, when a union makes demands for a new collective agreement, the matter is turned over for consideration to a Conciliation Board established by the government. Only after this process has been gone through is a strike legal. Even then, it is possible for a case to be presented to an arbitrator, whose word will be final, if both parties agree, if the workers involved are employed in a public service industry, or if the President of the Republic so decrees.

Since the National Revolution, most labor conflicts have been resolved without recourse to strikes. For instance, a few weeks after the Revolution, the Sindicato de Industria y Comercio submitted a list of demands to the employers of La Paz which were settled by the Conciliation Board.[8] Other cases were resolved by arbitration, as when, in November, 1953, President Víctor Paz Estenssoro decreed that an arbitration award made in the milling industry would become effective in spite of the opposition of the employers.[9]

Strikes did occur from time to time. For example, in March, 1953, an attempt by the Banco Popular del Perú in La Paz to reduce its staff was met by a strike of bank clerks. However, the situation was finally settled in an amicable manner.[10]

A frequent cause of dispute, particularly in the mines, was the behavior or alleged behavior of foremen, super-

visors, and managers. The workers frequently complained
that they had been insulted or bullied by some managerial
person, and not infrequently these claims resulted in work
stoppages. There is no doubt at all that discipline declined
greatly after the Revolution both in the mines and in manufacturing industry.

The unions took an active part in matters which had previously been regarded as being purely the concern of management. In government industries, notably the mines and
the government's petroleum company, Y.P.F.B., officials
were named after the Revolution to the post of *control
obrero*. They were named not only in the national headquarters of these industries, but at a local level as well. The official job of the *control obrero* was to consult with the management concerning any matter which directly related to
the workers and their well-being. However, the author has
heard much complaint from managerial people that the
control obrero frequently either tried virtually to take over
management, or spent his time largely in stirring up complaints among the workers.

The unions were frequently consulted on problems arising
in various industries. For example, in 1956, the railroads
were generally reorganized by the government, and in this
the unions played a key role. They drew up a plan for the
reorganization which was seriously considered and to a
large degree adopted by the Ministry of Transport. In 1957,
when the freight rates were reduced on government railroads, the unions helped work out the new schedules.[11]

The political struggle among various tendencies in the
labor movement continued after the First Workers Congress.
Although most of the old P.I.R. and P.O.R. trade union leaders joined the Movimiento Nacionalista Revolucionario in
1953 and 1954, the old feuds between them did not die.
These animosities came to a head during and after the Second Workers Congress of the C.O.B., in June, 1957.

There were four distinct factions in the Second Workers

Congress. One was composed of delegates of those unions controlled by elements which had formerly been members of the Trotskyite P.O.R., as well as the Miners Federation and some other groups dominated by Juan Lechín and original M.N.R. members. The second faction consisted of unions led by ex-members of the P.I.R. These were the two principal groups, but there were also smaller elements consisting of current members of the P.O.R. and the Partido Comunista de Bolivia.

Three issues dominated the congress. The first was the adoption of a statement of principles for the C.O.B. The ex-P.O.R.-Lechín group presented a resolution which, though pledging support to the thesis of "co-government" by the M.N.R.-C.O.B., denounced the Right Wing elements of the M.N.R. party and demanded a larger role for the unions. It also denounced "Yankee imperialism," and urged the ultimate establishment of a single South American nation. It saw a third World War as virtually inevitable, urging that the Bolivians and other Latin Americans should take the greatest possible advantage of this fact.

The second resolution, presented by the ex-P.I.R. group, was more moderate in tone, though it also urged a larger role for labor in the conduct of the Revolution. It called for a continuation of United States aid for Bolivia, but insisted that this should be for economic development and not in the form of food. Finally, it presented the international situation in terms of a relaxation of tension between the Great Powers.

A third resolution, calling for the establishment of a workers and peasants government in place of the M.N.R.-C.O.B. co-government, was introduced by the delegates belonging to the P.O.R. Those few delegates who belonged to the Communist Party generally supported the position of those who had been their comrades in the P.I.R., and now were opposing Lechín.

After much discussion, a vote was taken on the three resolutions. It was 260 for the ex-P.O.R.-Lechín motion, 190 for the ex-P.I.R. motion, and a few scattered votes for the P.O.R. position. After winning this victory, the group in control of the congress decided to "purge" the Executive Committee of the C.O.B., a move which provided the second great cause of conflict in the Second Workers Congress.

The Lechín group decided that a "homogeneous" executive committee should be elected to conduct the affairs of the C.O.B. They therefore excluded from membership in the executive representatives of some of the largest unions in the Central Obrera Boliviana, including the chauffeurs, construction workers, factory workers, and several smaller groups which had formerly been represented.

The third issue before the Second Workers Congress was the proposal for a general strike against the Stabilization Program, which had been in effect since December, 1956, and for a wage increase to compensate the workers for real wage declines which had occurred since that time. On this question there was virtual unanimity during the sessions of the congress, though grave conflicts occurred thereafter.

Immediately after the congress, the unions which had been in the minority there began passing resolutions declaring that they would not take part in the general strike, which had been set for July 1. These included the construction workers, railroaders, factory workers, petroleum workers, and several others. Even the Commercial Employees Federation of La Paz, led by ex-Trotskyite Edwin Moller, repudiated the walkout over Moller's protests. As a result of these declarations, and of energetic action on the part of President Siles, the general strike did not occur.

At the same time that they were refusing to obey the strike order of the C.O.B., the ex-P.I.R. trade union leaders lined up with President Siles in the open conflict which had developed between him and labor leaders of the other faction, including Juan Lechín, Nuflo Chávez, and Edwin Moller. They declared their support of the President, and even their support of the Stabilization Program, although reserv-

ing their right in the future to seek certain wage adjust-
ments in a peaceful way.

Finally, the leaders of the dissident unions refused to
participate in any further meetings or activities of the C.O.B.
until the Executive Committee elected at the Second Workers Congress resigned. They accused all the members of the
Executive Committee, except Lechín and Mario Torres (who
represented the miners), of being *líderes sin bases* (leaders
without rank-and-file support). They claimed that the Second Workers Congress had been packed by the ex-P.O.R.
group with spurious delegates, some of whom had been
named to the C.O.B. executive. The dissident union leaders
pointed out, for instance, that the man who represented the
Millers Federation was in fact a paid employee of the C.O.B.,
and that the representative of the Rubber Workers Federation (the membership of which was located in the jungles of
Eastern Bolivia) was a La Paz lawyer. The dominant group
in the C.O.B. retorted, quite correctly, that since its foundation the C.O.B. had had the policy of accepting credentials
of people resident in La Paz to represent groups in distant
parts of the country who could not send one of their own
number to be present at C.O.B. meetings. They added that
even without this type of delegate—who was also to be
found in the ranks of their opponents—the ex-P.O.R.-Lechín
group had a majority in the C.O.B. congress.[12]

The dissident unions set up a temporary committee which
for some time functioned as a rival to the C.O.B. A number
of unions which had not at first joined the minority bloc at
the C.O.B. congress applied for admission to the new committee, including the Federation of Commercial Employees
of La Paz, the home organization of C.O.B. leader Edwin
Moller.

The conflict became vitriolic. *Intransigencia,* organ of the
National Peasants Confederation and spokesman for the ex-
P.O.R.-Lechín faction of the C.O.B., thus described the ob-
jectives of the opponent group, in its issue of July, 1957:

They seek to impose Stalinists and supporters of Stabilization. The Chief of State, as never before, urges the same thing, and seeks a change in the make-up of the C.O.B.

They are not dealing with "reorganization for reorganization's sake." All these things should be analyzed, the trade union movement must be studied profoundly, so that traitors will not pass into history by any other name.

On the other side, *El Ferroviario*, newspaper of the Railroad Workers Confederation, in its issue of July 23, 1957, printed the following in a box on the front page:

Our answer to those who represent no one: In an apocryphal C.O.B. meeting convoked by the pseudo-leader—who claims to be a miller (miller of calumnies)—and who is known by the name of Orlando Capriles, some had the temerity to attack the railroad workers, charging them with being traitors. We know that they call us traitors because we are not an easy instrument of the Trotskyites embedded in the C.O.B., who thanks to an unsuccessful strike wished to obtain personal prestige which they have never had before. Because we are loyal interpreters of the wishes of our members, we could not precipitate the workers on an adventure. Because we are Bolivians, we are with the People of Bolivia and not with the opportunists.

The split during the Second Workers Congress and the weeks succeeding it was the first major division in the labor movement during the National Revolution. Personal rivalries of leaders, long-time political differences dating from the period when many union leaders were members of the P.I.R. and the Trotskyite P.O.R., conflicting opinions concerning the policies of President Hernán Siles, were among the causes of the scission in the Central Obrera Boliviana.

The split in the C.O.B. grew increasingly wide during 1958. In March, President Hernán Siles threatened to resign as a result of attacks upon him from the Lechín camp, but agreed to rescind his resignation after the workers' unions of La Paz went out on general strike "to force him to reconsider." During this crisis, meetings were held in the principal mining towns in support of the President, and some of these meetings were broken up by Lechín's followers, at the cost of some bloodshed.[13]

On April 10, 1958, President Siles's supporters in the miners' unions took the offensive. The La Paz newspaper *La Nación* reported on May 10 the minutes of a meeting held a month earlier to form the Bloque de Reorganización de la F.S.T.M.B. Delegates from thirty-two local miners' groups—including the large unions of Huanuni, Quichisla, and Colquiri and a number of smaller unions, as well as minority elements in other locals—attended this meeting, which declared war on Lechín, Mario Torres, and other leaders of the Federación Sindical de Trabajadores Mineros de Bolivia.

In a proclamation, the delegates founding the Bloque accused Lechín and others of corruption, tyranny, and demagoguery, and then announced a number of resolutions. The group agreed not to recognize any longer the incumbent officials of the F.S.T.M.B., to call a special congress of the federation to elect new officers, to have the Bloque function ad interim as a rival to the federation, and to urge the government to freeze the funds of the federation.

The Bloque insisted that its purpose was to strengthen the unity of the miners with other segments of the working class. It also insisted that it "obeyed no political directives," but it promised "to defend by all possible means the Government of the Revolution, because it is a Government of workers, peasants, and the middle class," and the Bloque's proclamation ended by "declaring a state of emergency in the unions affiliated with the Bloque to put them on guard against a conspiracy which is in preparation."

With the formation of the Bloque de Reorganización de la F.S.T.M.B., the forces supporting President Siles made considerable inroads in the camp of Lechín. This was the first serious challenge to Juan Lechín as supreme leader of the miners to be made in more than a dozen years.

Undoubtedly one of the principal causes for the crisis in the labor movement after the middle of 1957 was the growing realization of the responsibility which rested on the movement for cooperation in the economic reconstruction and expansion of the country. During the first five years of the Revolution, the unions had had things pretty much their own way, and the workers had begun to realize that they must give a good deal as well as receive if the National Revolution was to be a success.

There is no doubt that there had been abuses on the part of the trade unions during those first five years after April 9, 1952. There was a relaxation of discipline in virtually all enterprises. It was difficult if not impossible to dismiss a worker, even though he had flagrantly violated necessary working rules, or even though he had been guilty of stealing. In many instances, agreements signed by the unions proved to be scraps of paper.

One can cite many instances, but a single one will suffice. One of the country's largest public utility enterprises contracted with the government to construct a large new installation. Before undertaking the task, the company sought assurances from the government and the union that it would be able to dismiss the workers taken on particularly for this job, once the work had been accomplished. It got such assurances in writing. However, when the work was done, the union protested against the dismissing of the extra workers, who now had nothing to do, and the labor court upheld the protest, forcing the company to continue these workers in its employ. After much negotiation, it was agreed that the firm could fire half the workers, and in the future could dismiss any taken on for temporary jobs. This second agreement was signed by the national union, the local union, the government Labor Inspector, and the company. However, when the next incident arose in which the company sought to dismiss temporary workers, it was told that it could not do so. This time, it took the matter to the Minister of Government, and won the case, the Minister signing an accord to the effect that the company could discharge temporary employees. When the author was told this story, there had been a change in the post of Minister of Government, and the company was not sure whether the new incumbent would honor his predecessor's signature.[14]

Employers had other complaints. Many were forced by the government and the unions to take on workers they did not need. They objected that workers frequently refused to discuss improvements in techniques even when they might be advantageous to the workers. There were complaints that employers were forced to keep on their payrolls local union leaders who never put in an appearance in their plants.

Part of the trouble with labor relations during the years following the uprising of April 9, 1952, was the inefficiency of the Ministry of Labor. Not only was there a rapid turnover of Ministers during most of this period, but there was a large degree of turnover in lower personnel as well, since the salaries paid by the Ministry—some of the lowest in the whole government service—were not sufficient to attract and keep high-class personnel. There were relatively few technically trained people, and many of those who were trained—some of them in the United States—soon found themselves in positions where they were unable to use their newly acquired skills, due to the shifting sands of politics.

There is little doubt that the Ministry bent over backward to favor the unions during these years. The situation was complicated by the fact that there is no civil service in the Ministry, and the jobs there were largely political in nature. Due to the power of the unions, the Ministry officials hardly dared to alienate the union leaders.

However, by the middle of 1957 there were indications that the trade unionists were coming to realize that the grave economic crisis in which the nation found itself could not be overcome without their help, and that the success of the National Revolution itself was in danger. The clearest possible indication of this was the refusal of the unions to go out on general strike for wage increases as ordered by the Central Obrera Boliviana on July 1, 1957.

Certainly, with the power which they have, the union leaders also have a prime responsibility in the job of achieving the changes which the National Revolution is seeking for the economy and society of Bolivia. The future of the National Revolution will depend in large measure on the way the trade unionists—both leadership and rank and file—measure up to this responsibility.

Typical peasant cultivation in the Bolivian Highlands

Indians at work
in the mines

Hernán Siles in line to vote in the 1956 election

Víctor Paz Estenssoro signs the Agrarian Reform Law, August, 1953

Lake Titicaca

Construction work on the Cochabamba-Santa Cruz Highway

President Hernán Siles

Courtesy of the
Consulate General of Bolivia

President Víctor Paz Estenssoro

John Bennewitz,
U. S. Picture Syndicate

Víctor Paz Estenssoro takes the oath of office, April, 1952

Wide World Ph

The Fight Against Militarism

Militarism was long a curse in Bolivia. The Bolivian Army was notably unsuccessful in its principal task, defense of the nation's frontiers. It lost every war in which it engaged, including the last one with Paraguay in the 1930's. However, it was very successful in maintaining itself as the center of political power. It became an overgrown police force, serving to protect whatever regime happened to be in power, or upon frequent occasions, overthrowing that regime and putting another in its place.

The military started dominating Bolivian politics during the wars of independence in the first quarter of the nineteenth century. The first two Presidents of the country, Simón Bolívar and Marshal Sucre, were successful generals in the revolutionary armies. There existed in Spain and the

Spanish colonies no tradition of civilian dominance over the military, and from the beginning of the struggle for independence the soldiers in most of these new nations doubled as politicians.

Once independence from Spain had been achieved, the principal remaining centers of authority in Bolivian society were the Church and the Army. The conservative classes in the new Republic, the landowners and the merchants, looked to these two institutions to prevent the revolutionary movement from going beyond the achievement of independence and thus menacing their privileged position in society. With the drastic limitation of the power of the Church which occurred during the latter half of the nineteenth century, the relative importance of the Army became even greater than it had previously been.

The decree of July 24, 1953, which re-established the Army after the National Revolution, outlined the history of the Army during the nineteenth century:

The initial nucleus of the Bolivian Army was constituted of groups of chiefs and officers of the Spanish Army who, born in America, but educated in the feudal spirit of the Colony, abandoned the cause of the metropolis to join the patriotic ranks, together with a few soldiers enlisted during the course of the war; . . . Once the Republic was constituted, these chiefs and officers, allied with civil landlords, or themselves masters of lands and Indians, continued the colonial tradition of exploiting the great majority of the country for the benefit of the minority;

. . . Although the native landlords had sufficient power to keep the mass of peasants and artisans in servitude, they lacked ideological unity and internal consistency, which induced them to use military factions in intestine feuds of a sectarian nature, thus provoking military *caudillismo* which has sprinkled our history with barracks uprisings and *coups d'état* throughout the last century.

. . . as a result of this situation and the constant struggles between factions of the dominant group, the preparation of national defense was abandoned, and consequently the training of the Armed Forces, which resulted, among other things, in the defeats of the War of the Pacific and later the failure of the Acre Campaign.[1]

The result of all this was that there grew up a tradition in Bolivia that the Army was the ultimate arbiter of politics. Plots and counterplots were routine in the Bolivian Armed Forces. It became almost habitual for politicians who were on the outs with the current administration to seek to make contact with disgruntled or ambitious Army officers, in an attempt to organize a military *coup* to depose those in power.

During most of the nineteenth century the nation was ruled by a series of military *caudillos,* who fought their way to the top of the Armed Forces and thence to the presidency. The presidency of the Republic virtually became the highest step in the military hierarchy.

With the Liberal Revolution at the beginning of the twentieth century, the nineteenth-century Army was dissolved, and a new one was organized. The July 24, 1953, decree described this new Army:

. . . to organize this new Army, the Liberals brought successive foreign military missions, which, inspired by the medieval caste tradition, were ignorant of our people's idiosyncrasies, to which the structure of a truly Bolivian Army should conform;

. . . During the twenty years of the Liberal regime, that Army appeared to be a well-organized institution, but in reality it fulfilled efficaciously the function of an instrument of oppression at the service of the dominant group, while national defense was abandoned.

. . . although the mining interests had seized political power from the landlords in 1898, they respected their economic power, their possession of lands and Indians, which facilitated the return of these landlords to the political struggle under the name of Republicans who, favored by the economic crisis of 1920, broke the unity of the Liberal Party and took power.

. . . The Chaco War demonstrated the absolute inefficiency of the Army, created by the large mining interests as an instrument for the protection of the national territory, which, in spite of individual acts of heroism and the valor and spirit of sacrifice of the people, repeated the experience of the War of the Pacific. . . .[2]

Although some progress was made in the direction of civilian control of the government during the first three decades of the twentieth century, the tradition of Army intervention in politics was revived as a result of the Chaco War in the 1930's. In the middle of the conflict with Paraguay, the Army overthrew President David Salamanca and put another civilian, José Luis Tejada Sorzano, in his place. Subsequently, power was solidly in the hands of the Army. Of the nine presidents serving between the overthrow of President Tejada Sorzano in May, 1936, and the triumph of the National Revolution in April, 1952, six were military men. The three civilians who served as chief executive during this period held the position on the sufferance of the leaders of the Army.

Military uprisings overthrew President Tejada Sorzano in May, 1936, his successor, Colonel David Toro in 1937, President Peñaranda in 1943. The withdrawal of Army support from President Villarroel in July, 1946, resulted in his overthrow and hanging at the hands of a street mob. The Army again took over from the Constitutional President, Dr. Mamerto Urriolagoitia, in May, 1951.

Although there were new ideological currents stirring within the Army after the Chaco conflict, the military continued to serve as a bulwark of the economic and social *status quo* during most of the period between the Chaco War and the 1952 Revolution. The Army constituted the backbone of the regimes in power between 1946 and 1952, and was frequently used during this period—and before it— to discipline the turbulent mine workers and coerce the peasants.

In addition to the Army, which just before the 1952 Revolution comprised some 18,000 men and officers, there was the Carabineros, a militarized national police force, patterned on that of Chile. Its principal job was maintenance of order in the countryside. There was a certain amount of rivalry between the Carabineros and the Army, although until the Nationalist Revolution of 1952 the Carabineros did not play an independent political role.

Class and race distinctions were marked in the pre-1952 Bolivian Army. The officers were career men, drawn mainly from the urban middle classes, and trained in the country's military academy, located on the outskirts of La Paz. Officers found frequent opportunities to augment their somewhat meager salaries through holding civilian posts or obtaining extra income through other licit and illicit means.

The rank and file was made up of Indian conscripts, for whom it had become traditional to present themselves at the nearest Army barracks for their one year of service when they reached or thought they reached the age of eighteen. The discipline of the Army was severe, and the conditions for the enlisted men were poor.

The Bolivian Army was badly equipped. Its effectives consisted principally of infantrymen, plus some cavalry and a very small air arm. The Army possessed few if any tanks and little other heavy equipment. It did have some artillery, which might have changed the result of the April 9, 1952, uprising, if it could have been brought effectively into action.

Thus, the balance of strength between the government's forces and a group, of comparable size, of civilians armed with small arms was more nearly even in Bolivia than in perhaps any other South American country. Knowing this, the Army leaders generally took precautions to see to it that arms were kept out of the hands of civilian political groups. Until 1952, therefore, power remained in the hands of the Army.

The role of the Army in pre-revolutionary Bolivia was noted by the Keenleyside *Report:*

The Members of the Mission do not presume to advise on substantive military questions, but they are aware of the existence of a critical attitude on the part of competent military advisers concerning the present defense establishment and planning of Bolivia, especially the prospective increase in the air arm and other proposals such as the formation of a parachute unit. Nor does the army, in spite of recent attempts to diversify its activities, employ its manpower in engineering, construction or other economically useful work to the extent that would be desirable.[3]

The uprising of April 9, 1952, largely destroyed the existing Bolivian Army. The circumstances of the conflict made it possible for the new M.N.R. government to make a clean sweep of the old Armed Forces.

One of the first acts of the new regime was to retire antagonistic elements from the Army. Not only were 80 per cent of the officers and noncommissioned officers retired, but most enlisted men were sent back home. Many M.N.R. leaders felt that the existence of the Army was a menace to their regime. The M.N.R. had defeated it in open battle and naturally did not trust its remnants to defend the regime of the party which had routed it. The M.N.R. leaders did not have much more trust in the officials of the Carabineros, who had conspired with them to overthrow the government they were pledged to uphold, so this corps was reduced to very small proportions.

President Víctor Paz Estenssoro summed up his government's attitude toward the old Army and the regime's general military policy in his report to Congress in July, 1956. He said:

With the power of the State in the hands of the people through its political vanguard, the M.N.R. had to replace the old massacring army, organized and educated for the defense of the oligarchic interests, and to substitute for it a new one, destined for the defense of the political and economic sovereignty of the Fatherland, placed at the service of the ideals and interests of the workers, peasants, and people of the middle class, and disposed to cooperate in a program of development of the national economy, for the benefit of all Bolivians.

The first logical step was the elimination of those in active service, the chiefs and officers implicated in grave crimes against the economy of the nation and the lives of the citizens, crimes committed in the service of the feudal mining oligarchy. Those chiefs and officers were replaced by men who had supported Busch and Villarroel, and who were at the time of the Revolution out of service or relegated to posts where they commanded no troops.

The Military Academy, whose members had fought perfidiously against the people in the April days, was closed, to be opened again, reorganized, in 1953, with the name and spirit of the Martyr President Colonel Gualberto Villarroel. Now applicants from all social classes can enter the Military Academy, without any other requirement than ability, and the spirit of caste which formerly prevailed has been suppressed.[4]

During the revolt, arms had been distributed to workers of La Paz by the rebel Carabineros. In the mining areas the miners were able to use the dynamite, which they were accustomed to manipulating for other purposes, as a weapon of war, and succeeded in getting control of the mining camps with comparative ease. During the previous decade the miners had unsuccessfully attempted several uprisings, in the process of which they had seized guns from the police and soldiers. Many of these remained hidden in the camps and were used on April 9, 1952.

Once the April 9 uprising was successful, these *ad hoc* workers' militia groups were organized on a somewhat more systematic basis. Each local trade union established its militia, and these bodies were given a modicum of training in the handling of weapons and in the elements of military discipline. The government armed them with weapons taken from the disbanded Army's stores, and other arms were seized from the houses of the landlords.

At the same time, during the first year it was in power, the M.N.R. government carried out the policy of establishing peasants' unions and organizing the members of these unions simultaneously into local units of the M.N.R. These local agrarian groups throughout the country formed their own peasant militia, also armed by the government.

Thus the government of the National Revolution came to depend for its military backing on the armed force of its worker and peasant supporters. During the first years of the Revolution, the various militia units took their business very seriously and were conscientious about their training programs, though as time wore on the enthusiasm of the militiamen tended to decline.

The author visited one of the militia headquarters in the vicinity of Ucureña (in the department of Cochabamba) in 1954. What was once the house of the landlord had been converted into the headquarters of the unit. The peasants on the estate took turns in standing guard there and were ready for action.

The militia demonstrated its usefulness to the government on several occasions. When a group of rebels seized the city of Cochabamba and the person of the Minister of Mines Juan Lechín, in November, 1953, peasant militia from the nearby rural areas marched on the city and soon recaptured it for the government. When there was a threat of a *coup* against the government shortly before the 1956 election, militiamen were brought to La Paz and were stationed on the rim of the Altiplano above the city.

Although called to arms several times to defend the government of the M.N.R., the worker and peasant militia was surprisingly peaceful. With the armed force of the nation in their hands, the militiamen seldom used it irresponsibly. Discipline was good. There were few instances of drunkenness and violence among them. Order was kept in the cities and towns in spite of the large number of men carrying guns.

The existence of the worker and peasant militia, and the M.N.R. government's dependence upon it, caused a great deal of controversy in the early months of the National Revolution. The Partido Comunista and the Trotskyites waxed romantic about the existence of the militia and saw in it the hope of what they euphemistically called "a workers and peasants government." On the other hand, the unarmed middle classes of the city were very apprehensive of the militia, while the right-wing opposition denounced the government's reliance on it as sure proof that the M.N.R. was "Communist."

Leading figures in the government were also uneasy about their utter dependence on the armed workers and peasants. If the Communists or Trotskyites succeeded in getting control of any sizable part of the labor movement, they would be able to exert military as well as economic and political pressure upon the government. Even without political instigation, there was always the danger that unfounded rumors might bring the Indian militiamen down on the capital and other cities with results which might well be catastrophic.

For a year and a half after the National Revolution a controversy raged concerning the re-establishment of a full-fledged national army. Strong elements within the M.N.R. opposed its reconstitution. They feared that in Bolivia the Army would inevitably meddle in politics and felt that it was better not to have one. Furthermore, many trade union and peasant leaders feared a reduction in their power over the government would result from the re-establishment of an army.

However, others had a new vision of what role the Army could assume in the nation's affairs. They felt that the Armed Forces could become a school, which could be of immeasurable aid in teaching the Indian masses to play their new part as citizens of Bolivia. They argued that since the Indians were accustomed to presenting themselves for military service, this period of service should be used to teach them elementary lessons in hygiene, reading and writing, and even agriculture, and that the Army could perform a significant function in the government's program of economic development.

President Víctor Paz Estenssoro sided with the group in favor of re-establishing the Army, and it finally won out. On July 24, 1953, a decree was issued by President Paz Estenssoro, reinstituting the Army. Its long preamble recounted the history of the Bolivian Army, at least as seen by the M.N.R. leaders. It then proclaimed that:

The Government of the National Revolution has the duty of substituting for the old Army, organized and educated for the defense of oligarchic interests, an Army destined for the defense of the political independence of the country, the guarding of the frontiers, the service of the interests and aspirations of the workers, peasants, and people of the middle class, and cooperation in the program of using the natural resources of Bolivia for the benefit of the Bolivians;

. . . thus, it is necessary to build a new type of organization for the National Army and to set up new norms for the education of chiefs and officers, opening the doors of the institution to the sons of the classes who constitute the majority of the population and educating them in accord with the new functions which the Armed Forces must fulfill.[5]

The structure which the new Army would have was indicated in Article 2 of the decree of July 24, 1953:

The new juridical structure will include a body of fundamental laws, dispositions, and regulations which will replace the present ones, which are of foreign inspiration, and they will establish the organization and functions of the Armed Forces in accord with the peculiar characteristics of the nation and the material possibilities of the State. Its new technical structure will qualify its members not only for the fulfillment of their specific functions, but for the defense of the political and economic independence of the Fatherland, guarding its frontiers, and serving the interests and aspirations of the majority of the people, thus making the Armed Forces an instrument which contributes to the development of the economy of the country, so as to improve the welfare of the Bolivian people and make the Army an effective force for the defense of the nation.[6]

Article 6 of the decree provided for the careful selection of the officers of the new Army:

Both military academies must be constituted fundamentally of elements of the middle class, working class, and peasantry, which in addition to the technical training relating to the military art, will be educated to respect and protect the national sovereignty and the aspirations of the people, and to defend the riches of the country against the ambitions of the oligarchy.[7]

At the end of 1953 the military academy in La Paz was reopened. The new cadets were recruited on the basis of their social background and their political loyalties. Of them, 20 per cent were drawn from the sons of peasants, 30 per cent from the sons of city workers and miners, and 50 per cent from the sons of middle-class M.N.R. members of at least six years' standing. Officers of the old Army who were M.N.R. members or had worked closely with the party in the past were reinstated and undertook the task of rebuilding the Army.

This screening of the officer corps of the new Army was not the only means adopted by the government to prevent it from becoming once again a menace to constituted authority. The military budget was kept low, a close rein was kept on the new Armed Forces by the civilians, and the Carabineros were kept at equal strength with the Army. Furthermore, much of the Army was kept a safe distance from the capital. By 1956 there were eight thousand men in the new Army. Two thousand of these were kept busy in colonization and road-building projects in the Eastern part of the country; another three thousand were occupied in agricultural programs in the Altiplano. Only three thousand soldiers were kept in garrisons in various parts of the country.

President Víctor Paz explained in considerable detail the philosophy and orientation of the new Army in his Message to Congress in July, 1956:

The High Command of the New Army has developed a doctrine which takes into consideration in a realistic manner our geographical, historical, demographic, economic and financial, social and political peculiarities. Once this doctrine was defined, it was given form and life, military instruction being adapted to the reality of our situation, and being embodied in various regulations approved between 1952 and 1956. These established the norms for the Armed Forces in terms of tactics and discipline. . . .

Once the economic and political power of the mining firms and the feudal landlords had been liquidated by means of nationalization of the mines and the agrarian reform, which constituted the fundamental bases for the national rebirth, Bolivia undertook the next step, development and diversification of its economy. The New Army, identified with the national destiny, and possessing organized human resources, could not be absent from this battle in which the Bolivian people was engaged. It must dedicate part of its energies to productive work, which becomes part of its specific functions. Armies at the present time, in order to be useful, must have enormous quantities of materiel which is complicated and costly and must be backed up by a vigorous national economy. A nation which is economically weak cannot enjoy the luxury of a modern army. In taking part in the collective effort to develop and diversify the national economy, the New Army of Bolivia is engaging in its normal duties, because it is contributing to the creation of conditions which in the future will permit the country, if it is necessary, an efficient army, with all of the arms required by modern war.[8]

Part of the attempt to keep the Army in a position of subordination to the civilian authorities and have it participate in the process of economic development has been its use in colonization projects in the Eastern part of the country. This program has kept the soldiers a long way from La Paz, and at the same time has kept them engaged in useful work in the government's Economic Development Program. Specially selected volunteer recruits were put into the Army's new Colonization Battalion and were sent to the Department of Santa Cruz to clear the forests, build roads, and construct housing and other facilities for colonists from the Altiplano. Members of the Colonization Battalion have also been given the chance of settling in these colonies themselves, once their term of service was completed. By 1957 only a handful, however, had actually moved into the colonies.[9]

This colonization work has been only part of the constructive program of the Army since its re-establishment in 1953. Much time and energy have been devoted to road building. The Military Engineering Service has laid out two routes for a projected road to connect with the Beni River, which will in time open up a sizable part of the interior to contact with the principal populated areas of the country.

The Sappers' Battalion has been used to repair and improve the Mataral-Villagrande-Lagunillas road. Another group of sappers has been used to open a cattle trail from Chaparé to Mojos, to make it easier to supply cattle to the city of Cochabamba.

Even the troops stationed as garrisons in various cities have been used on a wide variety of public works projects. In July, 1956, President Víctor Paz reported, "They have cooperated in street cleaning, the installation of telephone lines, the construction of public buildings, of airports, as well as the construction and repair of barracks and homes for officers. For this purpose, a brick and tile factory has been established, which will also sell to the public."

The Army's Hydraulic Service, which was set up principally to supply water to the military garrisons, has extended its services and has provided water to other branches of government and to private consumers. From May, 1952, to March, 1956, it sunk 114 wells, with a capacity of over 100,-000 gallons per hour, in the Departments of La Paz, Cochabamba, and Tarija. This Service provided a drinking-water supply for the city of Trinidad in the Beni section of Eastern Bolivia.

The Instituto Geográfico Militar not only continued the work of surveying the whole country upon which it was engaged before the Revolution, but made its services available to the government oil firm as well. Between 1952 and 1956 the Instituto graduated 46 trained topographers.[10]

The country's small Air Force was retained and raised in status by the revolutionary government. An Air Force academy, the Colegio Militar de Aviación "General Germán Busch," was established for the first time on May 31, 1952. President Víctor Paz reported to Congress in July, 1956, concerning this school.

This military college has changed the old system of training aviators only among officers already graduated from the Army's military academy. Now it accepts cadets who are trained in aviation while they are receiving military instruction, and who emerge as sub-lieutenants. By the end of last year, 22 pilots and 20 Air Force officers had graduated. In the present year, there are 87 cadets in the school, and it's estimated that 25 new military pilots will graduate this year.[11]

The Air Force, like the Army, has been used mainly in the program of economic development. The principal element of the Air Force has been the Transportes Aéreos Militares (T.A.M.), which has provided regular service to outlying parts of the country which for commercial reasons were not reached by regular civilian airlines.[12] The T.A.M. has been subject to some criticism, however, on the grounds that it frequently runs lines competitive with those of the commercial companies, and charges much lower rates than the latter are able to do.

At the same time that the military forces were being re-established, the Carabineros were drastically changed. The National Police School was reorganized and rechristened "Academy," and emphasis was put on training for specialized police work. During the four years of Víctor Paz's administration, 115 new sub-lieutenants were graduated from the Academy, which is financed by the returns from fines levied by the police.

The detective force of the Carabineros was also reorganized. At the same time a National Identification Service was established by bringing together a number of provincial and departmental bodies of this nature. A foreign expert in detection was brought in to help to refurbish this part of the police force.

The police were also used in carrying out the economic and social program of the revolutionary government. A contingent of officers and men was put at the disposal of the National Agrarian Reform Council to serve as a Rural Security Service. The General Directorate of Police and Carabineros also established facilities for training some officers as topographers, so that they could help in the work of surveying and dividing the estates subject to the agrarian reform. A group of police was placed at the disposal of the government oil firm, Y.P.F.B., to establish a security service for its camps and industrial plants. Finally, a hacienda was taken over by the government for use by the Carabineros to grow food for the organization's members.[18]

In the whole process of reconstructing the military and police forces, the Bolivian Government received aid from the United States. A police mission was established as part of the Point Four program, to help train the Carabineros in modern techniques of police work. The United States Military Mission provided material, equipment, and teaching personnel for the Escuela de Armas "General Ballivián," the

Bolivian War College. It also provided help to the Bolivian Military Engineering School, the noncommissioned officers' school, and the Instituto Militar Geográfico.[14]

Thus, the military policy of the revolutionary government since the re-establishment of the Army has been designed in the first instance to create a force which would be subordinate to civilian authority. Also, within the limited financial resources made available to the Armed Forces, the attempt has been made to increase their technical efficiency. Finally, all parts of the Army and police have been used to further the social policies and program of economic development of the regime.

In spite of all efforts to build up an Army which would not attempt to challenge the power of the civilian regime, there was evidence by the middle of 1957 that the old tradition of military intervention in politics was not completely dead. The author was in La Paz early in August, 1957, when a crisis occurred in the Army's affairs. A shake-up in the Army command was conducted under the direction of President Siles, and a group of officers unhappy about these changes presented a memorandum—which reached the press —protesting the shake-up. Although the offending officers were severely reprimanded, and no overt move was made to topple the Siles government, the incident provided disconcerting evidence that certain elements in the Armed Forces were not wholly inclined to accept the authority of the constituted regime.

With the re-establishment of the Army, the government seemed to be following a policy of trying to maintain a balance among the militia, the Carabineros, and the Army. There was no attempt to disarm the peasants' and workers' groups, and the government was in a position to use them as a counterweight against the Army in case it should attempt an anti-government move. At the same time, the Army and Carabineros would be useful if any sizable group of armed union members turned against the government. Certainly the perennial problem of militarism had not been completely solved, but the M.N.R. regime was less subject than any of its predecessors to the pressure and the whims of the leaders of the Armed Forces.

9 . . .

The Search for Economic Independence

Independencia económica was from the beginning one of the slogans of the Movimiento Nacionalista Revolucionario. The precise meaning of the term was sometimes a bit vague, but in essence it can be summed up under two heads: placing Bolivia's principal means of production in the hands of Bolivians; and reducing the extreme dependence of the country on international markets. The M.N.R. government has sought to achieve these ends.

Its success during the first six years was limited. Although the key tin-mining industry had been partly nationalized, and the single most important source of foreign exchange was thus in Bolivian hands, another key potential source of foreign exchange, petroleum, had been put largely under the control of foreign companies. Although important steps had been taken toward agricultural self-sufficiency, a sizable proportion of the urban population of the country was in 1957–1958 being supplied with foodstuffs gratis by a foreign government. Although important measures had been taken to provide the country with a more diversified and stable economy, less subject to the shocks of the international market, the government of Bolivia was in 1957 more dependent than ever before in its history on aid from foreign sources.

Unfriendly critics have made the most of this apparently paradoxical result of the rule of the nationalist M.N.R. party. However, the fact is that, although in short-run terms Bolivia was at the beginning of 1958 further from economic independence than on the day of the National Revolution, the social changes and Economic Development Program of the M.N.R. government were laying the groundwork for a period of growth and diversification of the economy which would make it possible to provide the Bolivian people with a level of living which they had never known in the past, and would do away once and for all with the excessively high degree of dependence on one or two export products which had characterized the Bolivian economy since the coming of the Spaniards.

One of the principal objectives of the revolutionary regime has been to develop other sources of foreign exchange, in addition to the traditional mining enterprises of the Altiplano area. Its efforts in this direction have been concentrated on four different aspects of the economy: development of the petroleum industry; exploitation of rich iron resources in the Eastern part of the country; development of tropical agricultural products, some of which might be exported; and achieving progress for the country's grazing industry through making it more readily accessible to domestic and foreign markets and improving the breed of cattle grown in the Eastern part of the country.

The most spectacular economic success of the M.N.R. government has been in the petroleum industry. During the

Paz Estenssoro administration most of this success was registered in the operations of the government oil firm, Yacimientos Petrolíferos Fiscales Bolivianos, although the basis was also laid for further expanding the oil industry, through the granting of concessions to foreign oil companies, a process which reached its climax during the Siles regime.

The oil industry in Bolivia dates from 1922, when the Standard Oil Company of New Jersey acquired the concession originally given to Richmond Levering & Company, for exploration and exploitation of oil resources in the departments of Chuquisaca, Tarija, and Santa Cruz. The Standard Oil Company remained in charge of the oil industry in Bolivia until 1937. During this period, the highest output obtained was some 26,000 cubic meters of crude oil, reached in 1935. Standard also built two small topping plants for the refining of petroleum in Camiri and Sanandita, the maximum output of which was 26,000 cubic meters in 1935.

In 1937 the government of Colonel Toro canceled the Standard Oil Company's concessions, expropriated its equipment in Bolivia, and established a government firm, the Yacimientos Petrolíferos Fiscales Bolivianos, to take over the industry. It was not until 1942 that an agreement was made between the Bolivian Government and the Standard Oil Company concerning the payment for the expropriated property, which resulted in the Y.P.F.B.'s coming into possession of the exploration maps which Standard had developed during its operations in the country.

During the fifteen years between expropriation and the National Revolution, considerable progress was made in the oil industry, though this progress was not sufficient to keep up with the nation's increasing demand for petroleum products. Y.P.F.B. crude output rose to a peak of 108,000 cubic meters in 1949 and thereafter declined to 84,000 in 1952. Exploration work continued, with 62 wells being dug during this period, and equipment for drilling purposes was augmented. Refining activities also increased, reaching a maximum of 99,000 cubic meters in 1949 and declining to 71,000 in 1952.

An Export-Import Bank loan for $8,500,000 granted in 1947 was of material assistance in financing the construction of two refineries, in Cochabamba and Sucre, which work was completed after the National Revolution, and in building pipelines to connect these refineries with the producing fields.[1]

The Paz Estenssoro government had as one of its first economic objectives the increase of Y.P.F.B.'s output. In July, 1952, plans for this were completed, and orders were given for new equipment for the government oil firm. Actual increase in output dates from August, 1953.[2]

One of the first measures taken by the Y.P.F.B. was to increase its exploration activities. In 1953 a special Geological Department was established within the Y.P.F.B. In 1954 an Exploration Manager was established, with headquarters in La Paz and an operating office in the Southern part of the country. As a result of these activities, a number of exploratory wells were drilled, and at least one new oil field was discovered.[3]

The Economic Commission for Latin America's report on the Bolivian economy summed up the advances made by the Y.P.F.B. between 1952 and 1956 thus:

The discovery in 1953 of the Sararenda field in the Camiri area made possible a strong increase in production, which rose to 504,000 cubic meters in 1956 (six times that of 1952). Total consumption of petroleum derivatives increased rapidly (more than 20 per cent in the last three years), reaching 331,000 cubic meters in 1956. Imports, which in 1952 reached their high point of 133,-000 cubic meters, were practically eliminated after 1954. Furthermore, exports of crude petroleum increased and exports of derivatives were begun in neighboring countries, which reached 67,000 cubic meters in 1956. The work of exploration and perforation was also intensified, and oil structures were found at

Itapirenda and Buena Vista near Camiri and at Toro, to the North of Bermejo. Seismologic, geophysical, and aerial photography work was also increased. Better perforation equipment made possible the boring of sixty wells and seven exploratory wells between 1953 and the middle of 1956. Refining rose from 71,000 cubic meters in 1952 to 450,000 in 1956. Oil pipelines were built from Cochabamba to Oruro to La Paz and from the Camiri field to Yacuiba. An oil drum factory was also established, which resulted in more ample warehousing and distribution facilities. Finally, the Y.P.F.B. improved its organization and its technical personnel considerably during this period.[4]

As a result of all this, the Y.P.F.B., which in 1952 produced 1,200 barrels of oil a day (only 800 barrels in 1953), was by the middle of 1957 producing around 10,000 barrels, which was about the utmost then possible with the transportation facilities available. The country was consuming approximately 7,000 barrels of petroleum a day, leaving some 3,000 for export. A pipeline was under construction from the oil fields to the city of Santa Cruz, which would result in direct delivery of about 1,500 barrels a day, leaving some 5,500 for the rest of the country.

Arrangements had already been made by the middle of 1957 for the construction of a pipeline from the Bolivian oil fields to the Chilean port of Arica, which would for the first time make the country's oil available to the general world market. This pipeline, which was to have two spurs, one connected with the existing pipeline to La Paz, the other going from Cochabamba to Sica Sica in the Department of Oruro and thence to the Coast, was planned to have a capacity of 50,000 barrels a day.[5]

The Arica pipeline involved reaching an agreement with Chile. Bolivia first argued that it had the right to build the pipeline on the basis of a treaty signed at the end of the War of the Pacific, whereby Bolivia was given free port facilities in Arica. However, since the possibility of an oil pipeline was not even considered at the time this treaty was

signed, a specific arrangement was necessary for the purpose. The discussion of this proposal in the Chilean Senate
gave rise to a good deal of demagoguery and the assertion of
some senators that the pipeline would be "an invasion of
Chilean sovereignty," but the agreement was finally ratified.
It was expected that the pipeline could be constructed and
go into operation by sometime in 1959.

Plans for the oil pipeline call for its construction in two
stages, the first of which will result in a capacity of 6,000
barrels a day, and the second of which will make it possible
to take 50,000 a day from the Bolivian oil fields to the Pacific
Coast. It has been estimated that the first stage will result in
a return to Bolivia in foreign exchange of $7,000,000, and
the second will bring in $60,000,000 a year.[6]

The M.N.R. government's attempts to develop the oil industry were not confined to the re-equipment and expansion
of the Y.P.F.B. Serious and successful attempts were made to
interest the international oil companies in the exploitation of
the country's petroleum resources. In order to do so, it was
necessary to overcome prejudices and fears dating from the
1937 expropriation and reinforced by the expropriation of
the tin-mining companies in 1952. This had been successfully accomplished by 1957.

The first foreign oil firm to become interested in concessions in Bolivia was that of Glenn McCarthy, who had made
and lost several fortunes in oil operations in the United
States. The McCarthy enterprise, which had difficulty raising the amount of capital in the United States which was
necessary for its Bolivian operations, did bring in some
drilling equipment, and discovered several wells which,
however, proved to be richer in gas than in oil. When
McCarthy finally proved unable to fulfill the terms of his
concession, he was given four months in which to comply or
forfeit his claims under the agreement. Meanwhile, McCarthy had negotiated with the Tennessee Gas Company and
finally, with the approval of the Bolivian Government, trans-

ferred his interests to that firm. The Tennessee Gas group was represented in the negotiations by its attorney, Henry Holland, who until a few months before had been Assistant Secretary of State for Latin American Affairs.[7]

It was difficult to interest the larger American and British oil firms in Bolivian petroleum until the legal status of concessions was changed, since after 1937 all oil reserves were considered national property and could not be conceded to other firms than the Y.P.F.B. The Paz Estenssoro government, with the aid of Point Four, contracted for the services of the law firm of Travieso, Davenport, Evans and Fernández, to draw up a new Petroleum Code. This Code was finally promulgated in 1956 and paved the way for granting concessions to foreign firms.[8]

The Economic Commission for Latin America's economic survey of Bolivia outlines the terms of the Code:

> The Petroleum Code, although maintaining the direct, inalienable and unprescriptible dominion of the nation over deposits of petroleum, asphalt, natural gas, and other hydrocarbons, and declaring all exploration, exploitation, refining, and manufacture, transformation or transport of hydrocarbons to be public utilities, permits the intervention of private capital in petroleum activities, which can be carried out through concessions or contracts between the State and private firms.[9]

According to Jorge Fernández Solís, member of the law firm which drew up the Code and subsequently lawyer for the Bolivian Gulf Oil Company whom the author interviewed on August 1, 1957, the general objective of the Code was to establish the "fifty-fifty" basis for distribution of the returns from oil operations which had first been introduced in Venezuela during the late 1940's. Although this fifty-fifty arrangement is not stated in so many words in the Code, it was thought by those who drafted it that the various royalties and taxes provided in the Code would add up approximately to such a division of the profits of the industry, as between the companies and the government.

The Code divided the territory of Bolivia into four zones, the third of which was subdivided into three sub-zones, and the last of which was reserved exclusively to the Y.P.F.B. The Y.P.F.B. reserve is in the part of the country in which the government firm already has established its operations, and which is best known from a geological point of view. Limits on the size of any single concession are set between 150,000 hectares and 750,000 hectares, depending on the zone in which it is located; and though one firm may get more than one concession, the total area held under all concessions by a single firm may not exceed 500,000 hectares insofar as Zone 1 is concerned, 1,500,000 hectares in Zone 2, and 3,000,000 hectares in Zone 3.

Firms seeking concessions must pay a guaranty deposit varying from five cents a hectare to twenty cents a hectare, depending on the zone. Exploration contracts only run for four years, and cannot be extended, in Zone 1; they run for four years with a possible extension of two more years in Zone 2, and for six years with two possible extensions of two years each in Zone 3. During this period it is provided that the concessionaire shall invest twenty to eighty cents per hectare in exploration activities, or if he fails to do so, he must pay this much to the State.

Once oil is found, exploitation contracts run for forty years under the Petroleum Code. During the period of exploration, the concessionaire will pay a tax to the State of two to five cents a hectare, depending on the zone. During the period of exploitation, the concessionaire will pay in Zone 1 an initial tax of forty cents per hectare and an annual tax of from fifteen cents to a dollar per hectare, depending on the age of the concession. These taxes are less on land in Zones 2 and 3. In addition, the concessionaire with producing wells will turn over to the government a royalty of 11 per cent of the crude oil taken out of the ground and will pay a fixed tax of 30 per cent on the liquid profit from its operations in Bolivia.

Since one of the principal criticisms of the old Standard Oil concession before 1937 was that the company had tended to keep Bolivian oil as a reserve instead of actually seeking to expand production, there is provision in the 1956 Petroleum Code against repetition of this situation. A concessionaire may not wait more than six months after the granting of the concession to begin active exploration work. Once oil has been found, the company must, during the first seven years it is taking out oil, continue to drill not less than one well for every 100,000 hectares in its concession, with a total depth of 5,000 meters (about 16,400 feet). During the succeeding eight years, the concessionaire must drill two or more such wells, of a total depth of at least 10,000 meters (about 32,800 feet), for every 20,000 hectares in the concession.[10]

Although there is no mention of it in the Petroleum Code, previous treaties between Bolivia and Brazil provide that Brazilian companies must participate in the exploitation of oil in certain areas, including a part of Zone 1, as well as part of the area allocated to the Y.P.F.B. Negotiations to this end were begun in 1956, but by the middle of 1958 had not borne fruit. On the Bolivian side, there was reluctance on the part of the government and the Y.P.F.B. to enter into an agreement with a firm owned and controlled by a foreign government. The obvious Brazilian firm to help develop Bolivian oil resources in the allotted areas was Petroleos Brasileiros, the Brazilian Government oil monopoly, since there did not seem to be any large group of Brazilian private investors who would be willing to go into this venture. Hence, the Bolivians balked.[11]

On the other hand, charges were made by Senator Lourival Fontes of Brazil that the real reason for the hesitancy of the Bolivians was "that United States oil interests and specifically former Assistant Secretary of State Holland had influenced Bolivia against implementation of the treaty with Brazil for oil exploitation in the Santa Cruz area." Mr. Holland denied this charge.[12] In any case, by the end of 1957 no arrangement had as yet been made for opening the area reserved to Brazilian interests for exploitation and exploration.

However, a sizable number of other concessions had been granted during 1956 and 1957. The most important of these was to the Bolivian Gulf Oil Company, a subsidiary of the Gulf Oil Company in the United States, which not only got a concession in its own right, but also a contract with the Y.P.F.B. for helping in the exploitation of part of the area reserved to the government company and construction of a pipeline from Cochabamba to Arica. Other concessions of varying size were granted to the Shell Prospecting Company, Andes Oil Company (a subsidiary of the United States Puroil interests), and the Chaco Oil Company (subsidiary of the Tennessee Gas Company). Other concessions were given to the Bolivian Petroleum Company, a subsidiary of the Drilling and Exploration Company of the United States, which in addition to working on its own concession was providing services to other companies operating in Bolivia; and the Bolivian American Oil Company, a firm associated with the Cuban Petroleum Company.[13]

As of the middle of 1957, none of the Standard Oil companies had obtained a concession. However, it was known that representatives of the Standard Oil Company of Ohio had had representatives in Bolivia, studying the possibilities of applying for such a grant.

Virtually no political opposition was raised within the M.N.R. to the granting of these oil concessions. There was general agreement that it was a pressing necessity to develop petroleum so as to provide a source of foreign exchange in addition to the ailing mining industry, and it was also recognized that the quickest way to do so was through the granting of concessions. There seemed to be a general conviction that the Petroleum Code gave assurance of fair participation by Bolivia in the returns from the exploitation of the industry.

However, there was some indication of opposition from outside the ranks of the M.N.R. Articles began appearing in the press in the middle of 1957 attacking the policy of concessions, on the grounds that with the growth of the petroleum industry, Bolivia would once again find that her principal foreign exchange earner was in the hands of foreign-dominated companies over which the Bolivian Government and people had little control. One of the stranger aspects of these criticisms of the M.N.R. government's oil policy was that they were made by many of the same people who violently attacked nationalization of the tin mines.

It seems likely that the M.N.R. government moved with haste in granting concessions in 1956–1957 for several reasons. First, there was desperate need for a new source of foreign exchange. Second, there was a certain amount of pressure exerted by the United States Government—or at least the Bolivian Government might well think that there was. In this connection, the action of Henry Holland in resigning as Assistant Secretary of State for Latin American Affairs and turning up a few months later as a lawyer for oil interests seeking concessions in Bolivia has been criticized —particularly since he had been Assistant Secretary at the time the new Petroleum Code was written, with the help and advice of United States Government officials. Holland's action lends itself to interpretations not only in Bolivia but elsewhere which would seem to indicate a closer connection between the State Department and its policies on the one hand, and the oil companies and their interests on the other, than actually existed.

In the light of these circumstances, the Bolivians could not be blamed for regarding the sudden appearance of Mr. Holland so soon after his resignation from the top United States diplomatic post concerned with Latin American affairs as "pressure" of a rather obvious sort. How seriously the Bolivians regarded the actions of Holland is illuminated by the fact that when he arrived in La Paz in April, 1957, he was received at the airport by functionaries of the Ministry of Foreign Relations as well as by the President of the Y.P.F.B.—not to mention the Chargé d'Affaires of the United States Embassy.[14]

There was considerable Bolivian resentment of Mr. Holland's seeking oil concessions so soon after resigning his government post. The La Paz newspaper *El Diario,* on May 20, 1957, commented:

> Mr. Holland is again visiting us—whether to conclude the previous deal or to present new proposals, we do not know. Public opinion—surprisingly lenient in Bolivia—is, however, unable to approve the moral position of a former Assistant Secretary of State with so many previous ties in Bolivia due to his official position, now exercising the profitable activities of a private lawyer amongst us. It seems to indicate contempt for public opinion in Bolivia.

Aside from these issues, however, there is much to be said on the merits of the case for the policy which the M.N.R. government has adopted with regard to petroleum. Bolivia certainly does not possess the resources necessary to develop an oil industry on a big scale in the near future. The financial condition of the Bolivian government in 1956–1957 was not such as to attract large loans from the International Bank or the Export-Import Bank, even supposing that those institutions would have been willing to lend for the purpose. The only way in which the oil resources of the country could be brought into use quickly was through recruiting the large oil companies, which have the capital and technical know-how to do the job. Any other course would have meant the postponement, in all likelihood for a generation or more, of the full-scale exploitation of Bolivian oil reserves.

The conditions under which the oil companies have been

given concessions are not particularly onerous for Bolivia. They would seem to assure the country a sizable share in the return from the industry, though one might have wished that the fifty-fifty principle had been written more clearly into the Petroleum Code. The Code would seem to assure that the Bolivian Government and people will be partners in the foreign oil concessions in a way that they certainly never were in the Big Three tin-mining companies. Furthermore, a sizable role, particularly in the provision of petroleum for domestic needs, but also in the export field, is reserved for the government's own oil company, the Y.P.F.B., in striking contrast to the tin-mining situation during the first half of the twentieth century.

Finally, it might be well to note that the critics of the M.N.R. government are unduly pessimistic about the possibilities of other aspects of the Bolivian economy. Although petroleum is likely to become a large, and perhaps the largest single source of foreign exchange in the not-too-distant future, the rehabilitation of the mining industry will in all likelihood make its contribution to the country's foreign exchange budget rise instead of fall, and it is probable that still other sources of foreign exchange will be found. Furthermore, the M.N.R. government's work in developing other aspects of the nation's economy is likely to make the country as a whole vastly less dependent on the sale abroad of any one product than it was before 1952. Thus it seems highly dubious that the Bolivian economy will ever again depend in such a life-and-death manner as before 1952 upon the operations of a small number of foreign-owned enterprises. The oil policy of the Paz Estenssoro and Siles governments will serve to make the Bolivian economy considerably stronger and more diversified than it has ever been in the past.

Another field in which the M.N.R. government has been anxious to recruit the aid of foreign capital has been the exploitation of the nation's extensive iron resources along the Brazilian frontier. These reserves, believed to be among the world's largest, were already being exploited in the middle 1950's on the Brazilian side of the border near the city of Corumbá. The greater part of the iron range is believed to be on the Bolivian side of the river. Plans of the government in 1957 called for the establishment of a mixed company in conjunction with foreign steel firms for the development of these resources. It was believed that a ready market could be found for this iron ore in Argentina, perhaps in Brazil, and even in countries farther afield.[15]

The Siles government also was seeking to encourage the exploitation of other minerals. Gold mining was one of the most important projects, and late in 1957 there was discussion in the Bolivian Parliament of granting new concessions to United States enterprises in the field. These concessions caused a good deal of dissension, particularly upon the part of the Lechínist deputies and senators, who criticized them for being too liberal. Although there is probably justification for these complaints, the concessions were ratified by Congress.[16]

Equally as important as developing petroleum and mineral resources which could provide additional export items has been the M.N.R. government's program of developing the agricultural and grazing resources of the country, a program designed to make Bolivia more self-sufficient in foodstuffs and agricultural raw materials, as well as to provide possible new exports. This "Program of Economic Diversification," as it is generally called in Bolivia, has had three basic aspects: provision of adequate means of transportation to link producing areas with actual or potential consuming regions; encouragement of development and settlement of the Eastern two thirds of the country; and establishment of processing plants for the purpose of creating a readier market for some types of agricultural products, as well as other manufacturing establishments to meet local needs.

The Program of Economic Diversification inevitably imposed hardships on the people of Bolivia, as economic development programs always do in underdeveloped countries. President Paz Estenssoro commented on this aspect of the program in his Message to Congress in July, 1956:

> To carry out this plan it was necessary to have funds available in foreign exchange which Bolivia could not easily acquire in view of its semicolonial situation. As a result, there was no other way open than to sacrifice a part of the imports for consumption in order to acquire machinery, implements, and other capital goods.
>
> The Government of the National Revolution chose this road, fully aware of the sacrifice which it signified for all, the governors and the governed, and the political risks it implied. It did so, because with a high feeling of responsibility, it looked for the fundamental solution of the nation's problems, even though this resulted in momentary unpopularity.
>
> The sacrifice has been less than it might have been, thanks to American aid, initiated with the visit of Dr. Milton Eisenhower. That aid gave us food products and also certain sums of dollars for the importation of tractors and other elements necessary in the program of diversification.

A fundamental part of the Economic Development Program of the M.N.R. government has been the construction and improvement of the country's highway network. Some idea of the increase in this activity under Paz Estenssoro can be gathered from the fact that expenditures of the General Directorate of Highways increased from 60,000,000 *bolivianos* in 1951 to 988,000,000 *bolivianos* in 1956.[17]

The most important single project completed by the revolutionary government was the Cochabamba-Santa Cruz highway. This road, which was commenced by the administrations which preceded the M.N.R. in power, served to provide a land link for the first time between the Altiplano and valleys where most of the Bolivian people live, and the great Eastern part of the country, which has been sparsely populated and possesses vast resources which have lain all but untapped. The completion of this highway made it possible for the first time to begin to put to use the agricultural and grazing possibilities of the Santa Cruz region.

The first studies for this road were made as early as 1944, but the actual construction work moved slowly before 1952. In 1950 the project was put in the hands of the Thompson, Cornwall construction firm. The road was only 45 per cent completed when the M.N.R. government came to power, but by September, 1954, it was finished and was officially opened to traffic in a ceremony attended by leading Bolivian Government officials, as well as by Henry Holland, at that time Assistant Secretary of State for Latin American Affairs, Senator Bourke Hickenlooper, and officials of the Export-Import Bank.[18] In September, 1955, the work of asphalting the highway was begun, and by August, 1957, all but twenty miles of this job had been completed.

Under the direction of the Bolivian Development Corporation, the M.N.R. government carried out a program of constructing lateral roads connecting with the Cochabamba-Santa Cruz highway. By the end of the Paz Estenssoro administration, 207 kilometers (about 140 miles) of such roads had been built.[19]

The economic importance of the Cochabamba-Santa Cruz highway has been exceedingly great. The opening of the new highway has made available to the rest of Bolivia an area which is a potential producer of sugar, cotton, and a variety of other sub-tropical and tropical foodstuffs and agricultural raw materials. Some indication of the increase in traffic over the Cochabamba-Santa Cruz highway is shown by figures presented by President Paz Estenssoro in his Message to Congress in July, 1956.

Trucks on Cochabamba-Santa Cruz Highway

	1953	1954	1955	1956 (6 months)
From Cochabamba to Santa Cruz	2,869	6,026	8,522	3,186
From Santa Cruz to Cochabamba	3,058	5,960	7,900	3,441

Another highway of first-class importance on which construction was pushed by the M.N.R. government is the Orán-Tarija road, built by the Mixed Bolivian-Argentine Highway Commission. In 1953 some 32 miles of this road were opened to traffic, and by 1956 about 14 miles more were opened between Río Bermejo and Los Pozos. A further 15-mile piece of the road was contracted for in June, 1956, to be completed within thirty months. Studies were also completed for the extension of this road from Tarija to Potosí up in the Altiplano.[20]

The revolutionary government also undertook the extension of a highway down into the Yungas, the valley area near La Paz. The first step of this project was to extend the existing road 25 miles further into the valley. The next step into North Yungas will reach "a zone of ample valleys, with rich lands suitable for cultivating rice, yucca, coffee, cacao, and other tropical products," as President Paz Estenssoro described it.[21]

The Directorate General of Highways also continued the policy of building local roads to connect with existing highways. During the four years of the Paz administration, approximately 465 miles of road were constructed. Thirteen bridges were built on already existing roads.

The Army was used in the planning and construction of highways. It built part of the Montepunco-Puerto Villarroel road, running north from the Cochabamba-Santa Cruz highway toward a key river port, which has access to the cattle and rubber producing regions in the Department of Beni. The planning of the road had been completed by the end of the Paz Estenssoro administration, preliminary construction had been completed on 54 miles, and 25 miles had been entirely completed. The Army was also used to build a road from the mining zone of Tupiza to the agricultural region of Las Carreras, thus making easier and cheaper the transport of foodstuffs to an important mining area. This road was some 25 miles in length.[22]

In August, 1955, a considerable boost was given to the road program of the Bolivian Government by the establishment of the Servicio Cooperativo Interamericano de Caminos. This Point Four organization has as its principal task the maintenance and improvement of existing roads, and in July, 1956, it had some 2,000 miles of highway under its supervision.[23]

The construction of the Cochabamba-Santa Cruz highway made possible another important development project of the M.N.R. regime—the beginning of colonization of the Eastern section of the country, particularly in the Department of Santa Cruz. This program was put under the control of the Bolivian Development Corporation, with the establishment of the Department of Migrations as part of the Corporation. A National Commission of Migration was also provided for, with representation of various ministries concerned with the problem, as well as of international groups dealing with it.

The objectives of the migration program were stated by the Bolivian Development Corporation as follows:

a. To transport population to chosen areas in the Department of Santa Cruz.
b. To prove that the transplanting of population is possible.
c. Through the errors which are invaluable capital of an experiment, to seek a workable policy in migration.
d. To transport laborers to an area needing economic development, and transform them into permanent residents of an area where they would live by agriculture or industries which they would install.
e. These pilot projects would be the means of attracting a current of migration which in the beginning would be directed, but would soon become a normal personal and family movement.
f. To sow those crops which are appropriate to the region on a sufficient scale to feed the colonists; and to provide short-term financing for the whole project, since the country cannot de-

pend for long on foreign aid or long-term capital expenditures for the development of this colonization program.

The new Army constructed after 1953 played a key role in this colonization program. A Colonization Division, composed of four battalions, was established. In the beginning, in May, 1955, some 1,200 soldiers were in the first two battalions set up. In 1956 the number was increased to 1,800 men, but it was reduced to 800 conscripts as the result of the Stabilization Program of December, 1956.

The procedures used in the Colonization Division were described by the Bolivian Development Corporation thus:

a. The soldiers enrolled in this service are carefully chosen after a medical examination and a tuberculosis test. This site to which they are to go is explained to them, so that they may make a perfectly free choice as to whether they are to go into the Division. The great majority of those chosen are taken from the Altiplano and the valleys and only a small proportion from the East.

b. The military system is an attenuated one, the great majority of the soldiers' time being devoted to work. Military organization itself is more flexible so as to fulfill the purposes of the group.

c. Maximum United States aid is needed, so as to mechanize the work as much as possible . . . without exaggeration it can be said that the work has been done exclusively by hand, a forest of trees 15 meters or more high having been cleared, covering about 950 hectares.

d. Food for the soldiers has been calculated in a scientific manner for men doing heavy work, so as to avoid illness and death among them. At the present time the death rate is 1.5 per cent, and desertions are not more than 3 per cent.

e. Work is done in individual parcels of 17 to 20 hectares which will be given to peasants who transfer there. Along with the parcel of land, the peasant is given a house typical of the region, some implements and domestic facilities, seeds, as well as technical direction, medical assistance, drugs, and so on. The Colonization Division has fields which are sowed for the feeding of the soldiers during their year of work. All of this has a price, of which the Development Corporation absorbs 50 per cent and the peasants will pay 50 per cent during a period of not more than three years. . . .

f. Financing has been done by the Development Corporation, insofar as extra pay for officers and men is concerned, as well as medical aid for soldiers, clothing, and foodstuffs which are not produced in the zone.

g. The Ministry of Defense, in addition to paying the salaries of officers and men corresponding to their ranks in the Army, carries some other incidental expenses.

h. Titles to the plots of land given peasants are granted by the National Agrarian Reform Service, after the peasant has worked his land for three years.

In addition to the projects of the Colonization Division, the Bolivian Development Corporation has organized and supported five other colonies, two of which have had foreign colonists. By July, 1957, there were 1,885 people in all these colonies. Some 36 miles of roads had been constructed, and 344 houses had been built.

The Bolivian Development Corporation reached the following conclusions concerning the first two years of the colonization program:

a. The Plan of Internal Migration is well conceived and will be rapidly amortized.

b. After two years the results of the program are promising.

c. It is necessary to grant the program more economic aid and help for improving techniques of production, because otherwise from the strictly economic and social point of view the immense human resources of, for example, the Colonization Division, are not being used in the most efficient way.

d. It is necessary and urgent to make a serious study of the tropical products which can be sowed in that zone, considering on the one hand the market price and on the other, the possibility of short-term production.

e. It is fundamentally necessary to establish the National Migration Commission or another organization of this type in which will be represented Point Four, the United Nations, the National Agrarian Reform Institute, the Ministry of Agriculture and Colonization, the Ministry of Peasant Affairs, the Ministry of National Economy, and the Bolivian Development Corporation, which after studying the problem can draw up a national colonization plan, including areas in the Cochabamba Valley, the Department of La Paz, and the Department of Beni [as well as Santa Cruz-R.J.A.], where there are good lands available for colonization.[24]

In addition to the colonization projects, which have as their objective the establishment in Santa Cruz of a sizable peasant population, capable of growing foodstuffs not only for itself but to supply the cities in the Altiplano, the M.N.R. government bent its efforts toward extending irrigation projects which could be used for specialized types of production. Existing works in the Cochabamba region were enlarged so as to irrigate an area of 4,000 hectares, in addition to the 6,000 being watered before 1952.

In 1954 the Development Corporation began studies on a large irrigation project in Villa Montes, to the East of the city of Santa Cruz. By the end of President Paz Estenssoro's term of office, some $970,000 and 650,000,000 *bolivianos* had been spent on this project. It is designed in its first phase to irrigate some 5,000 hectares, and ultimately to take care of 5,000 hectares more. The purpose is principally to grow cotton for the Bolivian textile industry. The land of the region is said to be particularly good for cotton, but it is also thought to be able to produce soybeans, vegetables, and fruits.[25]

Considerable attention was also paid to the development of the nation's grazing industry. Before the Revolution, the Development Corporation had maintained a small Grazing Center at Reyes in the Department of Beni which, however, possessed only 60 head of native Bolivian cattle, and was ill-equipped to do the job of breeding and experimentation which was needed. The Corporation, under M.N.R. direction, began by importing 14 head of zebu cattle from Brazil, which were supplemented in 1954 by 150 cows and 40 breeding bulls of the same race. By 1955 the number of head of cattle in the Corporation's breeding farm had increased to 610. By 1956 the Reyes center had 960 head of zebu cattle and 80 crossbreeds of zebu and native stock. In that year 50 young zebu bulls were auctioned off to local grazers, and it was hoped in 1957 to have another 300 available. In addition, the government imported 120 head of zebu for sale directly to local cattle breeders.

To aid in fencing off cattle lands in both Beni and Santa Cruz, the Development Corporation imported during the Paz Estenssoro administration some 44,000 rolls of barbed wire. Another 12,177 rolls were brought in by the Servicio Agrícola Interamericano, the Point Four institution operating in the field.

The S.A.I. also took the principal responsibility for the construction of a laboratory for the development of vaccine against hoof-and-mouth disease in Ovejuyo in the Department of La Paz. A laboratory for making vaccine against diseases of hogs was also established through S.A.I. help, and the National Bacteriological Institute signed an agreement with the S.A.I. to produce these vaccines on a large scale.[26]

Another part of the development program of the M.N.R. government consisted of the construction of processing industries, to handle products of the Cochabamba and Santa Cruz regions and to begin to supply the country with products which had hitherto had to be imported. The two most important projects of this type were the sugar refinery in Santa Cruz and the milk products factory in Cochabamba.

As early as August, 1952, the Ministry of Economy asked for bids for the building of a sugar refinery according to specifications provided by the Bolivian Development Corporation. The French firm, Compagnie de Fives-Lille, received the contract to build this refinery, capable of producing 18,000 tons of sugar, and an alcohol distillery. With the help of United Nations experts, the Development Corporation chose for the site the region of Guabirá in the Department of Santa Cruz.[27]

The milk-processing plant, constructed near the city of Cochabamba, in the middle of one of the country's principal centers of milk production, was built by the Bolivian Development Corporation with the cooperation of U.N.I.C.E.F. and Point Four. Its construction began in September, 1956.[28] The project was due to be completed late in 1957, but there remained to be solved the problem of insufficient production of milk to supply the new plant.

A somewhat similar project of the Development Corporation, though not associated with agriculture, has been the cement plant which it built in Sucre. The construction of the plant was carried out by a German firm.[29] Its completion will bring the country a good deal closer to self-sufficiency in cement products than hitherto, and should be a considerable boost not only to building, but to other parts of the development program.

Another aspect of this planned diversification designed to serve both agriculture and industry was the provision of electric power. The Bolivian Development Corporation hoped in time to be able to establish a nationwide electric grid, of which municipal plants, some built by the Corporation, those of the Bolivian Power Company (serving La Paz and Oruro), and those of the mining companies would all be a part. As a first move in this direction, the Corporation sought to develop more efficiently the resources of the existing municipal electric plants in various parts of the country.

The principal step toward fulfilling this program taken during the first five years of the M.N.R. government was the strengthening of the Cochabamba municipal system, with the provision of enough Diesel motors to meet the city's needs more or less adequately until 1959, and the commencement of a large hydroelectric project to serve the

Cochabamba region thereafter.[30] This hydroelectric plant will be able to supply 16,000 kilowatts of electricity when it is completed.

The government also signed agreements with the Bolivian Power Company, that the latter should set up two new electric plants for mining operations, providing a potential of 7,833 kilowatts, and another plant for more general use at Sainani near Oruro, providing 10,000 kilowatts. In sum, the installed capacity of the country increased from 141,929 kilowatts in December, 1951, to 175,966 kilowatts in June, 1956.[31]

The Program of Economic Diversification, launched by the Paz Estenssoro administration, was seriously curtailed, at least temporarily, by the Stabilization Program of December, 1956. As part of a general attempt to balance the government's budget and to bring the demand for goods and services more nearly into equilibrium with their supply, many of the development projects were temporarily suspended or were seriously reduced.

The Stabilization Program called for the temporary cessation of all projects of the Bolivian Development Corporation which were not at least 75 per cent completed. As a result, the hydroelectric project near Cochabamba, the irrigation project beyond Santa Cruz, and some of the road-building projects came to a halt for the time being. The size of the Colonization Battalion was reduced by half, and so far as the colonies already established were concerned, it was decided to maintain them on a stand-by basis, but not to begin any new ones or increase the size of existing ones. Temporarily, peasants who wished to migrate to the colonies were discouraged from doing so. The parts of the diversification program which were continued included the paving of the Cochabamba-Santa Cruz road, the construction of one other minor road, the building of the cement factory in Sucre, and the completion of the sugar refinery near Santa Cruz.[32]

The slowing down of the development program engendered a great deal of bitter political opposition. Moreover, at least some of the experts of the International Cooperation Administration came to the conclusion that to hold up the work toward diversifying Bolivia's economy was a poor way to curb inflation. As a result, most of the program was renewed in January, 1958.

Another step taken in late 1957 and early 1958 which was of great importance for the future economic development of Bolivia was the elaboration of a Three Year Emergency Plan of Economic Development. During the Paz Estenssoro administration and the first year of the Siles government the regime's Economic Development Program had been conducted without much organized central direction. Each project had been treated on its merits, and there was little effort to establish a systematic arrangement of priorities.

In all probability, the M.N.R. government lacked during its first years in power the proper information on which to base an overall development plan. All too little was known about the economy as a whole, and there was little way to decide which things should come first and which should be left for the future. However, in 1957 two reports were prepared, surveying exhaustively all aspects of the Bolivian economy, and these reports made available for the first time the requisite information for the drawing up of a detailed plan. One report was prepared for the International Cooperation Administration by Mr. C. Zondag, the other by an international group of experts for the Economic Commission for Latin America.

The purpose of the Three Year Emergency Plan of Economic Development was to isolate those problems which constituted the most serious bottlenecks for future development, and to try to attack them in a comparatively short period of time. It was felt that only then could an overall development plan, taking into account the needs of every sector of the economy, be undertaken.[33]

Thus the M.N.R. government had sought to carry out its plans for "economic independence" through a varied program of developing the country's resources and diversifying its economy. In the opening up of one of the most important of the nation's resources, petroleum, it had chosen to accept the aid of the large international oil companies, on terms which it felt would provide Bolivia with a fair return for exploiting this valuable fuel. In doing so, the government hoped that the exploitation and export of oil would in fairly short order end the dire shortage of foreign exchange with which the country had been cursed ever since the Chaco War and the beginning of the decline of the tin industry.

At the same time, it launched its program of developing a transportation system which would create a truly national market for the country's agricultural production, while at the same time trying to diversify and extend that production by opening up new areas in the East and in the valleys. Finally, the M.N.R. government sought to make a beginning in the provision of processing facilities for the country's agricultural products, and sufficient electric power for both agriculture and manufacturing.

10 . . .

The Crisis in Industry

Logically, one might suppose that the manufacturers of Bolivia would have given the National Revolution their blessing and their support. The leaders of the M.N.R. had always conceived of their party as one representing "the workers, peasants, and people of the middle class." The M.N.R. government made possible for the first time a truly national market for the products of Bolivian industry. It was anxious to encourage the development and diversification of the nation's economy, which should logically redound to the benefit of the country's manufacturing interests.

However, the industrialists have by and large been bitterly opposed to the regime of the Movimiento Nacionalista Revolucionario. Upon occasion, they have even gone so far as to plot, in a rather ineffectual way, its overthrow. The reasons for this are to be found in the history of the development of Bolivian industry, particularly in the period after the Chaco War.

Industrialization began in a more or less serious way in the early 1920's, but by the time of the National Revolution, thirty years later, Bolivian manufacturing was still of relatively minor importance in the country's economy. In 1954 some 55,000 workers were officially recorded as being employed in manufacturing, of whom only 20,000 were employed in "registered" establishments, recognized by the government as being factories. There is little doubt that the majority of the manufacturing goods consumed in the country were still being produced by handicraft methods.

The Economic Commission for Latin America, in its report on the Bolivian economy, has given the following figures on employment in registered Bolivian industries as of the year 1954:

Employment in Bolivian Industry

BRANCH OF INDUSTRY	WHITE-COLLAR WORKERS	MANUAL WORKERS	TOTAL	TOTAL WAGES (IN THOUSAND *Bolivianos*)	AVERAGE WAGE	VALUE ADDED PER WORKER
Foodstuffs	428	2,834	3,262	466,886	143.1	447.3
Beverages	678	1,828	2,506	404,273	161.2	1,066.9
Tobacco	30	119	149	32,970	221.3	5,715.6
Textiles and Related Products	509	5,770	6,279	1,144,036	182.2	655.6
Leather	266	1,819	587	332,056	159.3	515.1
Wood and Furniture	76	511	735	78,570	133.8	276.9
Paper and Derivatives	117	618	158	128,544	174.9	481.9
Rubber	28	130	923	37,427	173.6	387.8
Chemicals	119	724	1,598	224,659	243.4	571.2
Cement, Glass and Ceramics	183	1,415	620	260,304	162.9	417.4
Metal Industries	96	524	97	100,759	162.5	245.1
Others	26	71		20,082	207.0	1,582.7
TOTAL	2,636	16,363	18,999	3,220,586	177.1	650.8[1]

These figures indicate the limited development of Bolivian manufacturing. They also show the concentration of industry in a few fields: textiles, foodstuffs, beverages, leather, and cement. Finally, they give some idea of the relatively small plants which characterize Bolivian secondary industry.

The reasons for this limited development of Bolivian industry are several. It is probable that the unsettled political conditions which marked Bolivian history after the Chaco War served to stifle whatever interest there might have been among foreign firms in establishing branches in Bolivia. Much more fundamental was the fact that the Bolivian market was extremely small. The total population of Bolivia probably does not exceed 3,000,000 to 3,500,000 people, and before 1952 only a very small part of this total population was in the market for anything which industry had to sell. It has been estimated that "the market" in Bolivia before the National Revolution did not amount to more than 500,000 to 600,000 people, in the cities and larger towns.

The result of this situation was very small consumption of manufactured goods per capita. The Economic Commission for Latin America's report gives figures comparing consumption per capita in Bolivia and that in another South American country in a considerably more advanced stage of development, Colombia. According to these figures, Colombia in 1953 consumed approximately 16.6 meters of cotton cloth per person, whereas Bolivia used only 6.8 meters in 1954; Colombia consumed three meters of silk and artificial fibers and Bolivia only one; Colombians drank 35.5 liters of beer and Bolivians only 11; Colombia used 72.3 kilograms of cement per person and Bolivia only 10.7.[2]

An additional factor in the backwardness of Bolivian industry was the shortage of foreign exchange, which acted as a hindrance to bringing in new and more modern equipment for Bolivian manufacturing. Between 1950 and 1955 only about $4,000,000 a year was spent for this purpose, representing about 13 per cent of the value of Bolivian manufacturing output during this period. This compares with expenditures on capital equipment by Colombia during the same period of the equivalent of 24.9 per cent of industrial output.[3]

However, of greater importance than any of these factors was the situation in which Bolivian industry had been functioning ever since the Chaco War, and particularly during the 1950's. Manufacturing industry had been allowed to import raw materials at favorable exchange rates, ever since the *boliviano* began slipping seriously in value after the Chaco War. By the middle 1950's the special exchange rate given to Bolivian manufacturers for the importation of raw materials had created a highly artificial and even bizarre situation. In 1956, for instance, industry was still able to import raw materials at an exchange rate of 190 *bolivianos* to the dollar, whereas the "free market" rate was as high as 13,000 to the dollar.

This led to various unhappy results. In the first place, there is no doubt that the favorable rate of foreign exchange was abused by many manufacturers and was used as a means to facilitate the escape of capital from the country. Manufacturers would request amounts of foreign exchange much in excess of what they really intended to use to import raw materials for their plants. The excess dollars would then be deposited in banks or invested in other ways in the dollar area.

In the second place, the favorable exchange rate created a situation in which the manufacturers were all but oblivious to cost and efficiency factors in the management of their plants. Since they received raw materials at ridiculously low cost, they could afford to tolerate all kinds of inefficiency in management and on the part of their labor force. They could without difficulty pay workers for doing nothing, and they had little incentive to improve the organization or the equipment of their plants.

In the third place, Bolivian manufacturers could sell

everything they could turn out. The artificial exchange rate contributed to this situation, and the inflation did the rest. Inflation assured them of ever-increasing prices in *bolivianos* for their products. Although prices were running away, so were wages and salaries, and the manufacturers' markets in the cities and larger towns of Bolivia suffered little if at all from the inflation. Furthermore, the inordinate cheapness of their raw materials made the prices of the Bolivian manufacturers' products very low in terms of the currencies of neighboring countries.

The result was that during the 1950's a large part of the output of Bolivian industry was being sold abroad, surreptitiously. Although the manufacturers themselves claimed that they were not smuggling goods abroad, they certainly were selling large quantities of produce to small smugglers, who made a business of selling them in Peru, Chile, Argentina, and Brazil.

The upshot of all this was that the Bolivian manufacturers forgot how to be entrepreneurs. Not only did they adopt a careless attitude toward the management of their enterprises, they made little effort to sell their goods. They did not have to do so; the goods seemed to sell themselves. A number of Bolivian manufacturers have agreed with the author on this point and have gone further, to point out that the *Turco*, that ubiquitous Arab peddler who in times past had taken nationally manufactured goods as well as imported products into the furthest reaches of the country and had beat up trade in the most isolated areas, had virtually disappeared by the 1950's.

Under these circumstances, there was little real incentive for the manufacturers to try to expand or modernize their enterprises. There was no reason, since they were getting a very good income both in *bolivianos* and in dollars from their factories as they were, why they should put aside funds for expansion, when they could use them for consumption and apparently never suffer the consequences.

Indeed, the industrialists were living well. They were able in one way or another to get their expensive cars, build their fine houses, take not infrequent trips—official and otherwise —to foreign countries, and send their children abroad for an education. They seemed to live in the best of all possible worlds.

However, this situation could not go on forever. The National Revolution itself was a severe jolt to the complacency of the manufacturers. With the events of April 9, 1952, the labor movement became the pillar upon which the new government rested. One of the most important parts of the labor movement was the Confederación Sindical de Trabajadores Fabriles, made up of the nation's factory workers.

There is little doubt that in relations between the unions and the factory owners after April 9, the unions had the upper hand. More interested in political than in economic questions, the union leaders frequently made a bad situation worse by circumscribing those few industrialists who were seeking to make their factories more efficient, who were trying to adopt labor-saving machines and methods. The unions forced the employers to take on more workers than they needed. Discipline in the factories deteriorated. Disputes between employers and unions were almost always settled in favor of the latter. Demands for wage increases were insistent.

The reaction of the industrialists to this situation was in many cases to denounce the government privately and, when possible, publicly. This was certainly the procedure of the principal spokesmen for Bolivian industry, and although there were exceptions, industrialists who tried to meet the new situation by refurbishing their entrepreneurial skills, they did not get the public attention which the others received.

With the Stabilization Program of December, 1956, a full-blown crisis faced Bolivian industry. A single rate of exchange was established, and overnight the industrialists' privilege to import goods virtually for nothing disappeared. Most of the industrialists—though they were warned some time in advance of what was to occur—did little to meet this situation. They were, in fact, taken by surprise, since they did not believe that the government was serious in its announced intentions.

The immediate result of the Stabilization Program was disastrous for manufacturing industry. Not only did the contraband markets in neighboring countries disappear, but the Bolivian market was severely restricted as a result of the limitation on wages imposed by the Program. Furthermore, the Bolivian manufacturers were now faced with surreptitious introduction of foreign-made goods into Bolivia by the same channels which had formerly taken their goods abroad, since these foreign manufacturers were suddenly cheaper than locally produced goods of the same kind.

The official spokesmen for industry met this situation with but one demand: the right to fire workers whom they now did not need. This right the government would not give them. Although it did say that the work force of any plant could be reduced to the number of workers employed at the end of 1954, the Siles administration refused to give the manufacturers *carte blanche* to dismiss any number of workers they desired. Quite rightly, the government said that before they would talk about this possibility, the employers must take steps to try to put their own house in order.

Some manufacturers did do so. Some time before the inauguration of the Stabilization Program the Bolivian Government had obtained through the International Labor Office the services of an expert on industrial productivity. He was successful in working with several dozen of the country's smaller industrialists and helping them to rationalize their production, organize the machinery and chain of production in their plants more efficiently, make better use of their labor force. The result was a very heartening one for these firms, several of which were able within a few months to turn a deficit into a sizable profit.

However, the spokesmen for Bolivian industry, and in particular the Cámara Nacional de Industrias in La Paz, indignantly refused to take this line of attack on the problem seriously. They made official charges to the Bolivian Government and to the International Labor Organization that the I.L.O. productivity expert was a "Communist" and "sided with the workers," and they refused to have anything to do with him. In conversations with the author some of these same industrialists insisted that the increase of labor productivity was no concern of theirs, that it was up to the workers themselves to increase their output.

The trade union leaders, particularly the second-rank officials, took a rather different attitude toward the problem of labor productivity. During a Labor Seminar organized by the International Cooperation Administration, the International Labor Organization, and the Bolivian Ministry of Labor, in La Paz in July, 1957, the trade unionists there expressed vital interest in the problem of increasing productivity. They realized, after the failure of the July 1 strike movement, that the only way in which the standard of living of their unions' members could be increased was by raising the level of output of the Bolivian economy. There seemed to the author to be a real willingness to cooperate with the employers and the government in trying to come to grips with this problem.

There is no doubt that the problems of Bolivian industry will have to be met by cooperation of all three parties—the industrialists, their workers, and the State. There is also little doubt that during the first few months after the Stabilization Program went into effect, there was little effort made by any of the three parties to try to establish the bases for such cooperation.

The long-run prospects for Bolivian industry have been made a good deal brighter by the policies of the government of the National Revolution. The Agrarian Reform and Economic Development Programs promise to make possible the creation for the first time of a national market, and once the foreign exchange shortage is overcome, the prospects for re-equipping existing industries and building new ones should be bright.

However, these possibilities cannot become actualities unless the manufacturers do their share. This involves two basic moves: reorganization of production; and an active program to develop a market for the goods produced by Bolivian industry.

There is no doubt that much could be done in Bolivian industry to use available equipment to better advantage. Most plants have "just growed," without any very great consideration being given to placing machinery in the most advantageous way and organizing the supply of materials most propitiously. It should be possible, through the United States Point Four Mission or through the United Nations Technical Assistance Mission in Bolivia, to supply a handful of experts who could advise the Bolivian industrialists on how to make their plants more efficient. Of course, the industrialists must first be willing to accept such advice.

The problem of excess labor is not an insurmountable one, and could be dealt with in several ways. It has been suggested, for instance, that with the assistance of the Servicio Cooperativo Interamericano de Educación, apprenticeship and other training courses could be organized for many of the workers involved. Since the employers must have these people on their payrolls in any case, progress would be made if they could be employed in obtaining or improving skills, in the period which will lapse until they can be adequately absorbed into production.

The overall problem of excessive workers is not very large in absolute terms. At most, it probably involves three thousand workers, who should in a reasonably short time be absorbed in expansion of existing industries and the establishment of new ones. The government, when this expansion of industry begins to take place, will undoubtedly have to relax its stern attitude toward the dismissal of excess employees, thus making it possible to shift them to places where they can be more usefully employed.

The excess labor problem, in any case, is being settled by some of the employers who are least vociferous in complaining about it. The author visited one factory where a considerable reduction in staff had been accomplished by the expedients of not filling jobs left vacant and of keeping a close watch on stealing by employees, catching those who stole red-handed, and dismissing them—with the Ministry of Labor's approval.

The expansion of Bolivian industry depends a great deal on the ability of Bolivian manufacturers to acquire new markets. Until 1957 the manufacturers apparently had thought very little about this problem. The author addressed a meeting of the Cámara Nacional de Industrias in August, 1957, and, in his discussion he laid considerable stress on the possibilities for expanding the market for Bolivian manufacturers among the Indians and in the smaller towns and villages. Many of those present regarded this as virtually a new idea, which they were encountering for the first time, and which was worthy of consideration and action. Such action is likely to net the Bolivian industrialists new markets of which they have not dreamed.

There is no doubt that the M.N.R. government's policies, and particularly the Agrarian Reform Program, have created potential markets greater than Bolivian industrialists have ever before enjoyed within the country. The possible effects of changes in agriculture on the Bolivian economy were foreseen by the Keenleyside *Report,* written more than a year before the National Revolution.

The static nature of Bolivian agriculture has tended to impede —if not to arrest—the ordinary course of economic development.

The impulse to modernization of economic life is usually provided by the export of raw materials or food, the proceeds of such exports being gradually used for the purpose of overall social investment in highways, railroads, power plants, etc. At the same time, an expanding industrial and urban population offers markets for food and other agricultural products. This stimulus to agriculture tends to lead to more intensive and more effective production, creating a food surplus. But, on the other hand, the growth of agricultural income creates new purchasing power and effective demand for the products of local industry. Gradually capital is invested in an ever-widening range of domestic manufacturing and a mature economy is attained. The economy as a whole is transformed into an integrated market system with interlocking, partly new, circuits of exchange.

It is easy to understand, therefore, that the failure of Bolivian agriculture to respond to the classical economic stimuli represents a serious impediment to the progress of supplementary industrial activities at a rate sufficiently rapid to permit substantial improvements in income per head of the population. . . .[4]

The effects of changes in agriculture had already begun to be felt by late 1956. The Economic Commission for Latin America's report on the Bolivian economy has noted this effect:

In Bolivia other factors will tend to give great dynamism to demand; above all, the profound transformations in the social field, and in the distribution of income, thanks to a considerable degree to the agrarian reform, which in practice is already resulting in a gradual incorporation of the rural population into the monetary economy and new forms of consumption. . . . The low levels of actual consumption and the tendencies toward redistribution of income would thus indicate that the need for manufactured consumers' goods will tend to increase in the future much more rapidly than the total income. Thus, once the immediate crisis is overcome, industry will have to face a growing and diversified demand for consumers goods; in other words, the problem will change from one of a small industrial sector seeking to partially fill the needs of a small part of the population to an industry which will face an increasing demand on the part of the whole population of the country.[5]

Even before the agrarian reform decree of August 2, 1953, the Indian peasants began to have a money income which they never had enjoyed before. Through the peasant unions, contracts were negotiated with landlords which provided for the peasants to receive wages for working on the land-lords' acres. With some of the land passing into the hands of the peasants, they had income from selling their produce, and at the same time, in many instances, continued to earn wages for working that part of the land which had not yet been divided.

The first evidences of the entry of the Indian into the market were already visible before the Stabilization Program went into effect in December, 1956. Many hundreds, per-haps thousands, of Indians had purchased bicycles; others had bought radios—even in areas where there was no elec-tricity. Some had bought glass to put windows on their huts for the first time. Although these developments were on a small scale, they were indicative of what was to come.

As the agrarian reform progresses, and more land comes into the hands of the Indian peasant, he will in all likelihood have increasing amounts of money income to spend. He will become increasingly anxious to buy the city man's goods. This will be the industrialists' big opportunity.

The kind of industries which might be developed in Bo-livia were indicated in the Keenleyside *Report* before the National Revolution:

In view of the scarcity of capital, and more particularly of for-eign exchange, it is desirable that in the development of industry priority should be given to such branches as, while requiring a relatively small capital outlay, are able to effect substantial sav-ings in foreign exchange, needed for further development work. Emphasis has been laid above on the urgent need of encouraging domestic production of food and agricultural raw materials such as cotton and wool. The next logical step is to encourage the processing of domestically produced raw materials . . . thus there is need for sugar and oil mills, sawmills, cotton and wool spinneries and similar plants. The possibility of domestic refining of ores should be further considered. Immediately after, and even simultaneously with, these developments, the creation of enterprises capable of producing processed raw materials needed in general development work should be encouraged. Typical examples are cement factories, the existing capacity of which stands in need of expansion; local production of bricks and tiles should also be expanded. Encouragement of industries producing simple goods for popular consumption (e.g., textile and shoe factories, household goods and furniture factories) should follow closely.[6]

However, the industrialists themselves have an important part to play in the development of this Indian market. For one thing, the Indians are unaccustomed to having much money income, and many of them will undoubtedly spend their *bolivianos* on things which will have no impact on the economy of the cities. There is, for example, the tradition among the Indians of celebrating certain holidays with a maximum of drink and festivity, and many hundreds of millions of *bolivianos* will undoubtedly be spent on these fiestas.

The industrialists have an educational job to do among the peasants. They will have to let the Indians know what there is to buy with their newly won *bolivianos*. They will have particularly to take textiles, shoes, simple household implements, and other products to the Indian women who, as in most societies, will be able to bring pressure on their husbands to spend their *billetes* on something other than traditional festivities.

In order to do this, the manufacturers will once again have to learn the art of salesmanship. They can no longer be content to sit in their factory offices and await their customers. They will have to go out and sell, take the goods to the consumer, and be able to sell them at prices which will be attractive.

That this is possible, there is little doubt. A few industrialists had already undertaken sales campaigns in 1957, with notable success. There was evidence on every side that much more could be accomplished in this direction. One of the industrialists attending the meeting of the Cámara Nacional de Industrias which the author addressed recounted an experience he had had in a small town in an isolated part of the Altiplano. A truckload of wares had been brought from La Paz to the town market by some enterprising entrepreneur, and the goods on the truck were sold almost as quickly as they could be unloaded. The people at the market, mainly women, were starved for goods to buy.

Sales campaigns by the industrialists will have a snowball effect. Once the Indians become aware of what they can buy with their *bolivianos*, they will be anxious to get more money. They will thus be interested in improving their output of agricultural products, so as to have more to bring to market, more income with which to purchase manufactured goods. The industrialists can thus play an important role in overcoming the Indian peasant's traditional resistance to change, and his tendency to cultivate only what wheat or corn or potatoes are necessary to feed himself and his family.

Thus the development of industry and agriculture are interdependent. The pushing of sales of industrial goods in the countryside will stimulate the production of foodstuffs and agricultural raw materials for the cities, and thus will relieve the excessive dependence of the urban areas on imported agricultural products. At the same time, the development of peasant agriculture will be a boon for the industries of the cities, providing them with an ever-expanding market.

The government also has an important role to play in the development of industry, a role to which it did not pay enough attention during the first five or six years of the National Revolution. With the revival of industry, there will undoubtedly be an increasing demand on the part of the manufacturers for machinery and other capital equipment to refurbish and expand their factories. The government should be in a position to meet this demand.

Several industrialists to whom the author has talked have urged the necessity of setting up some kind of institution for the financing of industrial expansion. These industrialists were suspicious of the government and dubious about its being willing to undertake the establishment of such an institution; they urged that it be established by the industrialists themselves. However, if developments in other Latin American countries are any indication, this is a role which the Bolivian Government could well perform.

In all probability the best way to approach this problem would be through the Bolivian Development Corporation. Although when the Corporation was originally established, it was conceived of as an organization which could make loans to, invest in, and otherwise help manufacturing industries, it never assumed much importance in this field. Its efforts were concentrated on road construction, electric power, and agricultural development.[7]

The fact that the official government agencies had failed to play the role expected of them before the National Revolution was highlighted by the Keenleyside *Report:*

At the present time the government's main efforts to aid economic development in the country are channeled through the Bolivian Development Corporation . . . the Commercial Department of the Central Bank, and the two State banks of Mining and Agriculture. . . . For reasons which cannot be analyzed in detail here, these institutions have failed to perform, except to a very limited extent, the functions with which they were originally entrusted. The Bolivian Development Corporation, according to the intention of the charter, should use its funds only in self-liquidating projects and should encourage the purchase by private interests of successful projects established by it. In fact, its assets have became frozen in loans to the government for road construction and for a number of other projects which have not proved self-liquidating. The Corporación has become a holding company saddled with assets of doubtful value. . . .[8]

However, it would seem logical for the Bolivian Development Corporation to set up a department specifically designed to aid manufacturing. Following the example of the Chilean Development Corporation, it might well use a variety of methods in forwarding industrialization. It might in some cases extend loans to industries—in foreign currencies or in *bolivianos*, depending on the case; it might seek out foreign firms which would be willing to go into partnership with Bolivian enterprises needing increased capitalization; it might itself invest directly in such firms; or in some cases it might set up industries which it might later sell to Bolivian private enterprise. The Chileans have used all these methods of operation.

Of course, for some years shortages of foreign exchange are likely to hamper Bolivian industrial development, as they will the growth of all other aspects of the economy. However, when this problem has been overcome—through the development of the oil industry, the revival of mining or some other means—there should be in existence some institution like the Development Corporation, which can in an orderly way channel some of the foreign exchange in the direction of needed industries.

This will be of particular importance when the time comes to move from consumers' goods industries into light machinery and similar producers' goods. This will be a new field, in which Bolivian industrialists will have had little experience, and some aid in mustering capital and technical skill will in all likelihood be necessary.

Thus the crisis in industry which has marked the first years of the M.N.R. regime, and was particularly acute during 1957, will in all likelihood prove to be a passing phase. The crisis calls for a return by the Bolivian industrialists to being aggressive entrepreneurs, for the continuance and stepping up of the agrarian reform, and for a wise policy on the part of the government of encouraging industrialization. If such policies are followed in the future, Bolivian industrialists should profit, as did their Mexican counterparts, from the ending of feudalism and the entry of their country into the economic and social life of the twentieth century.

Inflation and the Stabilization Crisis of 1957

The specter of inflation haunted the National Revolution from the beginning. Prices had been rising ever since the Great Depression, though between 1931 and 1952 increases had been relatively gentle. The rapidity of the inflationary spiral had varied at different periods. After 1952 the tendency of the value of the *boliviano* to decline got out of hand, and inflation assumed agonizing proportions.

Difficulties began in 1931 when Bolivia, faced with a drain on her foreign exchange, went off the gold standard, suspended payment on her foreign debt, and began the policy of financing government deficits through borrowing from the Central Bank. During the Chaco War of 1932–1936 the government was forced to raise much of the money needed to conduct the conflict by borrowing, but the inflationary pressure was somewhat relieved by the fact that investment fell off drastically.

Between the Chaco War and World War II, the same process continued, due to the fact that government expenditures rose more rapidly than the tax revenue to cover them, and prices rose more rapidly than they had during the conflict with Paraguay. During World War II internal inflationary pressures were augmented by foreign influences which intensified still further the rise in Bolivian prices. Finally, in the years preceding the National Revolution, an unfavorable trade balance and devaluation of the currency, combined with continuing government deficits financed by borrowing, brought about a continuance of the upward movement of prices.[1]

The advent of the revolutionary government served to intensify the already decided drift toward inflation. The Economic Commission for Latin America's report on the Bolivian economy explains why this was the case:

The essential elements of the Bolivian economy have not changed, and the country continues to depend on export of tin and a few other minerals, the productivity of agriculture remains low, the development of industry is incipient, and other traditional features remain. But in each of these activities and in the direction of the country changes have taken place which have altered the fundamental picture of the economy. To the external factors which in the past brought about price increases and the traditional factors tending towards disequilibrium and inflation have been added during the last five years aspirations towards social egalitarianism, a nationalistic mining policy, a hitherto unknown influence on the part of the trade unions, a radical redistribution of the land, and a program of public investment which demands resources superior to the financial possibilities of the government. The combined action of all of these forces at a time when the situation in foreign markets for the principal export products has not been favorable, has resulted in an aggravation of internal disequilibrium and an intensification of the inflationary process.[2]

According to the E.C.L.A. report, the annual increase in the cost of living in La Paz between 1952 and 1956 was 147.6 per cent. Ths is the most rapid increase in prices in Bolivian history, comparing with a 50.7 per cent annual increase between 1936 and 1939, and the rise of 18.3 per cent per annum between 1945 and 1952. In 1954 and 1955 the inflation was intensified. Prices rose 99 per cent in the former year and 69 per cent in the latter. In 1956 they went up 196 per cent during the first ten months of the year.

The worst price increases were in foodstuffs, followed by clothing. The prices of services rose more slowly in 1953–1954 than did other items, but in 1955 and 1956 they, too, rose very rapidly. Only rents remained more or less stable during all of this period, having been frozen by the government in 1953.

Price inflation was accompanied by a large increase in the circulating medium—2,000 per cent between the end of 1952 and October, 1956. The increase in money supply was much more rapid in 1956 than in preceding years.

Of course, the increase in prices and in currency circulation was accompanied by a catastrophic decrease in the foreign exchange value of the *boliviano*. In 1952 the free market rate of the *boliviano* was more or less stable at between 210 and 215 to the dollar. By the end of October, 1956, the *boliviano* was selling in the free market at between 10,000 and 11,000 to the dollar.[3]

There were various causes for this tremendously rapid increase in prices and decrease in the value of the *boliviano*. One of the most important was the situation of the mining industry. Not only was it faced with a serious decline in international market prices—from $1.21 per pound of tin in 1952 to approximately ninety cents in most of the succeeding period—but also it had problems of decreasing production of most of the minerals it mined. Furthermore, the mining industry had greatly increased expenses, particularly in relation to its social welfare program and its company stores for workers. The result was that the Corporación Minera de Bolivia borrowed very heavily from the Central Bank, such loans rising from 2,163,000,000 *bolivianos* in 1952 to 84,095,000,000 *bolivianos* during the first six months of 1956.[4]

During the first four and a half years of the revolutionary regime, there was also a tremendous expansion of government borrowing from the Banco Central for purposes in addition to subsidies for the mining industry. Advances were also made to the "autonomous" institutions of the government, such as the COMIBOL and Y.P.F.B., and to the departmental and municipal administrations. Between December, 1952, and October, 1956, these loans mounted from 7,521,400,000 *bolivianos* to 204,604,100,000 *bolivianos*.[5]

At the same time, there was a great increase in credit to private commercial and industrial institutions. Advances from the commerical banks for this purpose rose from 1,434,-400,000 in December, 1951, to 11,907,400,000 *bolivianos* in June, 1956. At the same time the Central Bank had increased its loans to the private sector of the economy from 697,300,-000 *bolivianos* on the first date to 5,990,800,000 on the second. The total increase to the private sector had thus been from 2,131,700,000 to 11,907,400,000 *bolivianos* in four and a half years. The average annual increase during this period was 46.56 per cent.[6]

There is little doubt that the multiple exchange rate which continued to characterize the Bolivian economy even after the Stabilization Program of 1953 also contributed to the inflationary pressure and the decline in the exchange value of the *boliviano*. The E.C.L.A. report has summed up the influence of this system of exchange:

. . . the diversity of foreign exchange rates contributed to the formation of a structure of relative internal prices—and their relation to markets in neighboring countries—which resulted in diversion from the internal market of sizable amounts of goods, and speculation in articles of prime necessity. Furthermore, the subsidy of imports of articles of prime necessity established by the exchange system brought about a disruption of national production of these articles.[7]

Since importers of raw materials and foodstuffs were given the benefit of the artificially established "official" exchange rate of 190 *bolivianos* to the dollar, which particularly in the later years of the inflation meant that they received these goods virtually for nothing, this created a situation in which goods produced from these raw materials were substantially cheaper in Peru and other neighboring countries than the national products of those countries. This fact stimulated contraband sale of Bolivian goods across national frontiers, as has been seen.

The effect of inflation on normal economic activity in Bolivia was well described by the Keenleyside *Report,* even before the Revolution:

In Bolivia, where inflation is already an old and familiar phenomenon, it seems certain that it has reduced voluntary savings, more than it may have increased forced savings. The ordinary channels of voluntary savings have been clogged by lack of use. Businessmen avoid the holding of liquid balances in local currency; the bond market—never highly developed—has atrophied; there is a general desire either to transform money into foreign currency (capital flight) and real assets, or to use it for short-term speculative purposes.[8]

Thus what had occurred in Bolivia during the first four and a half years of the M.N.R. regime was that an increasingly large amount of spending power had been seeking to purchase a declining amount of available goods and services. Under these conditions, a rapid increase in prices was inevitable.

By the end of the Paz Estenssoro administration inflation had got out of hand. One of the early jobs of Paz Estenssoro's successor, President Hernán Siles, was to come to grips with this problem. He did so in December, 1956, when he launched the famous Stabilization Program.

This was not the first time that the government of the National Revolution had undertaken a Stabilization Program. Under Paz Estenssoro an attempt had been made on May 14, 1953, to put a brake on inflation, by a modification of the system of five different rates of foreign exchange for the United States dollar then in operation, and other measures.

The 1953 Stabilization Program was outlined in the Memorandum presented by the Government of Bolivia to the Mission headed by Milton Eisenhower, on July 19, 1953. It said (pp. 35–37):

The Stabilization had two purposes:

a. To liquidate the multiple exchange rates.
b. To wipe out the budgetary deficit.

Consumption had to be reduced in order to create a new, healthier balance between consumption and production. This could only be obtained by decreasing the demand for money. . . . If the new price level is higher than the new wage level, and both are frozen at the moment of the Stabilization, the real purchasing power of the public will decline.

Deflation is always an unpopular measure, and it is especially unpopular when it is accompanied by an increase of 150 per cent in the price of bread.

The new, unified rate of exchange is Bs. 190 for the dollar. One of the decrees authorized the importers, the industrial and agricultural producers to include in their costs all additional expenditures resulting from Stabilization. Thus the price level increased by about 100 to 150 per cent. The same decree established the maximum prices for basic food necessities.

Every salaried person was granted a flat "cost of living allowance" of Bs. 4,000 per month. This means an average salary increase of about 70 to 80 per cent. The rich got relatively less than the poor, but the latter need it more, especially because the flat increase covers, at the maximum, the price increases of the most important food items only.

All additional wage increases have been suspended for a period of six months. Thus, prices and wages are frozen at their new levels.

The new rate of exchange resulted in substantial additional expenditures for the national budget, too. Although some direct taxes had already been considerably increased before the Stabilization, their yield could not balance the new deficit. The government took the following additional measures:

a. The Bolivian Mining Corporation will pay an additional tax of Bs. 35 for each dollar it receives.
b. The importers of "semi-essentials" and nonessentials will have to pay an additional customs duty of 50 and 100 per cent respectively, calculated on the C.I.F. value of the merchandise.

These new, extremely heavy taxes have already begun to show results. They allow the government to hope that the 1953 budget will be balanced, for the first time since 1946.

The hopes of the Paz Estenssoro government for the effects of its Stabilization Program proved illusory. The foreign exchange value of the *boliviano* continued to fall, even more sharply than before. Prices continued to skyrocket. The unreal situation of the Bolivian economy became increasingly complicated and chaotic.

The economic measures undertaken by President Siles were recommended to him by an American, George Jackson Eder, who had been brought down by the United States International Cooperation Administration to study the price situation and suggest steps to bring the economy back onto a more even keel.

Eder did not make himself popular. The measures which he recommended were extremely drastic, and in the months that followed the launching of the Stabilization Program, Mr. Eder frequently felt called upon to defend his recommendations to the press and public. In doing so he erred on the side of brusqueness and brought upon himself the charge from the opponents of the program of "foreign intervention" in the internal affairs of Bolivia. The author remembers attending a meeting of the Central Obrera Boliviana where one of the ex-Trotskyite leaders of that organization commented that the Bolivian Revolution had had its Thermidor, with the launching of the Stabilization Program, and that the nation had the dubious distinction that its Napoleon was not even a citizen, that he was George Jackson Eder.

It is doubtful, however, if even a more tactful man could have defended the Stabilization Program without incurring some enmity from groups which felt their interests harmed by it. The measures taken in December, 1956, were Draconian and could not help but cause discontent in some quarters.

As announced by the Bolivian Embassy in Washington, in a press release of December 13, 1956, the Stabilization Program was as follows:

1. Adoption of an over-all balanced budget policy by the government, commencing with the 1957 budget. This will entail a 40 per cent cutback in government expenditures on imports and increased taxes on exports, imports, and domestic goods. Although some deficit will still remain, this will be covered by counterpart funds derived from sales to the public of U.S. aid shipments, largely agricultural commodities and equipment. Previously, Bolivian currency realized from sales of U.S. commodities to consumers was used to defray domestic costs of developmental projects within the country. The bulk of these funds will now be diverted to balance budgetary expenditures.

2. Elimination of the deficits of the major autonomous government agencies—the Mining Corporation, Mining Bank, the railroads, and the Petroleum Corporation (Y.P.F.B.). This will involve stricter limitation on their foreign purchases and discontinuance of their subsidized commissary system, which it is estimated has cost the government billions of *bolivianos*. Imports will be limited to those essential to their operations.

The commissary subsidization, in addition to contributing

in large measure to the general deficit of these agencies, has also added to black-market operations, since goods could be bought through such stores at a low price and then resold domestically or smuggled abroad for sale at a much higher figure.

3. Immediate elimination of all government price controls.
4. Abolition of all restrictions on private imports, exports, and exchange payments, other than payment of export taxes.
5. Imposition of strict controls over bank credit.
6. Discontinuance of subsidies on consumer goods.
7. Pricing of commodities received through U.S. assistance programs at a realistic world market price in terms of the new exchange rate. The government is convinced that effective application of this measure will discourage hoarding and halt illegal sales outside Bolivia of goods purchased at government-subsidized rates.
8. Cost-of-living increases for wage and salary earners to compensate for the anticipated increase in prices which will follow the proposed tax increases and the abandonment of price controls and consumer subsidies. This will be followed, in turn, by a one-year freeze on all wages.

This program obviously was a return to a wide degree of free enterprise in the Bolivian economy. It lifted many of the controls and restrictions of the government on the economy, and was designed to let the exchange rate of the *boliviano* and the internal prices of Bolivia seek their own levels.

At first glance such a program might seem absurd in a country with a dire scarcity of foreign exchange. The return to a free market in foreign currency would seem to doom the program from the start. However, it was largely successful, and the key to its success was to be found in another part of this same press release which said:

U.S. Government assistance includes an arrangement by which the International Cooperation Administration will make available $10 million to support the Bolivian stabilization program, and an exchange agreement in the amount of $7.5 million with the U.S. Treasury. Further support is being provided by the International Monetary Fund in the amount of $7.5 million.

Thus, the inevitable drain on the foreign exchange resources of the country resulting from a return in such a large degree to free enterprise was met, at least temporarily, by a fund of $25,000,000 made available to Bolivia. Without this fund, upon which the country could and did draw, the program could not have succeeded, since those anxious to convert their *bolivianos* into dollars were now perfectly free to do so, and would soon have exhausted the already depleted dollar reserves of the nation.

The effects of the program were immediate. Within a short time the *boliviano* fell from 15,000 to the dollar to 7,500 to the dollar, and during the following months again rose, but only to 8,500. Goods which had been hoarded by shopkeepers and producers began immediately to appear on the market, and shortages of consumers' goods—which had been chronic and acute—disappeared. Prices went up in short order by about 100 per cent and then began to decline. Prices of primary essentials particularly began to go down.

Different elements in the economy were affected differently by the Stabilization Program. One of the hardest-hit groups was the manufacturers, who had been turning over a large part of their output to dealers in contraband for surreptitious sale in neighboring countries. With the Stabilization Program, the manufacturers found that their raw material costs rose immediately from the 190 *bolivianos* to the dollar rate which they had formerly enjoyed to the 7,500 to the dollar rate. The prices of their goods skyrocketed, and they lost markets in neighboring countries, it now becoming advantageous for smugglers to bring manufactured goods into Bolivia, instead of taking them out. In addition, price increases resulted in a shrinkage of the internal market for manufactured goods.

The banks also suffered from the Stabilization Program. Their ability to extend credit to business and industry was severely restricted, with the result that within half a year after the beginning of the program many of the country's banking institutions were barely making enough money to carry their overhead expenses. Only one or two banks were making a profit.

The peasants probably benefited from the Stabilization Program. The prices of their goods went up along with everything else. Since the peasants were not sizable buyers of imported goods, or indeed of manufactured goods of any kind—tending to hoard their income—they did not feel the effect of the increase in these commodities to any great degree.

The effect of the program on those who had been the chief purveyors of foreign exchange before Stabilization was disastrous. Until Stabilization those enjoying the privilege of importing goods at an artificially low rate were in a position to turn around and sell at least part of the goods they imported to the general public at 15,000 *bolivianos* to the dollar prices. The chief beneficiaries of this were trade union leaders and politicians closely associated with the government. With the establishment of a single exchange rate, all these privileges disappeared, and people who had been getting wealthy with great rapidity soon found that lucrative sources of income were cut off.

The effect of Stabilization on the workers varied from case to case. The construction workers, who had not benefited from the *cupo* system, were at least as well off as they had been before Stabilization. Prices increased about 100 per cent, but so did their wages. Factory workers suffered a considerable decrease in their real wage, since their monetary income increased about a third, and their cost of living about a half.

Commercial employees of the big import-export houses gained through Stabilization. During the pre-Stabilization period the big houses had found that much of their trade was diverted into the hands of those holding *cupo* privileges. However, after December 15, 1956, imports and exports were again largely handled by the firms whose principal business that was. The employees of these firms shared some of the increased income of their companies.

The working-class group which was undoubtedly most hard hit was the miners. They had enjoyed a commissary system which permitted them to buy a wide range of goods at prices which had no relation to general market prices. Thus, some products in the company stores were selling at 1 per cent or less of what they would bring in the market. The miners were able, therefore, to purchase these goods and turn around and sell them at a large profit. It is not stretching the truth to say that many miners were working more for the commissary privilege than they were for the money wages which they received.

Of course, the situation of the miners was not uniform. In some of the more isolated mining camps, the workers had not been able to sell the goods they got from the company stores so easily. As a result, they tended to hoard them rather than sell them. When Stabilization occurred, these workers did not feel its effects for several months, since they had enough goods stored up so that they did not need to buy more.

Generally, however, the miners suffered heavily from Stabilization. Although their wages were increased as much as 500 per cent, prices of goods in their stores increased much more than this. The miners thus experienced a severe drop in their real wage.

With the exception of the miners, all urban workers had one gain from Stabilization which was overlooked by the trade union leaders and politicians. This was the fact that workers no longer had to wait in line interminable amounts of time to buy the simplest goods. Before Stabilization it had not been unusual for people to queue up at sundown in order to be in line to buy something from a butcher shop or food store when it opened the next morning. There were many who could not do this, and so there developed a regular business of standing in line. People would queue up with no intention of buying anything themselves, but rather for the purpose of selling their place in line to someone else in the morning. The current price for such a service just before December 15, 1956, was reported to the author to have been 2,000 *bolivianos*.

With Stabilization, as has been noted, commodities which had been hoarded returned to the market. Although goods were more expensive, they were to be had if one had the money to purchase them. So the lines disappeared. This was a tremendous boon to innumerable city workers, and was one of the principal arguments among them in favor of the Stabilization Program.

In the beginning there was not much opposition to the Stabilization Program. The working-class members of the Congress all voted for the authorization of special powers for the President to deal with the inflationary situation, powers which Siles used to launch Stabilization. When the miners threatened to go out on strike if their wages were not increased sufficiently to compensate for the loss of commissary privileges, President Siles declared a hunger strike, and within two days the miners dropped their demands, at least temporarily.

During the first months of 1957, however, opposition to the Stabilization Program mounted, particularly among the trade union leaders. In April, 1957, the railroad workers' and miners' organizations agreed that they would go on strike if they were not given wage increases to compensate completely for the rise in prices since December, 1956.

This strike program was brought before the Second Congress of Workers called by the Central Obrera Boliviana, which started on June 1, 1957. Although President Siles, who spoke twice before this congress, said that he would not concede to the demands of the workers' organizations and urged the workers not to go on strike, a resolution was passed unanimously to the effect that if compensatory wage increases were not given by July 1, a general strike would be declared throughout Bolivia on that day.

However, the trade union leaders assembled in the Second Congress of Workers had not correctly read the mood of their followers. Pressure immediately developed among the rank and file against the strike move. The Petroleum Workers Federation was the first organization to give way before this pressure and to announce that it would not participate in the walkout. It was followed within the space of a few days by the railroad workers, construction workers, telecommunications workers, chauffeurs, and most of the other important trade union groups.

Only the miners continued with plans for the walkout. President Siles then took the bit in his teeth, and a few days before the strike was scheduled to begin he made a tour of the principal mining centers near Oruro, speaking to the workers and urging them not to walk out. He was met by a huge crowd in the city of Oruro, which was strongly in his favor. He retired for the night to one of the nearby mining camps, where he heard before going to bed a radio announcement from a neighboring mining camp that if the President went there tomorrow, he would be shot by the armed miners. So President Siles went to the camp in question, he was greeted by cheering crowds of miners, and the local leaders of the union were nowhere to be seen. The upshot of all of this was that the miners, too, resolved not to go out on July 1.

There were many reasons for President Siles's victory. First of all, there had been a great deal of dissension in the Second Workers Congress, and one group represented there sided with the President immediately after the congress, against Juan Lechín and other union leaders who were strongly critical of the Stabilization Program.

In the second place, there was a widespread feeling among the workers that even if they were suffering under the Stabilization Program, this was a necessary sacrifice for the good of the country. Furthermore, many of the workers were in fact not any worse off—as we have indicated—than they had been before Stabilization. There was, too, the particularly wide approval of the program because it had eliminated the drudgery of standing in line.

Furthermore, President Siles possessed vast popularity among the rank and file of the unions and of the M.N.R. He had been the man who had actually led the fighting in La Paz on April 9, 1952. He was indisputably Number Two in the revolutionary movement, and Number One, Víctor Paz Estenssoro, was far away in London. Furthermore, Siles had a nationwide reputation for being an honest man, which could not be said of some of the trade unionists and politicians opposing him, many of whom were suspected by the rank and file of complaining more about their own loss of privileges as the result of Stabilization than about the situation of the workers. In addition, the President had wide popularity among elements which in the 1956 election had opposed the M.N.R.

Finally, the critics of President Siles and the Stabilization Program lacked an alternative program to that offered by the President. They had certain more or less valid criticisms of the stabilization effort, but they did not come forward with anything concrete to replace it.

One of the principal criticisms of the Stabilization Program made by its opponents was that it decisively slowed down the Economic Development and Diversification Program which had been started under the Paz administration. They argued that without the economic diversification of the country there was in the long run no hope of Bolivia getting out of the critical economic situation which she had suffered since 1952. New sources of foreign exchange and greater

ability to supply for herself the foodstuffs and light manu-
factures she imported were absolutely essential.

This argument had great merit. The author also doubts the
advisability of cutting down the Paz Economic Development Program. However, it was necessary that this program
be accompanied by a greater degree of overall economic
planning and coordination, so that the development projects
would not merely constitute a dispersed effort, without much
regard to what things were most essential for the country's
immediate future. The Siles administration, soon after the
July 1 crisis, set plans afoot for such a coordinated economic
development program. Furthermore, the projects already
started by Paz were renewed with the 1958 budget, drawing
very heavily on resources provided by United States counterpart funds.

It might also be noted that the Economic Development
Program was by no means completely ended. It was curtailed during 1957, but the colonization efforts in the East
were continued—though not expanded; the road-building
efforts of the Servicio de Caminos and on the Cochabamba-
Santa Cruz highway were continued; the agricultural programs of the Servicio Agrícola were continued. Work on the
sugar plant went forward. Although the author agrees that
the curtailment of economic development was bad in the
long run for the economic future of Bolivia, the fact is that
the curtailment was far from complete, and, in any case,
this charge does not constitute an alternative program.

Others of the opposition maintained that instead of the
Stabilization Program, which sought to stop inflation entirely, Bolivia needed "controlled inflation." However, no
one with whom the author talked, nothing which he read,
indicated that the opposition had any concrete concept of
just what "controlled inflation" meant or how it was to be
achieved.

The Stabilization crisis of June-July, 1957, was certainly
the first major threat to the revolutionary regime. It brought

for the first time a clear split in the ranks of the supporters of the M.N.R. government, and an open struggle for power and popular approval among the M.N.R.'s different elements.

Coinciding with the Stabilization crisis and virtually a part of it was the resignation of Vice President Nuflo Chávez. He had been put on the M.N.R. ticket in 1956 as the representative of the Left Wing, the group most closely associated with the trade unions and peasant organizations. As the controversy over Stabilization developed, it became clear that Chávez was on the side of those who opposed the Siles program.

The crisis in relations between the Vice President and the President came to a head as the result of a confidential report which George Eder presented to President Siles just before leaving the country. This report summed up the results of the Stabilization effort and made certain comments on the behavior of high members of the administration.

Eder was particularly critical of the Vice President. He accused him of ill-advised actions and perhaps worse in relation to the efforts of the government to renew payment on Bolivia's long-defaulted foreign debt—a measure necessary in order for the country to join the International Bank for Reconstruction and Development and receive loans from that institution. While the President was working out the details of this measure with the International Cooperation Administration and the United States Government, Chávez initiated negotiations of his own with certain American banking interests. Most observers agreed that Chávez had no ulterior motives in so acting, but Eder severely criticized his move.

The matter would have stopped there if the papers of La Paz had not obtained and published these critical parts of the Eder report. Thereupon Vice President Chávez sent to the President of the Senate, his friend Juan Lechín, a strongly worded letter of resignation, stating that his determination to give up his post was "irrevocable." He then decamped for his home department of Santa Cruz, where he stayed for more than a month.

During all of his "exile" in Santa Cruz, Nuflo Chávez was deluged with requests from his friends to reconsider his resignation. One of these came from Víctor Paz Estenssoro in London—and provoked a sharp reply from President Siles. Finally, two days before Congress reassembled on August 6, Nuflo Chávez sent another letter to Lechín, saying that he was withdrawing his resignation.

However, the matter did not end there. Pro-Siles congressmen insisted that the Chávez resignation was public knowledge and therefore must be debated by the body to which it was addressed. Their point of view was upheld by Congress, the debate was held, and Chávez's resignation was accepted. Thus, in a clear showdown in the political field, President Siles won out over his opponents.*

The President pushed his victory further, and reorganized the government party, the M.N.R. Late in July he made use of special powers which he claimed to have received from the last congress of the party to dismiss the members of the National Executive Committee and to appoint a new group, made up of people who had supported him in the June-July conflict.

President Siles also carried out a thorough reorganization of his government. Not only were most of the members of the Cabinet changed, but a new President of the Banco Central, Luiz Peñaloza, was appointed, and a new Mayor of La Paz was named. Peñaloza's nomination was particularly notable, because he had in January, 1953, led an ill-fated attempt by a group of M.N.R. members to oust Lechín, Chávez, and other Left-Wingers from the Paz Estenssoro government.

---

* It is perhaps not coincidental that after the ouster of Chávez, in the latter months of 1957, an "autonomist" movement developed in the Department of Santa Cruz. Members of this movement clashed with police and soldiers, and several people were killed.

The Stabilization crisis also brought a change in the labor movement. Most of the larger union groups refused any longer to recognize the authority of the National Committee of the C.O.B. which had been elected at the Second Congress of Workers. They set up a rival committee, which soon had the majority of the country's unions under its aegis. The full story of this development is told elsewhere in this book.

The result of the Stabilization crisis was to set Bolivia on a new path. The period of destruction of old institutions had definitely passed, and the job of constructing new ones to take their place had begun. Tin mine nationalization, the agrarian reform, and other measures had undermined or destroyed the economic and social fabric of pre-1952 Bolivia, but it was essential that new institutions be put in place of those which had been cast aside by the National Revolution. The Stabilization Program was a step in this direction.

It is understandable that certain elements inside of and allied with the M.N.R. should be opposed to the process of institutional reconstruction and should be against the Stabilization Program as calling a halt to further evolution of the movement started in April, 1952. Those ex-Trotskyites who had joined the M.N.R. after 1952 and still believed in "the permanent revolution" felt that the objectives of the April 9 uprising would not be achieved until the bases of a fully socialist society had been laid. They feared, and quite rightly, that the Stabilization Program was a clear signal that the dominant elements in the M.N.R. had no intention of taking the National Revolution in that direction.

In any profound social movement such as that of Bolivia there are events tending to separate different elements who in the beginning are able to go a considerable way down the revolutionary road together, but at crucial turning points in that road want to go in different directions. The Stabilization Program was one of these events.

If Stabilization were successful, the way would be open

for the building of the kind of mixed economy and society which the majority of the M.N.R., consciously or unconsciously, was seeking to construct. This would be a society in which agriculture would be in the hands mainly of individual cultivators, some large, but most of them middle-sized and small-scale operators, with the State having an important role in directing and encouraging agricultural production. It would be a society in which the State would control the largest part of one major extractive industry—mining—and a sizable part of the other, petroleum, and in which it would be in a position to direct a large share of the foreign exchange gained from these industries into channels which it felt would be best for the economic development and social welfare of the nation. It would be an economy in which manufacturing industry would remain largely in private hands, though the government would make a leading contribution by stimulating and guiding this important activity. It would be a society in which the equality of the nation's various racial groups would be assured, and government would be in the hands of those duly and democratically elected by the citizenry.

The Stabilization Program had the political significance which we have indicated because its success would remove one of the principal dangers to the political stability of the regime, a danger which might shift the leadership of the Revolution further to the Left in the direction of the "permanent revolution." Control of inflation would make easier the solution of most of the other problems facing the administration and would create an atmosphere more conducive to both domestic and foreign investment, which in turn would make more likely the development of an economy and society such as we have outlined.

Thus the Stabilization had general political significance for the future direction of the National Revolution. Its outcome depended in large part on the continuance of the outside financial aid which made its initial success possible.

Without the dollar Stabilization Fund which made free convertibility of the *boliviano* possible, Bolivia would be forced to return to something similar to the confused and anarchic situation existing before December, 1956.

12 . . .

The Opposition and the Revolution

The revolutionary regime of the Movimiento Nacionalista Revolucionario has been faced since its victory on April 9, 1952, with two kinds of opposition, that from the Left and that from the Right. Although both opposition groups taken together have represented a minority of the voting populace, they have been strong enough to annoy the M.N.R. government and keep it on its toes. The attitude of the M.N.R. regime toward the opposition has varied considerably in the two administrations of Paz Estenssoro and Hernán Siles.

The opposition of the Left consisted of the Stalinist and Trotskyite Communists. The Stalinist group was divided after 1955 between the Partido de la Izquierda Revolucionaria (P.I.R.) and the Partido Comunista de Bolivia.

The P.I.R. had supported the government throughout most of the six-year period between the fall of the Villarroel regime in 1946 and the victory of the M.N.R. in April, 1952. Although it had finally swung to the support of Víctor Paz Estenssoro in the 1951 presidential election, its change of sides did not come soon enough to prevent the disillusionment of most of the workers and many of the intellectual leaders in the party. The trade union leaders for the most part joined the M.N.R. after the 1952 Revolution.

José Pereira, a young teacher and recent university graduate and a leader of the P.I.R. youth group, led out of the P.I.R. those elements who sought to establish an official Communist Party. He visited behind the Iron Curtain during the last two months of 1949, and, according to the Chilean Communist Party paper *El Siglo*, January 18, 1953, soon after his return to Bolivia early in 1950 the Partido Comunista de Bolivia was formed in secret.[1]

Shortly before the Revolution of April 9, 1952, the secret party came out into the open when the youth of the P.I.R. broke away from the Partido de la Izquierda Revolucionaria to openly form the Partido Comunista de Bolivia. Subsequent to the Revolution, the P.I.R. held a national congress. The result of this congress was the decision to dissolve the P.I.R., after which the delegates reconvened to found a second Partido Comunista de Bolivia, which became known as the Partido Comunista No. 2. A few months later the two groups joined to form a single Communist Party.[2]

The leadership of the Partido Comunista was largely in the hands of university students or recent university graduates. It had some support in the mining unions and other labor organizations, but the Communist Party was no match in the unions either for the Movimiento Nacionalista Revolucionario or the Trotskyites.

Late in 1955 a number of intellectuals who had formerly been among the leaders of the P.I.R., but who had refused to remain in the Partido Comunista, called a new congress to re-establish the Partido de la Izquierda Revolucionaria. However, the principal former leader of the P.I.R., José

Antonio Arze, did not rejoin the organization. He died less than a year after it was reconstituted.

At the approach of the 1956 election, negotiations were opened between the Partido Comunista and the P.I.R. As a result of these parleys, the two groups put up a joint slate of candidates. However, they made a very poor showing in the presidential poll and did not succeed in electing a single member of Congress.

Both the P.I.R. and the Partido Comunista were strongly critical of the M.N.R. government. They sought to use what influence they had in the unions to cause dissension among the workers.

The Partido Obrero Revolucionario, the Trotskyite party, which had been allied with the M.N.R. and particularly Juan Lechín between 1946 and 1952, emerged stronger than it had ever been before from these years of trial. Among its principal figures were a number of trade union leaders of the commercial workers, peasants, bank clerks, and miners.

In the first few months of the Revolution, the P.O.R. adopted a sympathetic attitude toward the Revolution, and particularly toward the Left Wing of the M.N.R., of which Lechín was the recognized leader. This was shown by an interview with Guillermo Lora, chief spokesman for the Bolivian Trotskyites, which appeared in the United States Trotskyite paper, *The Militant,* on May 19, 1952. In answer to a question, "Is our party in the vanguard of this struggle?" Lora replied:

"Yes, and it supports the left-wing faction of the new cabinet. It should be said that we alone are capable of defending every progressive measure through the mobilization of the masses. It is now necessary to fight for the nationalization of the mines, the key industries, and the land. This struggle will be intimately connected with the development of the mass upsurge, with the involvement of new working class sectors in the struggle in such a way that it acquires nationwide scope, and finally with the constitution of a workers and peasants government."

Thus the Trotskyites looked upon the Paz Estenssoro government as comparable to that of Kerensky in Russia in 1917, one which should be supported as against the Right, but which should be pushed constantly to the Left, and which ultimately would be replaced by a P.O.R. regime euphemistically defined as "a workers and peasants government." The author heard this argument put forward a number of times by Bolivian Trotskyites during the first two or three years of the National Revolution.

After the first few months, the leadership of the P.O.R. became increasingly critical of the Paz Estenssoro regime, particularly after M.N.R. elements in October, 1952, seized control of the Central Obrera Boliviana, which the Trotskyites had virtually dominated up to that time. An article in the January, 1953, issue of *Lucha Obrera,* the official P.O.R. periodical, which was republished in *The Militant* on March 2, 1953, showed the hostility of the Trotskyite leaders toward the M.N.R. government. Predicting a collision between the Central Obrera Boliviana and the government, the article said:

> The most violent clash between the C.O.B. and the government is due to the fact that the latter has a Bonapartist character, which obliges it to veer between the imperialist pole and the proletariat. In its moments of greatest danger the government finds its support in the C.O.B. In its need to placate imperialism, it later attacks the C.O.B. and sabotages its activity. . . . The future of the C.O.B. depends upon its strengthening itself, converting itself into a form of proletarian power, and following the course indicated by the Partido Obrero Revolucionario.

Elaborating on the role which it thought the Central Obrera Boliviana should play, the Trotskyite periodical said:

> The insurrection of April 9 placed on the order of the day the question of the working class taking power. Thus the organism that was created as an expression of worker-peasant unity cannot

be a simple trade union center which concerns itself only with the economic demands of the masses. It must be understood that the C.O.B. constitutes a superior form of mass organization in a period of revolutionary upsurge.

In embryonic form the elements of power are stirring within it and are consciously expressed by the P.O.R.'s fraction. The development of these tendencies will profoundly transform the structure of the C.O.B. and will convert it into a workers' parliament which will have executive attributes.

Thus, the Trotskyites sought to convert the C.O.B. into a species of Soviet, indicating their preoccupation with the parallel which they thought they saw between the process of the Bolivian National Revolution and the Russian Revolution of 1917. However, the leaders of the M.N.R., even its trade union leaders, had no intention of having the Central Obrera Boliviana converted into a Soviet. Furthermore, the Trotskyite trade unionists themselves were not happy about waging open war on the revolutionary government. They found themselves increasingly opposed to the antagonistic attitude which the principal ideological leaders of the P.O.R. adopted toward the government of the M.N.R. This controversy inside the party was complicated by a struggle within the Fourth International, with which the Partido Obrero Revolucionario of Bolivia was affiliated.

After the death of Stalin, in 1952, the Secretary General of the Fourth International, known to the world as "Pablo," took the lead in pushing through that organization a motion calling for an attempt at reconciliation between the Trotskyites and Stalin's followers. Opposition to this move came from the leadership of the Socialist Workers Party of the United States, and their position was supported by most of the important sections of the Fourth International, including the powerful Lanka Sama Samaj of Ceylon, the world's most influential Trotskyite group.

The Bolivian P.O.R. was split by this issue. Most of the trade union leaders favored the position of the Socialist

Workers Party, while the ideological leaders among the intellectuals of the Partido Obrero Revolucionario supported Pablo. The upshot of this controversy within the P.O.R. was the withdrawal of most of the more important trade union leaders from the party. In 1954 these trade unionists joined the Movimiento Nacionalista Revolucionario, and in 1956 several of them, notably Edwin Moller, the outstanding ex-P.O.R. labor leader, were M.N.R. candidates for deputy.

Subsequently, there was a further split in the Partido Obrero Revolucionaria, two groups being formed, both using the party name. One of these was led by Guillermo Lora, who since the early days of the party had been its principal ideological spokesman. The other faction was led by Hugo González Moscoso, for many years the Secretary General of the party.

Both P.O.R. factions continued to be opposed to the M.N.R. government. Characteristic of the attacks of the Lora group on the revolutionary regime is an article which appeared in the August, 1957, issue of *Masas*, its mimeographed periodical. This article not only refers to the M.N.R.'s President Siles as a "rightist and agent of North American imperialism," but also contains an open attack on Juan Lechín, the Executive Secretary of the C.O.B. and leader of the Left Wing of the M.N.R. Speaking of the unsuccessful general strike of July 1, 1957, *Masas* said:

It was the duty of the Executive Secretary of the C.O.B. to say that "with good will the strike can be avoided." . . . Some days afterward he gave us the news that the general strike would be strictly economic and in no way would be directed against the Siles government. All of this in spite of the fact that the stabilization plan (which brings misery to the people and turns the country over to imperialism) is Dr. Siles's only program. The Executive Secretary has shown that in addition to being a bureaucrat, he is an ignoramus.

The González faction was equally against the M.N.R. regime, though it expressed its opposition in somewhat more moderate terms. Typical of its approach was the following, from its mimeographed periodical, *Lucha Obrera,* in its issue of July 25, 1957. After referring to Siles as "reactionary" and talking about his "offensive" against the Central Obrera Boliviana (the Stabilization Plan against inflation), it added that the general strike threat of July 1, although it had failed:

. . . has provoked the disappearance of Siles, who, trying not to lose any time, has been very active, while imperialism demands, imposes, and pushes an attack on the C.O.B. before the masses can mobilize. For this, he expells, suspends, isolates leaders. But all of this is ineffective. The M.N.R. is defeated everywhere and no one has any authority. No one obeys anyone. The leadership of the M.N.R. does not exist. Siles has no authority.

Lucha Obrera urged an end of the "co-government" of the M.N.R. and the C.O.B., and called for a "workers and peasants government," adding that the P.O.R. "with the experience of the strike, calls on the labor leaders with revolutionary sensibility to . . . impose a new program and a new leadership on the C.O.B., independent of the M.N.R., the government, and with new aims."

The right-wing opposition came to be concentrated around the Falange Socialista Boliviana after the 1952 Revolution. Previous to April 9, 1952, the right-wing and centrist opponents of the M.N.R. were divided into various parties. The most important was the Partido Unión Republicana Socialista, which had been the principal support of the governments of Presidents Enrique Hertzog and Mamerto Urriolagoitia. Other parties active during the "six years" included the Liberal Party, during the first twenty years of the twentieth century the dominant political organization of Bolivia; the Partido Social Democrático, founded by a group of young Christian and Marxist Socialists; and the

Partido Social Cristiano, a more frankly Catholic offshoot of the P.S.D.

The Falange Socialista Boliviana had stayed aloof from the regimes in power between 1946 and 1952. As a result, it was not tainted by the widespread revulsion against those groups that had supported Hertzog, Urriolagoitia, and the Military Junta, which occurred after April, 1952.

Those elements of the P.U.R.S., Liberals, Social Democrats, and Social Christians who remained more or less active in politics tended to rally to the Falange as the principal right-wing focus of opposition to the M.N.R. regime. This fact was reflected in the 1956 election, in which only the Falange and the left-wing opposition parties ran candidates against the M.N.R.

The Falange had its support principally among the middle classes of the cities, as the 1956 election returns clearly indicated. The Falange carried the middle-class sections of virtually all the cities, including La Paz. However, the party was very interested in reaching out for support among the workers and peasants. Although the Falange failed completely to gain any influence in the labor movement, it did claim in 1956 to have rallied some backing among the peasants, by appealing to their attachment to private property. They held their first "peasants congress" in that year.

The Falangista leaders claimed, subsequent to the 1952 Revolution, that they had left their fascist past behind them. They admitted the fact that they had originally been patterned upon the Spanish fascist party, but insisted that they were strongly devoted to democracy by the middle 1950's.[3]

The author is inclined to discount these assertions considerably. For one thing, in his conversations with Falangista leaders in 1956, these leaders stressed above all the need for "the restoration of discipline." Although they claimed to favor the agrarian reform, they laid great emphasis upon its "abuses." They showed little reticence about their plans for a "strong" government once they came to power.

The attitude the Falange took toward the National Revolution of the M.N.R. was indicated by a proclamation, "To the People of Bolivia," issued in March, 1957. This pronunciamento, which was signed by Mario R. Gutiérrez, the Falange's 1956 candidate for Vice President, said in part:

What has been the significance of the nationalization of the mines? Demagogy in the national economy. What of the agrarian reform? Anarchy in the countryside. What of universal suffrage? Democratic tyranny of the M.N.R. Where has this economic demagogy led? To the poverty of Bolivia, with the downfall of the economy. Where is that anarchy of production leading? To hunger for the people. Where is the illiterate tyranny leading? To the inversion of human values, to corruption of public morals, to the destruction of republican institutions and the cancellation of the fundamental rights of man. And this same so-called popular democracy does not lead to anything except a theoretical dictatorship of the peasantry which is exploited by the M.N.R. to keep it in power, against the conscious working class of the cities, of the mines, and of the countryside.

The government of the National Revolution took quite a different attitude toward the two types of opposition. Although the Movimientistas generally kept a sharp eye on the Stalinist and Trotskyite parties, to keep to a minimum their influence in the labor movement, and particularly among the peasants, it generally did not take physical measures against them. A few P.O.R. members were jailed in 1953, but they were soon released. So far as the author knows, no Communists were jailed by the Paz Estenssoro or Siles administrations.

This relatively mild attitude toward the left-wing opposition is attributable largely, it seems to the author, to the fact that this opposition did not represent any immediate danger to the regime, and was not trying to use the traditional *coup d'état* method of getting rid of the M.N.R. government. Since the Left was not using force against the regime, the latter had no reason to use force against this opposition.

The administration of Víctor Paz took a much sterner attitude toward the right-wing opposition. The principal leaders of the regime which the M.N.R. deposed sought refuge in exile soon after the April 9, 1952, Revolution. These included ex-Presidents Enrique Hertzog, Mamerto Urriolagoitia, and Ballivián, and the principal leaders of the Partido Unión Republicana Socialista. However, President Paz, in his report to Congress in July, 1956 (p. 137), noted that his government did not have any political prisoners in jail in the period immediately after the April 9 uprising. He maintained that his harsh policy toward the right-wing opposition subsequently was provoked by attempts by that group to organize *coups d'état* and plots against the M.N.R. government.

There is no doubt that during the four years of Víctor Paz's administration many opponents were jailed. Harsh treatment of the opposition by the Paz government is the most serious charge—in the author's opinion—whch can be brought against the M.N.R. regime.

Frequent protests were made by the opposition against their suppression by President Paz. One of these was a letter written to him and signed by a group of political prisoners, and was presented to the President by the Bishop of Oruro on January 20, 1954. It read in part:

We, the 660 political prisoners in the Concentration Camp of Uncía, have decided after a long and patient wait, to ask you for justice, and to inform you of the following:

In the Panóptico Nacional of La Paz, monstrous methods are used to break down the morale of prisoners. Prisoners are deprived of bed, food, and water, for an average of eight days. In one section of the prison, a faucet was left running behind a locked door, so that the prisoners who were virtually dying of thirst could hear the sound, with the result that at least one man,

Señor Ivica Kraul, lost his reason. The object of these tortures is to extract false confessions. For the first time many women are now being imprisoned for political reasons. The whereabouts of some of the women is not known, as is the case with certain army officers (some of whom are reported to be under the care of psychiatrists). We are guarded by common criminals and the lowest type of hoodlums.

All legal processes have been denied us. We do not know whether we are imprisoned because of formal accusations, or just because we are considered suspicious. Since we have no legal recourse, it is pointless even to try to obtain a writ of habeas corpus. Not only would our action be useless, but it would surely endanger the personal security of individuals acting in our behalf.

Not satisfied with the tortures and privations we suffered in the Panóptico Nacional and the Corocoro Concentration Camp, the government ordered that we be taken to Uncía. We believe the reason for this new move is that the government is executing a plan to incite miners and peasants against city dwellers, workers against their employers, tenants against landlords, consumers against store owners, Indians against whites, nationals against foreigners, etc. . . .

The writer has spoken to enough former residents of the concentration camps mentioned in this letter to know that much of what is charged here was true. There is no doubt that the Paz Estenssoro administration mistreated many of its opponents, keeping many in jails and concentration camps, where they were sometimes tortured, keeping others in exile. President Paz admitted, in the report to Congress of July, 1956 (p. 138), that his administration had had at one time 711 political prisoners in jail—after the revolutionary attempt of November, 1953.

The Paz Estenssoro administration also took drastic measures against the opposition press. This policy started with the newspaper *La Razón* of La Paz, owned by the Aramayo mining interests who, of course, were strongly opposed to the M.N.R. regime. During the first few days after the Revolution crowds gathered in front of *La Razón* building on Avenida Santa Cruz and threatened to destroy the paper's presses. Faced with this situation, the owners of the newspaper asked the government for protection. However, President Paz Estenssoro said that, although he would not oppose the opening of the paper, he would not guarantee it the kind of protection for which it was asking.

The owners of *La Razón* interpreted the position of the President as a negation of their right to freedom of the press. The fact that the paper was still closed in 1957 indicates that this was true. However, one can also perhaps understand the unwillingness of President Paz to risk a serious clash with his own followers in order to give protection to a newspaper which was dedicated to the overthrow of his regime.

Within a year after the Revolution, the newspaper plant of *La Razón* was taken over by Juan Lechín's Ministry of Mines and Petroleum. It continued to be the headquarters of the Ministry, and even when President Siles came to power in 1956 and offered amnesty and reconciliation to the opposition, he refused to allow *La Razón* to reopen. The sequel is told by *Hispanic American Report* of September, 1956:

After an inventory of "La Razón's" facilities was taken, the Chamber of Deputies passed a law authorizing expropriation of the newspaper for official use, but at month's end the bill had not been passed by the Senate. In the midst of the political upheaval labor chief Lechín suddenly resigned as Senate President, giving as reasons poor health and Senate failure to obtain a quorum. However, it appeared that the firm stand taken by moderates on . . . "La Razón's" expropriation was also a factor.

The newspaper remained closed, and its property remained in the hands of the government, in spite of lack of legal action to this effect. President Siles refused to permit *La Razón* to reopen. According to *La Prensa* of Lima (March 26, 1957), Siles argued that he "could not be expected to uphold Aramayo's right to publish a newspaper at the sacrifice of Bolivian lives. . . ."

Even more serious than the *La Razón* case has been the government's action in closing the newspaper *Los Tiempos* of Cochabamba. This paper did not belong to any of the mining magnates, and its principal "crime" was opposition to the M.N.R. government. *La Prensa* of Lima presented the anti-M.N.R. point of view on this case in an editorial, on March 26, 1957:

Mobs of so-called popular militia, led and urged on by the party in power, attacked and set fire to the printing plant of "Los Tiempos." After his property was destroyed, Demetrio Canelas himself was attacked. Following this he was victimized, persecuted, and imprisoned. He might even have lost his life had not the Inter American Press Association intervened with the Bolivian authorities on his behalf.

This treatment of the opposition press has brought the M.N.R. government a great deal of condemnation, particularly from the Inter American Press Association. *The New York Times* editorialized on November 4, 1956, on the action of the Association with regard to the Bolivian press. The I.A.P.A. declared that "there is no freedom of the press in Bolivia." *The New York Times* editorial went on:

It is a great disappointment to see Bolivia rightly condemned. Bolivia desperately needs the goodwill of the American nations, but it will never win a good press throughout the hemisphere as long as it permits assaults against newspaper plants and keeps outstanding newspapers such as *Los Tiempos* of Cochabamba and *La Razón* of La Paz closed.

A year later the Inter American Press Association again condemned the suppression of *La Razón* and *Los Tiempos*. According to *La Prensa* of Buenos Aires, of October 19, 1957, the I.A.P.A. report said in part:

There is no liberty of the press.

We may repeat with respect to Bolivia the phrase used in previous reports. The situation has not varied, since the injustices committed against press organs have not been corrected, nor have the damages done to their proprietors been recompensed.

The report went on to note that Demetrio Canelas, proprietor of *Los Tiempos* had returned to Bolivia in September, 1956, in conformity with the political amnesty of a few months previous, and had found the government inclined to recompense him. However, when he presented his demand for compensation to the President in official form, he was again deported. The report concluded by saying that although Canelas had again been invited back to Bolivia, he had not by October 4, 1957, actually received a visa to return.

A change of the government's policy toward the opposition was noticeable in the months preceding the election of 1956. Although he had issued partial amnesties to political offenders in December, 1953, March, 1954, December, 1954, and June, July, September, and December, 1955, President Paz declared a general amnesty for all political prisoners in March, 1956. Exiles were invited to return. The opposition parties were given full opportunity to reorganize their ranks, though the Falange Socialista Boliviana was the only one which really seriously attempted to do so.

During the election campaign of 1956 there was extensive freedom of campaigning in the cities, although *La Razón* and *Los Tiempos* were not allowed to reopen their doors. The author was in La Paz and Oruro a few weeks after the election, and saw many signs scribbled on the walls advertising the opposition candidates. However, there seems to be general agreement that the opposition parties did not have much chance to do effective campaigning in the countryside. This was undoubtedly due in part to the fact that the peasants were overwhelmingly in favor of the M.N.R., and not anxious to listen to Falange speakers, but the government probably did little to dampen the enthusiasm of its peasant supporters or make them willing to listen to the opposition.

The Siles government's policy toward the opposition was much milder than that of Paz Estenssoro. Siles invited all opposition members to come back and occupy their posts in Congress, and all but one of them, Major Elías Belmonte, did so. Siles again invited members of the opposition in exile to return to Bolivia. The President boasted that he did not have a single political prisoner in confinement.

The Inter American Press Association report of October, 1957, was not entirely correct in saying that there was no freedom of the press in Bolivia under Siles. Although *La Razón* and *Los Tiempos* did not reappear, an opposition press began to develop, particularly during and after the Stabilization crisis in the middle of 1957. Mimeographed newspapers of the Stalinist and Trotskyite groups strongly attacked the Siles regime. So did the printed newspaper of the Confederation of Peasant Unions, *Intransigencia*.

On the Right, the daily newspapers *Ultima Hora* and *El Diario* also became increasingly anti-government. The latter grew violent in its attacks on the Lechín wing of the M.N.R. However, it also began to attack the M.N.R. as a whole. On October 7, 1957, it published as an editorial a letter to the editor signed by Armando Sotelo Beltran, calling for reversal of government policy with regard to nationalization of the tin mines and the agrarian reform. *El Diario* became more and more critical of the M.N.R. government. On March 30, 1958, it published the text of a strong letter of Falangista deputy Jaime Ponce Caballero criticizing the government. On April 1, 1958, it attacked some actions of President Siles, to whom it formerly had offered lukewarm support, and on April 2, 1958, it carried a strong editorial censuring the government for not allowing political exiles to return. Meanwhile the Falange Socialista Boliviana was itself publishing a weekly periodical entitled *La Antorcha*. A wide degree of freedom of the press had been restored by President Siles, in spite of the fact that *La Razón* and *Los Tiempos* remained closed.

The principal criticisms which one could make of the civil liberties position of the Siles administration are three in number. The first is that it refused to allow the reopening of *La Razón* and *Los Tiempos*. The second criticism concerns Siles's action in October, 1956, three months after being inaugurated, in hustling a number of the principal leaders of the Falange Socialista Boliviana off to exile after what he claimed was an attempt to overthrow the government by violence. Finally, some question might be raised about the hesitancy of Bolivian consulates to grant entry permits to political exiles, even after President Siles said that they were welcome to return.

There are several general comments which should be made with regard to the lack of democratic liberties under the M.N.R. government. First of all, the civil liberties situation under Paz Estenssoro was not worse than it had been under several previous regimes. Unfortunately, Bolivia had frequently in the past been governed by dictatorial regimes which did not have the extenuating circumstance that they were regimes which enjoyed the wide support among the masses of the people which the Paz Estenssoro and Siles regimes have possessed.

Strong-arm government in the past, however, would not justify such government by a regime which claims to be democratic as well as social-revolutionary. The M.N.R. leaders have recognized this to the extent of apologizing for their attitude. They have maintained that they had no intention of suppressing the opposition, but were forced to do so by the fact that the opposition refused to give up the time-honored weapon of the *coup d'état* as the means of getting rid of the M.N.R. regime.

The best statement of the M.N.R. case was made by President Víctor Paz Estenssoro in his Message to Congress in July, 1956. He said (pp. 137–138):

> On April 11, 1952, after our victory, there was not a single political prisoner under confinement. In contrast to the counter revolution of 1946, in which Villarroel was sacrificed . . . the attitude of the new government was characterized by the generosity which characterizes the strong. On that day we pardoned our enemies and forgot a long account of persecutions, exiles, misery, and massacre. . . .
>
> The conspiracy of the oligarchy after the National Victory of April was continuous. In July and August of 1952 the first attempts were made, and on January 6, 1953, there was an attempted coup characterized by the action of some elements associated with the reactionaries and others from within the party who chose a forbidden path to show their dissension. On June 20 of the same year a terrorist plan was discovered, a method of political struggle unknown in our history, and typical on the other hand of the minority groups which thus seek compensation for their lack of popular support. On November 9 the key idea of the subversion was the assassination of the President of the Republic. Terrorism figured in the plots discovered in February and August, 1954, and in April, 1955.
>
> In each of these cases, the government published the documented proof of the planned *coup d'état;* photostatic copies of the plans, letters exchanged between the conspirators . . . and the confessions of the prisoners.
>
> The conspiracy in each case was financed by the old owners of the mines and the lands or by the unmentionable foreign interests which were promised concessions of national property. . . .

Although some of the explanations of President Paz as to the origins of the movements against the M.N.R. regime may be taken with a grain of salt, the writer is convinced that the opposition never was willing to give the government an opportunity to be democratic. This was demonstrated during the early months of the Siles administration, when the opposition attempted to provoke the government into taking strong police action which would augment its unpopularity with the middle class and perhaps engender sufficient opposition among working-class groups so that there would be a possibility of repeating the experience of July 21, 1946, when the government of President Villarroel was overthrown by the La Paz city mob.

The writer was witness late in August, 1956, to an incident similar to the more serious riot, two months later, which provoked the expulsion of Falangista leaders from the country. Ostensibly demonstrating against the high cost of living, the participants in this protest parade marched up and down Avenida Santa Cruz and then walked up the hill to Plaza Murillo, where they demonstrated in front of the Presidential Palace. The demonstrators shouted insults at the President and the M.N.R. and *vivas* for the Falange. Although the police interfered in no way with the marchers, the latter attempted to incite the soldiers on guard at the Presidential Palace to take action against them. They failed completely on this occasion.

The demonstration of October, 1956, was a good deal more serious than this. After a march similar to that described above, demonstrators attacked the government radio station, the newspaper *La Nación,* and several other M.N.R. centers. When the government took sudden measures against the Falange, the latter group alleged that the administration had *agents provocateurs* in the demonstrating crowd, who were responsible for the attacks on government and M.N.R. institutions. The writer has seen little evidence to bear out this charge.

The author again was made aware of the tendency of the opposition to rely on force to oust the M.N.R. regime when he was in Bolivia in August, 1957. Shake-ups in the Army gave rise to opposition hopes for a military *coup* against the government. Members of leading economic groups opposed to the M.N.R. went so far as to make up a Cabinet for the government which they hoped would take the place of the Siles administration.

Further evidence of the belief of the Falange in the *coup d'état* as a method of overthrowing the M.N.R. and seizing power appears in the Falange's proclamation, "To the People of Bolivia," issued in March, 1957. It said in part:

But the Falange was not alone. Another institution was equally broken and persecuted. The Army (and when we say the Army, we refer to all its members, active and retired) feels its institutional spirit in the face of humiliation and insult.

Hence the Army and the Falange fight in common for the redemption of Bolivia in union with the people, which, victim of deception and betrayal by the M.N.R., was resolved to avenge the indecorous selling out of its sacrifice and its blood.

People, Army, and Falange, today masters of a clear historic conscience, will reconquer the Fatherland, making all sacrifices and overcoming all obstacles. . . .

In view of the tradition in Bolivia of overturning governments by force, and in view of the continuing belief of the opposition in this method of changing regimes, the M.N.R. government could not be expected to extend to its adversaries all the rights of free speech, free press, and free assembly. One can and must criticize the excessive lengths to which the Paz administration went in dealing with its opponents, and the remnants of this in the Siles government, but one must also recognize that some defensive measures against conspiracy were necessary.

As deplorable as the government's strong-arm measures is the failure of the opposition to realize that the era of changing governments in Bolivia by *coup d'état* and revolt ended with the Revolution of April 9, 1952. Furthermore, the opposition demonstrated during the first months of the Siles administration that it was not ready or willing to live up to the democratic freedoms which it was demanding, and which President Siles gave evidence of being willing to grant in large degree.

In terms of its own interests, the failure of the opposition to confine itself to peaceful means of changing the regime could be suicidal. Since the defeat of the Army in the Revolution of April 9, 1952, the principal armed forces in the country have been the miners', city workers', and peasants' militia. If a rebellion should succeed in capturing or killing the President in La Paz, this would not, as in the past, mean the downfall of the government. Rather, it would mean that the armed workers and peasants would descend upon the capital, with the intent of taking revenge for the attack on the government and restoring the M.N.R. to power. The fate not only of the opposition leaders, but of all white men in La Paz, under these circumstances, would not be nice to contemplate.

There is no doubt that the record of the M.N.R. governments with regard to civil liberties has been much less than ideal. However, the Siles regime sincerely attempted to alter the worst aspects of this situation for the better in 1956. Siles reiterated his amnesty proposals in 1957. Perhaps the most remarkable fact is that a regime which has made as fundamental a change in society as has the M.N.R. government has been able to maintain as much freedom for the opposition as it has done.

13 . . .

The United Nations Experiment in Bolivia

The Bolivian National Revolution has coincided with one of the most interesting experiments which the United Nations Technical Assistance Board has engaged in anywhere in the world. Through a unique arrangement with the Bolivian Government, the United Nations has cooperated intimately in the work of transforming and modernizing the nation's economy.

The work of the United Nations in Bolivia began before the Revolution of April 9, 1952. In 1950 the government of President Mamerto Urriolagoitia invited the United Nations to send a mission to Bolivia to study the economy and make recommendations for how it might be developed. The mission was led by Hugh L. Keenleyside, at that time a Deputy Minister of the government of Canada, and subsequently

Director General of the United Nations Technical Assistance Administration. Carter Goodrich, who in 1952 and 1953 headed the United Nations program in Bolivia, has described the Keenleyside *Report* as follows:

> The resulting Keenleyside Report . . . is almost unique among the official documents of the international organization in the vigor and frankness of its comments. It recognized the need of diversification. It called attention to the weaknesses of mining and agriculture and to specific possibilities of development. It emphasized what it called "the paradoxical contrast" between the present poverty of Bolivia and the potential wealth which its natural resources should make possible. It expressed the conviction that "the explanation of this paradox . . . [is] to be found in the governmental and administrative instability that has consistently marked the history of that nation." [1]

The Keenleyside Mission suggested a novel approach to United Nations aid to Bolivia. In the words of the Mission's *Report* itself, this proposal was as follows:

> It is proposed that the United Nations assist the Bolivian Government in obtaining the services of a number of experienced and competent administrative officials of unquestioned integrity drawn from a variety of countries, and that the Bolivian Government appoint these officials on a temporary basis to positions of influence and authority as integral members of the Bolivian civil service. [2]

The Keenleyside *Report* defined the role of these "administrative assistants" thus:

1. To perform the duties and exercise the authority assigned to them in the Bolivian civil service.
2. To direct and assist in the training of Bolivian personnel with the object of developing as rapidly as possible a Bolivian civil service of experience, competence, and integrity.
3. To aid in ensuring that the terms of the proposed Agreement between the Bolivian Government and the United Nations . . . are carried into effective execution. [3]

Thus, it was suggested not only that a more or less permanent United Nations technical assistance mission be sent to Bolivia, but that the members of that mission have the status not of mere advisers, but actual officials of the ministries in which they were supposed to serve. This was the first time such an arrangement had been proposed. It paved the way for a unique experiment in the extension of technical aid and advice to an underdeveloped country by the United Nations.

The Keenleyside Mission was well aware of the significance of what it was proposing. It indicated this when it said:

The proposal constitutes a new development in the methods by which the United Nations endeavors to extend friendly, and unselfish but mutually beneficial assistance to one of its members. Because the aid is offered by the United Nations as a whole, and because the personnel involved—as in the case of the present Mission itself—will be drawn from a variety of national sources, there can be no question of any single external authority gaining undue influence in Bolivia.[4]

The actual negotiation of the agreement for the permanent mission was entrusted by the United Nations Technical Assistance Administration to Carter Goodrich, Professor of Economics at Columbia University, who had long been associated with the International Labor Organization. Dr. Goodrich went to Bolivia in September, 1951, and signed an agreement on behalf of the United Nations on October 1, 1951.[5]

In February, 1952, Dr. Goodrich returned to Bolivia to make plans for the arrival of the full mission. However, he did not confine his energies during this visit merely to official functions. He attempted to become acquainted with the situation of the country, and particularly to meet important political figures of all tendencies. Among others, Hernán Siles, then in hiding in La Paz, and in charge of the Movimiento Nacionalista Revolucionario activities inside the country, sought an interview with Goodrich. The two men talked for a considerable time, and this interview was to be of key importance after the Revolution of April 9, 1952.

Dr. Goodrich came to Bolivia once again, with other members of the United Nations Technical Mission, only a few weeks before the April 9 Revolution. As it turned out, he had to spend a good deal of his time during his first months in Bolivia in making sure that the Mission could stay and carry out its work.[6]

The first move of the United Nations Mission was to obtain permission from United Nations headquarters in New York to extend whatever emergency aid Bolivia might need as a result of destruction occurring during the fighting. The fighting was over on Friday, April 11, 1952, and on Sunday, April 13, Dr. Goodrich talked with Vice President Siles and presented the offer of emergency aid. This served to get the United Nations effort off on a good footing.[7]

There was still strong opposition in the M.N.R. and among the workers who supported it to the presence of the United Nations group. Víctor Paz himself had made some strong statements against the idea of the mission when the agreement was signed in October, 1951, and some of his supporters were not willing to let him forget these statements.

There were several reasons for this opposition. In the first place, the agreement providing for the presence of the United Nations Mission in Bolivia had been signed by the regime which the M.N.R. had overthrown. In the second place, the Mission was headed by an American, and there was a widespread belief that it was an "agent of Yankee imperialism," and would seek to undermine the Revolution which had only just begun.

An example of the opposition to the Technical Assistance Mission appeared in a Manifesto of the Central Obrera Boliviana, published in the first (May 1, 1952) issue of the C.O.B.'s paper, *Rebelión:* "The servile attitude of the previous government has imposed ignominiously upon us a foreign mission which came to govern us with extraordinary powers to place the Bolivian economy at the entire disposition of imperialist military plans."

The situation of the United Nations Technical Assistance Mission was largely saved by the contacts which Goodrich had had with Siles, Vice President in the new government, during his February, 1952, visit, and by the diplomacy of Dr. Goodrich himself. After a few months the agitation against the United Nations Mission subsided, and the United Nations employees were able to get on with their work.[8] Although Dr. Goodrich was criticized by some of his fellow Americans in the United States Embassy as being "too much of a politician," there is little doubt that the whole United Nations Technical Assistance Program in Bolivia would have been a failure, had he not been able to convince the M.N.R. leaders of his own and the United Nations' good faith and desire to help in the development of Bolivia.

A few weeks after the April 9 Revolution Foreign Minister Walter Guevara Arce finally notified the Mission that the government was willing for it to stay, but that the agreement between Bolivia and the United Nations Technical Assistance Administration must be revised. Such a revision was finally agreed to and signed in May, 1953. The revised agreement did not fundamentally alter the basis upon which the Mission operated in the country. Dr. Goodrich has described the changes which were made:

The Modified Agreement of May 2, 1953 . . . eliminated some of the extreme powers originally assigned to the "administrative assistants," changing their title to that of "technical consultant," but it retained their position as civil servants under contract with the Bolivian Government. . . . Moreover, in addition to their ordinary functions of counsel to the Ministers or other chiefs of agency, the members of the Mission were also to cooperate under their direction "in the execution" of agreed projects and "in the improvement or the reorganization" of the agencies to which they were assigned.[9]

Although the Trotskyites and Communists continued for some time to attack the Mission, and to attack individual members of it, its position was secure by the first anniversary of the National Revolution.[10] The satisfaction of the M.N.R. government with the United Nations Mission was shown by President Paz Estenssoro in his report to Congress in July, 1956:

The results of the Modified Agreement are excellent. We have obtained the services of first-class technicians and experts, who have collaborated in different studies and administrative and economic programs already in operation or planned. It is appropriate at this time to express our satisfaction with the form in which the Agreement is being fulfilled. The amount assigned by the Technical Assistance Program to our country has increased from $250,-000 in 1953 to $640,000 in 1956.[11]

Dr. Goodrich himself has described the kind of work which the United Nations Mission undertook during his period as chief:

. . . members of the Mission assisted in the reorganization of the Ministry of Labor and in bringing order to an exceedingly chaotic system of social insurance. An expert from the International Labor Organization made arrangements under which groups of foremen and workers from the mines and oil fields were given periods of training and experience in other countries. Mining engineers, and more recently a metallurgist and a mineral geologist, have advised on costs and methods of mining. They recommended further exploitation of the baser minerals of lead, zinc, and copper, for which market prospects appeared more favorable than for tin. They also investigated the undeveloped iron resources of Mutún, which have since attracted the attention of a United States company. On the advice of one of these experts, the Corporación Minera is introducing into the mines a system of bonuses for productivity. Another United Nations technician investigated the possibility that Bolivia might profitably smelt a part of its own ores instead of sending the concentrates to England or the United States. . . . Other experts advised on agricultural policy, on road development, and on the business methods of the petroleum industry. When the Bolivian Development Corporation received bids for the construction of a new sugar mill—the largest single contract to be let in many years— its president invited the United Nations to send down two experts to help judge the bids in order to ensure expertness and objectivity.[12]

The United Nations Mission cooperated with most of the programs of economic and social reform of the revolutionary government. It was particularly active in its aid to the Agrarian Reform Program. Before the writing of the Agrarian Reform Law the United Nations assigned Edmundo Flores, who had been working with the United Nations Misión Andina in neighboring Peru, to advise the Bolivian Government in this field. Flores was a Mexican, who had worked closely with the National Peasants Confederation, and who had a Ph.D. from the University of Wisconsin, where he had presented a thesis on the Mexican agrarian reform.

During the months before the issuance of the agrarian reform decree Flores served as adviser to the Agrarian Reform Commission. He sat in on the drawing up of the decree, and his advice was of considerable importance. Once the decree had been issued, Flores helped to set up the administrative organization for carrying out the agrarian reform, the Servicio Nacional de Reforma Agraria. He left Bolivia at the end of 1954.

A key role in United Nations aid to the agrarian reform has been played by the so-called Misión Andina. This Andean Mission has helped in the job of extending technical aid to the peasants who have received or are about to receive land under the Agrarian Reform Program. It has established a number of stations throughout the country. Dr. Goodrich has described the first and most important of these projects:

Another enterprise of the international organizations, the Andean Highlands Mission, under the leadership of the International Labor Organization, has been invited to take over the management and operation of a large landed property at Pillapi in the center of the region of dense Indian population near Lake Titicaca. Here it is attempting to devise a workable combination of individual and cooperative methods for the organization of agriculture. A blacksmith's shop has been set up to make improvements in the Indians' hand tools. Schoolhouses have been built, largely by the labor of the children and their parents, and are in use both day and night. A small medical center has been established. The hope is to make Pillapi a demonstration center for rural progress. One plan is to recruit groups of young Indian men and women who will come there for training in the rudiments of agriculture, health, and education and then return to their own communities to put their knowledge into practice.[13]

The project at Pillapi was on an expropriated hacienda consisting of nine different farms, with a total of 11,200 hectares. There were some four hundred Indian families on the hacienda. The work of the Misión Andina was hampered for some time by the government's slowness in expropriating the property and giving the Indians clear title to it. However, by January, 1956, this had been accomplished, and the project began to prosper.

Emphasis at Pillapi has been on agricultural activity, but the Mission also installed machine and carpentry shops, the machinery for the former being a gift of the American Federation of Labor. It established a small hospital-dispensary and several elementary schools. The peasants were particularly enthusiastic about the educational activities of the Mission, and cooperated in constructing the school buildings.[14]

The job of the Misión Andina at Pillapi was to encourage the peasants to use new techniques and get more production from their holdings. This called for considerable diplomacy. The Indians at first refused the offers of the United Nations people of better seeds and fertilizer, saying that they had always used their own methods and achieved good output and they saw no reason to change. So the head of Pillapi asked the Indians to let him plant with his methods land which they considered too poor to use. They agreed to this. When the output on the "waste" land turned out to be much better than their own production, the peasants were convinced and became eager to get the new seed and to use fertilizer.[15]

The author visited one of the projects of the Misión Andina at Playa Verde, near the mining camp of Huanuni. The Playa Verde project was set up as the result of an application for help made to the United Nations Mission by seven villages in the vicinity. The petition which the villagers submitted bore 347 signatures or fingerprints, and those signing it said that they spoke for some seven thousand people in an area embracing almost 2,600 square miles.[16]

The staff of the Playa Verde project, headed by a Swede (though most of the personnel are Bolivian) includes a doctor, two nurses, a veterinarian, a schoolteacher, an agronomist, and several general purpose workers. Each of the experts goes out to the sixteen haciendas and communities with which the project deals, to advise and help the Indians to improve their methods and output. In the beginning the Indians were suspicious, but after a few months they began to have more confidence and to come in to the headquarters of the project to seek advice on their own.

The Playa Verde project also conducts classes. Every day there are classes for the nearby peasant union leaders, to show them how to be better farmers and make it possible for them to pass on this knowledge to their confreres. The project also has a primary school of three grades, for children of nearby peasant communities. This school runs from 1:00 to 5:00 in the afternoon, and the children walk to and from classes, some of them coming from as far as seven or eight miles away. There are about seventy-five children in the school.[17]

The Misión Andina had two additional projects by the end of 1957, one at Cotoca in the Eastern lowlands, which we have discussed more fully elsewhere in this volume, and one at Otavi in the southern part of the Altiplano. Otavi was a hacienda dating from the early eighteenth century, on which were located some 2,200 families, all Quechua-speaking, who had "been easy prey to typhoid, tuberculosis, enteritis, tetanus, venereal disease, and glaucoma." Misión Andina was given control of this hacienda early in 1956 and attempted not only to help the Indians overcome their traditional handicaps of illness and illiteracy, but also to teach them new and better farming methods. The project, located in a lush agricultural region, was particularly well designed for the kind of work which the Misión Andina is trying to accomplish.[18]

The United Nations Technical Assistance Mission also sought to help the fight against inflation, which was a constant preoccupation of the M.N.R. government. It played a particularly significant role in drawing up the first Stabilization Program, attempted by the Paz Estenssoro government in 1953. Of this, Dr. Goodrich says:

. . . the eagerness of the new government to obtain help in its developmental projects made possible an adjustment of the program, and the very gravity of the economic problems led to an increasingly serious use of the members of the Mission. Of this, the stabilization program was a notable example. The difficult political decision could only be taken by the President and the cabinet, but the economic and technical preparation of the measures was mainly the work of the United Nations consultants in the Central Bank and the Ministry of Finances. A special mission of the International Monetary Fund cooperated on the exchange problem, and the measures were facilitated by a credit of $2,500,-000 provided under the rules of the Fund.[19]

Much of the effort of the United Nations technical experts in Bolivia was aimed directly at economic development. Not only was the United Nations consulted on various projects, not only did it contribute, through U.N.I.C.E.F., to the construction of the milk-processing plant near Cochabamba and to other development projects, it also helped in the government's colonization efforts in the Eastern part of the country. The Misión Andina maintains an experimental colony at Cotoca in the Department of Santa Cruz. In 1956 there were some two hundred people in this colony.[20]

The most important work of the United Nations in this direction was the survey of the Bolivian economy made by the Economic Commission for Latin America. This Commission, which operates under the aegis of the Economic and Social Council of the U.N. and has its headquarters in Santiago, Chile, sent a team of experts to Bolivia in 1956. They drew up a two-volume report which went into all aspects of the economy and drew up also a list of suggestions to serve as the foundation for a general development plan. It was partly on the basis of this document that the Planning Commission set to work in the middle of 1957 to draw up a Three Year Emergency Development Plan.

The work of the E.C.L.A. group did not end with the presentation of their report. During July, 1957, most of the members of the group which had written the report returned to La Paz and spent two weeks in holding a "seminar," to discuss their work and its implications for the future of the Bolivian economy. Leading figures in the Bolivian Government, as well as in industry, labor, and politics, and members of the United States Point Four Mission, were invited to attend the sessions of this seminar, where there was a free exchange of opinion between the E.C.L.A. experts and interested Bolivians on the various problems dealt with in the report.

The United Nations Mission has been truly international. Its members have included Americans, Canadians, Italians,

Mexicans, Venezuelans, and Australians, among others, and during the first two years of its activities some fifteen nationalities were represented among the twenty-six experts in the Mission.[21] The first head of the Mission was Dr. Goodrich, an American, who was succeeded by Sune Carlson, a Swede. When Carlson left, a Mexican, Gustavo Martínez Cabañas, served as Acting Chief of the Mission for several months, until succeeded by Dr. Alejandro Oropeza Castillo, a Venezuelan. An Italian was a consultant on social security; a former Labor Minister of Venezuela helped rewrite the country's Labor Code; a productivity expert loaned by the I.L.O. to the Mission was a German-Australian.

In another sense, too, the United Nations Mission has been a unique example of international technical assistance. Not only was the United Nations Technical Assistance Board directly involved in its operations, but U.N.E.S.C.O., the International Labor Organization, the Food and Agricultural Organization, and the World Health Organization have all played important roles in the work of the United Nations Mission to Bolivia.[22]

The international experts have worked in close collaboration with the ministries or other government agencies to which they have been assigned. The novel feature of the United Nations arrangement in Bolivia has been that the Mission's experts have been given positions in the hierarchy of the Bolivian Government organizations with which they were working and have had their offices in the headquarters of these governmental units. Every attempt has been made to integrate the United Nations experts as much as possible in the functioning of the Bolivian Government.

There is no doubt that the United Nations Technical Assistance Program has given invaluable aid in dealing with some of the most pressing problems of the Bolivian economy. After initial hesitation, the revolutionary government made the fullest use of the advice and information supplied by the United Nations experts, and the result has been one of the most interesting experiments in technical assistance which the United Nations has carried out anywhere in the world. There are undoubtedly important lessons which can be drawn from this experience for the organization's whole program of technical assistance.

Uncle Sam and the Bolivian National Revolution

The United States has made possible the success of the Bolivian National Revolution thus far. After some hesitation during the first year of the Revolution, the United States began in 1953 an extensive program of economic aid to Bolivia, aid which has been essential in feeding the nation's cities, in advancing the program of economic development, and in helping to combat inflation.

Few people would have predicted on April 9, 1952, that the United States would adopt this kind of an attitude toward a government controlled by the M.N.R. and carrying out the revolutionary program which has characterized the administration of the Movimiento Nacionalista Revolucionario. The past history of the relations of the M.N.R. and the United States had been stormy. A considerable effort on both sides has been necessary to transform the previous hostility into genuine friendship.

The nationalistic program of the Movimiento virtually guaranteed its being skeptical, if not hostile, toward the United States. Nationalism usually has to be "against" some other nation, and with the considerable United States investment in the Bolivian tin industry, and the preponderant influence which United States purchases of Bolivian minerals have on the whole economy, the North Americans were the most logical butts of aroused Bolivian nationalism. Furthermore, the members of the Movimiento, like many other Latin Americans, had never become quite convinced that the United States had lived down the record of active intervention in the internal affairs of Latin American states which characterized its policy in the earlier decades of the twentieth century.

Moreover, the general intellectual climate in Bolivia at the time of the National Revolution was conducive to hostility toward the United States. A very important element among the Bolivian intellectuals consisted of convinced Marxists, of one or another Leninist variety. There was wide acceptance, even in the ranks of the M.N.R., of the Leninist concept of "imperialism," and of the inevitability of "exploitation" of small, non-industrial nations by the powerful capitalist industrial countries. It was also accepted as an axiom that the United States would not be willing to tolerate, much less help, a revolutionary government such as that of the M.N.R., which was not only willing to expropriate important foreign-owned economic interests, but was determined to destroy the social, economic, and political influence of the semifeudal latifundists, who, according to the Marxist-Leninist argument, were the "allies" of the "foreign imperialists." This frame of reference for Bolivian-American relations was accepted not only by intellectuals, but by trade union leaders as well.

For its part, the United States Government had long been

suspicious of the Movimiento Nacionalista Revolucionario. Senator George Aiken has noted that during World War II, "The M.N.R. had a reputation as a dangerous group of radicals and malcontents." He added that in 1952, "The bad reputation which the M.N.R. had in wartime still clung to the party." [1]

During the Villarroel regime, when the M.N.R. participated in the Cabinet from time to time, the relations between the M.N.R. and the United States Government were particularly unfriendly. The United States hesitated nearly six months before recognizing the Villarroel regime, and brought pressure upon other American nations to do the same. Finally, recognition was only extended after the Movimiento Nacionalista Revolucionario had retired from the government.[2]

Although Ambassador Víctor Andrade, who was sent to Washington by the Villarroel government after the restoration of full diplomatic relations, made considerable headway in convincing official Washington that the Villarroel government and the M.N.R. were not as diabolic as they had hitherto been pictured, there was still considerable hostility in the United States capital toward the M.N.R. when the Villarroel government was overthrown in July, 1946. There was little lamentation in Washington when this event took place.

During the six years that the M.N.R. was out of power, there was further reason for United States concern about the Movimiento and its orientation. Many of the party's top leaders spent their years of exile in Argentina, and there was suspicion in Washington that they were being supported financially and morally by Perón, who during most of this period was vociferously opposed to the United States and all its works. Although such suspicions were largely unfounded, they undoubtedly helped to perpetuate the "black legend" about the M.N.R. This legend was accepted not

258 *The Bolivian National Revolution*

only in United States official circles, but among liberals and "Latin American experts" as well.

In spite of this initial hostility on both sides, relations improved immensely during the first five and a half years of the National Revolution. There are undoubtedly a number of reasons on both sides for this change of attitude. On the Bolivian side, there was the incontestable fact that in order for the nation to survive, let alone for the Revolution to succeed, the country sorely needed economic aid—and the only place it could be obtained in sizable quantities was the United States.

However, the change in the attitude of the M.N.R., and probably of the majority of politically conscious Bolivians, toward the United States has a much deeper explanation than mere opportunism. This more profound reason is well summed up by Bolivia's Ambassador to the United States, Dr. Víctor Andrade, when he says:

> The relationship between my own country of Bolivia and the United States since 1952 is heartening to all who hope some means can be found to avoid colonialism and imperialism and substitute for them cooperation which helps both the weak and the strong. This relationship today refutes a favorite Communist theory—that a strong capitalistic state always exploits weaker nations if it can.[3]

Many Bolivians who were hostile toward, or at least highly suspicious of, the United States in 1952 became convinced over the years that the Marxist-Leninist dogma of "imperialism" was not correct, at least with regard to the United States and the Bolivian revolutionary regime.

Ironically enough, the United States attitude toward the Guatemalan Revolution undoubtedly did much to convince many Bolivians of this. Although the general reaction of South Americans to what they conceived to be a revival of "Yankee imperialism" and "the big stick" at the time of the overthrow of the Arbenz government in 1954 was extremely hostile, the attitude of many Bolivians was quite different. Juan Lechín, for instance, hastened to point out to his miner followers that in contrast to United States hostility to the Communist-influenced regime of Arbenz, the United States had helped the indigenous revolutionary regime in Bolivia. Many Bolivians thus saw much more clearly than their neighbors that it was the Communist influence, not the revolutionary program, of the Arbenz government which the United States opposed.

Other Bolivians, seeking a materialist explanation for what they thought to be a change of heart on the part of the United States, professed to find it in a realization of the United States Government that the three and a half million poverty-stricken Bolivians of the pre-revolutionary period constituted only a minuscule market for United States goods. Those who argue thus say that the United States Government realized that the program of the M.N.R. regime was designed to bring the whole population into the market not only for locally made goods, but for imports— particularly United States imports—as well, and that the State Department therefore supported the Bolivian Revolution. The author has heard this argument advanced on several occasions.

On the North American side, there are also several explanations for the policy which has helped the progress of the National Revolution and won the good will of most of those Bolivians who were hostile at one time toward the United States. Paradoxically, perhaps, geography has played a role in this. The 12,000-foot altitude of La Paz has not made the United States Embassy in Bolivia a particularly delectable plum for amateurs in search of a diplomatic post. As a result, the conduct of United States relations with Bolivia since the April 9, 1952, Revolution has been in the hands of career diplomats, who have had an active sympathy for the aims which the M.N.R. governments have been attempting to achieve, though they might be privately critical of some of the means adopted in trying to achieve them.

There is no doubt, too, that United States officials in Washington, as well as in La Paz, have been very much aware of the importance of the Bolivian Revolution in the whole scheme of inter-American relations. They have known that the Bolivian case presented a rare opportunity for the United States to demonstrate that it is not inevitably on the side of military dictatorships and the defense of the *status quo* in Latin America; that it is willing to cooperate with a regime which is trying fundamentally to alter the outmoded social, economic, and political structure, and is doing so in a Latin American manner, not under dictation from another continent. United States officials—no less than Latin Americans—have been very conscious of the political impact of United States aid to Bolivia's Revolution and its contrast with the United States attitude toward the Guatemalan Revolution, in which Communist influence came to dominate.

Perhaps there was also a feeling among United States officials that more could be gained by going along with the Bolivian revolutionary regime, and trying to convince it of the necessity of modifying policies considered extreme in Washington, than by opposing it. In fact, the United States Government was able to bring considerable influence to bear in the years after 1952 which would probably have been impossible had the United States not made clear its friendship. Thus, it did get an interim agreement on settlement of the claims of the old tin companies in 1953, and several years later United States advice was a key factor in the writing of a Petroleum Code which is, from the point of view of the foreign companies seeking concessions, one of the most liberal in America.

Finally, many North Americans on the spot and in Washington became convinced that there was no viable alternative to the M.N.R. regime. An overthrow of the revolutionary government would not mean the establishment of a "safe and sane" regime, but rather would result in a chaotic situation which could only serve the interests of the Trotskyites and the Stalinists, not those of the Bolivian people or better inter-American relations. Any attempt to undo the nationalization of the mines or the agrarian reform would merely serve to convince large numbers of Bolivians that the only way to end the old semifeudal, semicolonial status of their country was to follow the lead of the Communists of one brand or another. So long as this continued to be true, therefore, the United States would have to help the M.N.R. regime economically and morally.

Although the American government indicated a more or less friendly attitude toward the revolutionary regime from its early days, a year and a half passed after April 9, 1952, before a United States program of aid began on an extensive scale in Bolivia. The United States was not willing to begin such a program until at least a preliminary arrangement had been made with the old tin-mining companies, in which a considerable amount of United States capital was invested.

At last, on November 6, 1953, an Economic Assistance Agreement was signed between the governments of Bolivia and the United States "in virtue of which the latter put at the disposal of Bolivia various amounts of dollars to carry out development projects and a quantity of consumers' goods to cover popular consumption needs. Bolivia promised to invest counterpart funds in *bolivianos,* coming from the sale of these goods, in programs of economic development approved in accordance with this agreement." [4]

Most of the United States aid to Bolivia has been dispensed through various Servicios, or joint Bolivian-American organizations under United States direction. Three of these—in the fields of agriculture, public health, and education—existed before the M.N.R. came to power. In addition there was established in 1955 the Servicio Boliviano Americano de Caminos to work on road building and maintenance. [5]

The oldest of the Servicios is the Servicio Interamericano

de Salud Pública, established in the early 1940's. In addition to arranging for the sending of public health personnel to the States and elsewhere for training, this Servicio has created health centers in Cochabamba and La Paz, the latter of which was handling some ten thousand cases a month in the middle of 1957. Its operations were much expanded after 1952, and it undertook a special study of occupational diseases, particularly silicosis, and greatly expanded its training program.[6]

The Servicio Agrícola Interamericano has carried on a wide range of activities. In 1957 it was maintaining four experiment farms and demonstration stations. One of these was a cattle farm, where the Servicio was developing new strains of livestock, breeding brood stock and demonstrating the new brands of cattle. Another was a combination cattle and pasturage station. One was a station for tropical crops and the fourth, for agriculture on the Altiplano. The S.A.I. also was running six substations, dependent on these four experimental farms. All these were for the purpose of giving demonstrations to the Indians, who were reported very anxious to observe what was going on there.

People engaged in this demonstration program have declared the Indians were eager to get new strains of seed and were by 1957 beginning to use them. Although it is too early to see the results in increased production, the Indians are swarming into the experiment stations to see and learn new methods of planting and cultivation.

The S.A.I. also began after the Revolution to establish an extension service program. By the middle of 1957 it had sixty extension agents in the field. It had sent a few of these agents for training in Chile, and others had been trained in Bolivian agronomy schools. The extension agents were doing the same general kinds of work as their counterparts in the United States—demonstrating new agricultural methods, youth work, home economics education. In the youth field, the "4-S" organization, patterned on the North American

4-H clubs, included some five thousand youngsters in its ranks by 1957.[7]

The Servicio Agrícola has also cooperated in the Bolivian government's efforts to open up the Eastern part of the country. In Santa Cruz it maintains a pool of about twenty tractors, all of which are kept busy most of the time. Some of these are being used for building roads from the main Cochabamba-Santa Cruz highway into nearby farming areas. Others have been rented to private farmers to help them clear land.[8]

Indirectly, the S.A.I. has also assisted the Agrarian Reform Program. Although it has not given direct aid in terms of providing or helping train topographers, or rendering similar technical advice, the program of supervised credit has been a distinct aid to the development of the Agrarian Reform Program.

The Servicio Cooperativo Interamericano de Educación, working in the field of education, has cooperated closely with the Bolivian Ministry of Education in a program for training personnel in Bolivia and the United States. It has also cooperated in the revolutionary government's policy of extending vocational and technical education, by contributing the foreign exchange costs of building and equipping the new Pedro Domingo Murillo vocational school in La Paz. It also started in 1957 a program for apprenticeship training of workers already employed in industry.[9]

The Servicio Cooperativo de Caminos, established subsequent to the Revolution, has undertaken a sizable program of maintaining and improving the country's roads, in addition to laying out routes for new ones. The importance of this Servicio was indicated by the Keenleyside *Report's* description of the road-maintenance facilities of Bolivia before the Revolution:

There is no organized and properly equipped road repair service, little or no competent staff at any level, from the simple road-

mender to the heads of departments, no equipment appropriate
to the needs and possibilities of the country, and above all, no
adequate funds for the maintenance of the road network. . . .
Moreover, there has been a steady decrease in the amount of
funds allocated to the roads for some years past, and this decrease
is in fact much more marked than the figures would indicate, for
it has been accompanied by a progressive and continuous rise in
the cost of living and the cost of manpower and materials. . . .
Efficiency is further reduced by the fact that, while there are only
a very few competent technicians, there is a great multiplicity of
agencies in charge of roads. . . .

Mechanical equipment does exist but is widely dispersed, badly
maintained, and very little used. . . .[10]

In 1957 the Servicio Cooperativo de Caminos had some
2,000 miles of roads under its supervision. It had some
$950,000 worth of road-building equipment available, one
of the biggest pools of such equipment in America.

Some idea of how much the work of the Servicios was
stepped up after the National Revolution can be obtained
from a comparison of the amounts spent by them before
and after that event. Between 1941 and 1951 the Servicios
spent over $3,000,000 in Bolivia; but between 1951 and 1957
they spent $15,000,000.

However, the work of the Servicios was not the total
United States effort to aid the Bolivian development program after 1952. Among the other activities has been a Civil
Aviation Mission, which has worked with the Bolivian air-
line, Lloyd Aéreo Boliviano, in training personnel, and
which has founded and helped maintain a school for this
purpose, the Instituto Aeronáutico Nacional in Cochabamba.
There has also been a Police Mission, which has aided in the
reorganization and specialized training of the Carabineros.

Training grants for medical students, miners, public officials, labor leaders, agriculturalists and agronomists, and a
variety of other Bolivian specialists and leaders have been

made available by the I.C.A. In 1956, 167 people were given such grants, and in 1957, 160 received them.

This training program has encountered two important difficulties. All too many of those sent for special advanced education in the United States have been unwilling to remain in Bolivia once they returned home. Although they have to sign an agreement not to seek a United States visa again for two years after their return to Bolivia, many of the doctors, engineers, and other specialists trained in the United States have sought employment in neighboring countries, and some have been able to return to the United States after the waiting period has elapsed.

The reasons for this are the sharp contrast between living standards in the United States and their native country, and the economic crisis of recent years. Extended residence in the United States has too frequently whetted the appetites of these visitors to remain, or at least not to return to the comparatively provincial atmosphere of Bolivia. Furthermore, the difficulty experienced by government employees, doctors in the state medical service, and other technicians in keeping their salaries abreast of price increases during the rampant inflation of 1952–1956 convinced many of these people of the necessity of leaving Bolivia.

This problem is not confined to those specialists and technicians who have received United States training. The inflation and economic crisis had the general tendency of draining off a sizable part of Bolivian professional and specialist personnel into nearby countries. This made the training program of the Point Four Mission doubly hard.

Another difficulty facing the training program was the lack of a civil service in Bolivia. Even before the Revolution, the Keenleyside *Report* had commented several times on this fact. It noted:

The instability of Government policies and administration does not arise solely from the frequent changes of the personnel in high office. It is due also to the failure of Bolivia to establish, or indeed to make possible, the development of competence and stability. Bolivia simply does not possess enough senior (or indeed junior) civil servants with ability and experience to handle the problems with which the administrative machine must contend. Yet until this problem is solved Bolivia cannot hope to obtain the raw material of skills and capital that are essential to its welfare and progress.[11]

A bit further on, the Keenleyside *Report* noted that:

The technical qualifications and practical capacity of many of the officials do not appear to reach a very high level. This is largely due to governmental policy with regard to public employment. There is no general system of merit selection or permanent tenure. Except in the Ministry of External Relations, there is no merit system of selection in the national service. Higher executives and administrators sometimes have law degrees, but they have little specific training or previously tested aptitude in public administration. Most of the professional posts in the public service (lawyers, engineers, accountants, teachers, and doctors) are occupied by persons who have acquired professional degrees, but other posts are usually filled without reference to formal training or other qualifications. The general standard of performance is consequently low. So far as tenure is concerned, ministers change frequently and the average length of service in many administrative posts is correspondingly brief. There is considerable overstaffing in some of the agencies in spite of the general shortage of trained personnel.[12]

This situation is one which did not change with the National Revolution. By 1958 there was still no civil service law in Bolivia, and salaries were still too low to attract the best personnel. Consequently, turnover in the government service continued to be rapid and efficiency remained low. All too frequently those government employees sent abroad for training returned to find themselves transferred to other jobs, or dismissed from the government service altogether. The Export-Import Bank has also made a contribution to

Bolivian economic development since 1952. It helped finance the Cochabamba-Santa Cruz road, toward which it advanced some $42,000,000.[13] The road, which had been started before the Revolution but had progressed very slowly, was finished in 1954, and plans called for its being completely paved by early 1958.

The International Cooperation Administration (previously called Foreign Operations Administration, Mutual Security Agency, and Economic Cooperation Administration), which administers the aid program to Bolivia, has sought to assist the country to build up a more efficient corps of public employees. With the help of the University of Tennessee, it organized a School of Public Administration at the University of San Andrés in La Paz. This school had a yearly budget of $421,000 and had several hundred students by 1957. Some students were being sent for advanced training to the University of Tennessee.[14]

With the signing of the agreement of November 6, 1953, a program of "general economic aid" was initiated, which in its first four years contributed $80,300,000 to the Bolivian economy. Of this, some $22,500,000 went, for wheat and flour imports from United States surplus stocks, 365,000 tons of these being brought in during this period. The grain and flour were sold in the Bolivian market, and the counterpart funds in *bolivianos* arising from these sales were spent by the Bolivian Government on development projects worked out in conjunction with Point Four officials.

United States aid to Bolivia reached a high point in 1957, after the adoption of President Siles's Stabilization Program, recommended to him by George Eder. During 1957 United States aid was responsible for underwriting approximately 40 per cent of the Bolivian Government budget, through counterpart funds. Biggest contributions were to the Corporación Boliviana de Fomento, United States aid covering 50 per cent of its deficit and virtually all its deficit in *bolivianos*.[15]

In addition to this underwriting of the Bolivian Government budget in 1957, the United States was giving extensive aid to back up the Stabilization Program. The International Cooperation Administration advanced $10,000,000 toward the Stabilization Fund, and the United States Treasury an additional $7,500,000.

There is no doubt that the United States aid program to the revolutionary Bolivian Government has greatly impressed the Bolivian people and has been widely appreciated by them. In the course of five trips which the author has made to Bolivia between August, 1952, and July, 1957, he has sensed a profound change in the attitude of the Bolivians, particularly in the attitude of the trade unionists and members of the M.N.R. Whereas in 1952 the typical position of these people toward the United States was one of suspicion and hostility, over the years this hostility diminished, and by 1957 it was reduced to a minimum.

This change in attitude can be measured in part by the change in opinion concerning the aid program itself. When the M.N.R. first came to power, the position of most trade unionists and many M.N.R. leaders was that they not only wanted to do away with official United States Point Four aid, but they wanted to cancel the technical assistance agreement made with the United Nations as well, on the grounds that this was "Yankee imperialism." By 1957 all open opposition to both the United States and United Nations programs had disappeared.

This fact was dramatically demonstrated during the crisis over the Stabilization Program in the middle of 1957. There was no suggestion, even from the most extreme elements within the M.N.R. who opposed the Siles program, that United States aid should be curtailed. Although there was severe criticism of the activities of George Eder, criticism of the American aid program was limited to proposals that its emphasis should be changed. Those in the group opposed to Siles urged that more attention should be given by the

United States aid officials to economic development projects, and less emphasis should be placed on the importation into Bolivia of foodstuffs and other agricultural products of United States origin. No responsible leader proposed that the aid program itself be ended or even seriously reduced, and several of these leaders with whom the author talked in July and August, 1957, expressed very strongly their belief that the aid program should be continued.

As of 1957 the United States Point Four Program in Bolivia had certainly been successful. It had prevented starvation in the Bolivian cities; it had aided in laying the foundations for future economic development, Bolivia's only hope of getting out of the severe economic crisis in which she found herself in the 1950's. It had done this through assisting in road construction, development of agriculture, training of specialists and technicians, and a variety of other ways.

However, whether or not the economic aid program to Bolivia will be a success in the long run will depend on whether it is continued until its fundamental objectives have been achieved, and whether the Bolivians, with the advice and help of the United States Point Four officials, are able to make good use of the aid.

The objectives of the program are twofold: to tide Bolivia over the crisis caused by the declining productivity of the tin-mining industry, until new sources of foreign exchange can be developed; and to help her obtain a more diversified economy, through the development of her agriculture and her manufacturing industries. United States aid should continue until these two goals have been achieved.

The prospects for rehabilitating the mining industry and finding a supplementary source of foreign exchange in petroleum are good, as is indicated elsewhere in this book. However, the realization of these prospects demands time. The re-equipment of the mining industry cannot get under way until the settlement of claims with the old mining companies, and after that at least two or three years will be needed. The exploration for oil only began on a large scale in 1957, and it will take five or six years before the export of oil will begin to take the place of mineral exports. Meanwhile, Bolivia will need continued help from the United States.

Economic development likewise cannot be hurried. The reorganization of agriculture as a result of the agrarian reform involves not only the redistribution of the land, but also arousing the interest of the Indian cultivators in new methods of production and instructing them in how to put these new methods into operation. The opening up of the Eastern part of the country involves a large program of road building, land clearing, settlement of people from other parts of Bolivia and abroad, which also cannot be done overnight. The development of manufacturing requires not only an alteration in the attitudes of many of the industrialists, but a concerted effort to seek out markets, a program for training workers for old and new industries, and considerable capital investment in new plants and the refurbishing of old ones. This, too, will take time.

So the prospect at the end of 1958 was that Bolivia would continue to need United States aid for some years to come. As the development program makes progress, and as the oil industry develops and the mining industry is re-equipped, the need for aid will undoubtedly decline. However, the necessity for technical assistance in the sense of training specialists and technicians will probably go on long after the need for help in the form of capital equipment will have ended.

15 . . .

The Significance of the Bolivian
National Revolution

The Bolivian National Revolution is the most profound
movement of social change in America since the beginning
of the Mexican Revolution of 1910. Like its Mexican counterpart, the Bolivian Revolution has differed from the typical
Latin American "revolution," which merely results in substituting the outs for the ins without fundamentally changing the life of the country in which it occurs. The Bolivian
upheaval which started on April 9, 1952, is profoundly alter-
ing the way of living of all classes in Bolivia, as the Mexican
Revolution did and is continuing to do. The Bolivian National Revolution presents some striking parallels and important contrasts with the Mexican phenomenon.

The revolutions of Bolivia and Mexico have been alike in
their fundamental objectives. Paz Estenssoro, Siles, Chávez,

Lechín, and other leaders of the Bolivian Revolution have had the same desire to integrate the largely Indian peasant masses into the life of the nation, through giving them land and education and making them fullfledged citizens, as did Zapata, Obregón, and Cárdenas in Mexico. In both countries, the agrarian reform has been the fundamental act of the revolutionary movement. There are considerable differences in the way the reform is being accomplished in Bolivia and how it was achieved in Mexico, but it is fair to say that the Bolivians, beginning their reform more than a generation later, have learned a great deal from the successes and the failures of the Mexican land redistribution.

Both revolutions have had the objective of asserting the national character of their respective countries. The right of the nation to be sovereign within its own boundaries has been stressed. The leaders of both movements have sought to bring under national control some of the principal sources of wealth hitherto in the hands of foreigners. In the Mexican case, nationalization was one of the last great reforms of the Revolution, whereas the Bolivian leaders have made it the first order of business. However, in both cases the motives were the same—the assertion of national sovereignty and the securing of a greater degree of control for the respective countries over their economic life.

The two revolutions have also shared the objective of economic progress and development. In the case of Mexico, the phase of economic expansion came after virtually all the fundamental social transformation had been accomplished, whereas in Bolivia economic development activities have been carried on concurrently with the work of redistributing the land and asserting national economic sovereignty.

The Mexican and Bolivian Revolutions have both been fundamentally American. Neither has been led by people owing their allegiance to any foreign government or to any foreign ideology. Although not unaware of ideological currents in other parts of the world, the leaders of both movements have been adherents of the widely popular school of political thought in Latin America that holds that Latin Americans must find their own solutions to their problems, not slavishly adopt those in vogue elsewhere. Both groups have believed that the problems of their respective countries owe their origin to those nations' specific geographical, historical, and economic circumstances, and that solutions consistent with the circumstances must be applied to resolve them.

However, there have also been striking differences between the Mexican Revolution and that of Bolivia. In the former, there was a period of about ten years of almost constant civil war and armed rebellion. In contrast, in Bolivia the actual fighting of the National Revolution was over in three days, and never recommenced. The Bolivian revolutionary regime has been faced with only a few abortive attempts to oust it by armed force. Furthermore, the armed supporters of the M.N.R. government, upon whom it has principally relied for military security, have proven themselves amazingly well disciplined. In contrast to the roving bands of armed peasants who were a constant menace to peace and security in Mexico for at least a decade, the armed Bolivian workers and peasants have engaged in very few outrages and have tended to keep their arms in reserve in case of emergency.

The principal reason for the relatively small amount of violence accompanying the Bolivian National Revolution is probably the existence in the leadership of the Bolivian movement of a well-organized and well-disciplined political party which knew from the beginning what it wanted to achieve and more or less how it wanted to achieve it. This party had a history going back more than a decade before the beginning of the National Revolution, had had previous experience in exercising governmental power, had known the bitterness of persecution and exile, and had built up a wide mass following. After taking power, it extended its influence to the great mass of the peasantry, who had been politically and militarily inert until April 9, 1952. In Mexico, in contrast, the National Revolutionary Party did not come into being until almost two decades after the Revolution began. In Bolivia the M.N.R. made the Revolution; in Mexico the Revolution made the P.N.R.

Another striking difference between the Bolivian and Mexican national revolutionary movements has been the attitude adopted toward them by the government of the United States. The Mexican movement began at a time when the United States was committed to the policy of the "big stick" and armed intervention in the internal affairs of its American neighbors. Furthermore, Mexico lay just across the border from the United States. As a result, successive United States administrations adopted a hostile attitude toward the Mexican revolutionary movement, and a decade and a half had passed before this attitude began to soften.

In the Bolivian case, in contrast, the United States Government hesitated only a few months before throwing its moral support and considerable financial aid behind the revolutionary movement. The changes in United States policy in preceding decades had paved the way for a more understanding attitude toward events in Bolivia than had been demonstrated toward the Mexican Revolution during its early years. There is little doubt that United States aid has played a significant role in making it possible for the Bolivian revolutionary regime to carry out its objectives.

As in the case of the Mexican upheaval, the impact of the Bolivian National Revolution is widely felt throughout Latin America. This impact is probably most forcefully experienced in the neighboring countries which have problems most like those of Bolivia—Peru and Ecuador.

The news of the Bolivian agrarian reform has spilled across national frontiers into Peru. When Indians on one side of the border have been given land, this has aroused the curiosity and desire of those on the other side, for whom national frontiers have very little meaning in any case. An official of the National Agrarian Reform Service told the author how Indians from Peru frequently presented themselves at his office in La Paz and demanded their landlords' land. To them, the international boundaries were of little import. They knew that their brother Indians a few miles away were being given the land, and they came to claim their share.

There is little doubt that Peruvian Government authorities, and most particularly the members of the Peruvian economic aristocracy, are well aware of this effect of the Bolivian land reform on "their" Indians. That this is so was reflected in the change of government in Peru which occurred in June, 1956.

For many decades, almost without a break, Peru had been ruled by military regimes which depended heavily on the agricultural and commercial aristocracy for moral and financial support. It is the author's conviction that significant elements among the Peruvian aristocracy had come to the conclusion by 1956 that changes of the kind which were occurring in Bolivia were inevitable in Peru sooner or later. They also reached the conclusion that it was better for these changes to come peacefully, as the result of the democratic electoral process, than by violent upheaval.

This is the true significance of the election of 1956. The predominant group in the aristocracy refused any longer to support a military dictatorship, and thus paved the way for the election of one of its own members, Don Manuel Prado, as President of the Republic and head of what is essentially a caretaker regime. He was elected with the support of the Aprista Party which, though much older than the M.N.R. of Bolivia, is its counterpart in Peru. There is widespread belief among elements associated with the Prado group that the next election, in 1961, will be won by the Apristas, all other things being equal. They are also convinced that the Apristas will be in earnest about their desire for an agrarian reform, education for the Indians, Indian participation in civic life. However, they hope that, coming to power democratically, the Apristas will carry out these reforms in a peaceful manner.

Ecuador, too, has been influenced by the Bolivian Revolution. This little nation, lying to the North of Peru, has a largely Indian population, living under a social and economic system similar to that of pre-revolutionary Bolivia and contemporary Peru, a system which has hitherto never been challenged, even by an opposition political party. However, in 1956 the newly elected Conservative President (coming from the Social Christian wing of the Conservative Party), Camilo Ponce Enríquez, shocked the nation by a promise in his inaugural address to start the process of agrarian reform in Ecuador. Thus the phrase which until that time had never been mentioned seriously in Ecuador, "agrarian reform," suddenly became respectable, and a matter of immediate concern. This, too, was in all likelihood a reflection of the Bolivian National Revolution, and of the realization by important Ecuadorean leaders that change was bound to come after what had happened in Bolivia.

However, not only Bolivia's immediate neighbors are watching closely the progress of her National Revolution. It is being followed throughout the hemisphere. Conservative elements abhor it; even some Leftists still oppose the M.N.R., influenced by the "black legend" which surrounded it during World War II. Other Leftist elements have the mistaken notion that what is transpiring in Bolivia is a model to be followed slavishly, regardless of what the local circumstances in their own country may be. Still others are looking to Bolivia for object lessons in the mistakes and triumphs of a typically Latin American social revolutionary movement.

There are numerous parties throughout Latin America which feel a peculiar affinity for the Movimiento Nacionalista Revolucionario and the revolution which it is leading. These are the parties which for convenience sake can be called the "Aprista" (taking the name from the oldest of them, the Peruvian Aprista Party) or national revolutionary parties. These include, aside from the Peruvian Aprista Party, the Democratic Action Party of Venezuela, the National Liberation Party of Costa Rica, the so-called Febrerista Party of Paraguay, and even perhaps the Popular Democratic Party of Puerto Rico.

All these groups, which represent the principal strength of the democratic Left in Latin America, are eager to carry out in their own countries a social and economic transformation in a broad sense similar to that in progress in Bolivia. They are revolutionary parties in the true sense of the word, since they wish to destroy the remnants of their countries' feudal and colonial past which have hitherto prevented these nations from becoming modern nation states. Like the M.N.R., they seek to change old social systems based on racial discrimination and class snobbery. They seek to alter economic systems based on large landholdings. They seek to diversify the economies of their countries, introducing as much industrialization as is feasible. They wish to lay the solid foundations for political democracy, ending the century-and-a-half tradition, which still exists in many Latin American countries, of Army domination of politics and change of government by *coup d'état.*

All these parties share with the M.N.R. the desire to adapt their programs and actions to the peculiar conditions of their respective lands. Thus, although they recognize affinity with one another, there is in no sense a common "party line." They seek to learn from each other's experience, but not uncritically to copy each other's strategy or tactics.

The national revolutionary parties conceive of themselves as spokesmen for the new industrial middle class, the workers employed in manufacturing, the white-collar workers, and the peasants. They are parties based on a body of principles and a program, rather than on a "cult of leadership" such as has all too often characterized Latin American political parties in the past. In these respects, too, the M.N.R. is a typical member of the group.

These national revolutionary or Aprista parties are particularly significant, because they are the major American alternative to Communism. There is little doubt that many, if not most, of the Latin American countries still need to have, or to complete, their national revolutions. They need to establish more egalitarian social systems, more modern and diversified economies, firm civilian control over the government, and modern political democracies. The national revolutionary parties are trying to find an approach to these problems adapted to the needs of Latin America and of their individual countries. If the national revolutionary parties fail to work out democratic methods appropriate for bringing their countries more completely into the general stream of twentieth-century Western civilization, more totalitarian approaches will certainly prevail. The Communists, at the moment of relatively minor immediate importance, though active in every one of the Latin American countries, are the group most likely to profit from the national revolutionaries' failure.

The Communists have been most successful in those nations without a strong national revolutionary party or some other party with a mass appeal, capable of meeting them on their own grounds and among the groups from whom they especially draw support. The Communists have been notably unsuccessful in those countries, such as Bolivia, Peru, Venezuela, Puerto Rico, and Costa Rica, where they have been faced with a national revolutionary party which has a chance of coming to power (or which actually is in power) and of carrying out some of the things which the Communists promise so lavishly, but have no intention of actually providing—strong trade unionism, land reform, social legislation, economic development, political democracy.

For nearly four decades now, the Communists have been saying that the only way in which the overdue social revolutionary changes can be brought about in Latin America is through following the path of Moscow—and more recently, Peiping. They have denounced as futile the insistence of national revolutionaries that Latin America must find its own path to social change.

This is why the Bolivian National Revolution is of such key importance for the whole hemisphere. In recent years, Bolivia has been the most important country in which a party of the national revolutionary orientation has been in power. Its government has attempted more thoroughly than any regime since the Cárdenas administration in Mexico (1934–1940) to destroy the economic and social bases of feudalism. It has pushed against almost insuperable odds to develop a more broad-based economy. It has sought to establish a society which will make real political democracy possible.

If the M.N.R. regime fails in Bolivia, if it should be violently overthrown, the effect on Latin America and the whole Western Hemisphere would be catastrophic. Many politically alert Latin Americans would conclude that the Communists were right, that it is impossible to carry out a fundamental revolution in Latin America on an American pattern, and without the political, economic, and moral support of the Soviet Union and its allies and puppets.

Furthermore, the defeat of the Bolivian National Revolution would inevitably redound to the discredit of the United States. The all-too-common tendency of the Latin Americans to see duplicity in whatever the United States does would be intensified. The considerable amount of economic aid which this country has given to the M.N.R. government would be quickly forgotten. The easily acceptable proposition that the United States was working both sides of the street, and in the showdown was more concerned with the interests of a few thousand North American investors in Bolivian tin than it was in the welfare of the three and half million Bolivians and in the fate of Latin America, would be widely believed. The fact that it was not necessarily true would not make it any less effective.

The future of the Bolivian Revolution depends in large degree on the continuance of United States moral and economic support of the M.N.R. government. We have a great deal more than an $80,000,000 financial investment in the Bolivian experiment. We have a tremendous amount of prestige and good will invested as well. All this will be lost—and in return there will not even be any lasting gain for the American stockholders of Patiño, Aramayo, and Hochschild —if the Bolivian National Revolution fails. The United States must continue its support of the Bolivian National Revolution until the exceedingly precarious foreign exchange position of the country has improved, and until the social and economic changes launched by the M.N.R. regime have had time to become permanent.

Bibliographical Note

Much of the material in this book is based on personal observation and on conversations with hundreds of Bolivians in all walks of life, as well as foreigners with more or less knowledge of what has been going on in that country. Those cited directly are noted in the footnotes at the end of this book.

In addition, the author has depended rather heavily on a number of books and reports, as well as certain periodicals. A full list of those quoted can also be culled from the footnotes. However, some of the written source material is worthy of special comment.

For those interested in a short but competent and readable general survey of Bolivia, Harold Osborne's *Bolivia: A Land Divided*, published in 1954 by the Royal Institute of International Affairs, is to be recommended. Its outlook on the Bolivian National Revolution is on the whole unfriendly. The author has relied on it for some of the historical references in the present volume.

The two-volume report of the Economic Commission for Latin America, first issued in mimeographed form in 1957 and entitled "El Desarrollo Económico de Bolivia," is a thoroughgoing investigation of the economy of the country. It is an invaluable source of statistics, as well as of observations concerning the past and present state of Bolivia's economy. Extensive use has been made of it in this volume.

Reference likewise has been made to the report of the United Nations Technical Assistance Mission which visited Bolivia in 1950, known generally as the "Keenleyside *Report*," after the Mission Chief. It contains a good deal of basic information on the Bolivian economy. However, since the *Report* was written before the 1952 Revolution, it skirts gingerly around the problems of land distribution and other matters which became the key issues of the National Revolution.

The author has relied heavily on the Message to Congress of President Víctor Paz Estenssoro, delivered just before he left office, in July, 1956. President Paz reported very widely on all aspects of the work of his administration, providing many facts and figures not otherwise available. He also presented the point of view of the Movimiento Nacionalista Revolucionario on a broad range of economic, social, and political problems.

A volume by President Víctor Paz Estenssoro, consisting of his collected parliamentary speeches, entitled *Discursos Parliamentarios,* and published by Editorial Canata in La Paz in 1956, has also been used. It is particularly helpful in determining the historical position of the M.N.R. before taking power.

A pamphlet containing collected speeches of Bolivian Ambassador to the United States Víctor Andrade, entitled *Bolivia— Problems and Promise,* has been a source of information concerning activities of the M.N.R. government, as well as its official position on a variety of matters. It was published by the Bolivian Embassy in Washington in 1956.

Of a rather different nature is *El Marxismo en Bolivia,* the report of the majority of a Commission established by the Third Congress of the Inter American Confederation for the Defense of the Continent. This self-styled "anti-Communist" group tends to see Communism in everything which has been done in Bolivia since 1952. However, the report contains quotations from a number of documents which are used in some parts of the present book.

Certain publications have been particularly helpful in connection with individual chapters of this book. Carter Goodrich's pamphlet, *The Economic Transformation of Bolivia*, published in 1955 by the New York State School of Industrial and Labor Relations, has supplied much information on United Nations activities in Bolivia since 1952. The same is true of Dr. Goodrich's article on "Bolivia and Technical Assistance," in the April, 1954, issue of *Foreign Affairs*, and Agnese Lockwood's "Indians of the Andes— Technical Assistance on the Altiplano," in *International Conciliation* for May, 1956.

For the chapter on the opposition and the National Revolution the author perused a great deal of material published by both the left-wing and right-wing opponents of the M.N.R. regime. Much of this contains more rhetoric and accusation than facts, but of particular use, and cited in these pages, is Alberto Ostria Gutierrez, *A People Crucified: The Tragedy of Bolivia*, first published in Spanish, and issued in an English translation early in 1958. The author has also used Demetrio Canelas's pamphlet, *Bolivia After Three Years of Revolutionary Dictatorship*, published in English in November, 1955; and a mimeographed Letter from Inmates of Uncía Concentration Camp to the President of Bolivia, dated January 20, 1954.

On the government's educational program, the volume *Código de la Educación Boliviana*, published in La Paz by the Ministry of Education in 1956, has been the chief source of information.

The texts of most of the key decrees of the National Revolutionary government, as cited in the present book, are translated by the author from a publication of the Government of Bolivia issued on the third anniversary of the Revolution in 1955. This is entitled *La Revolución Nacional a Través de sus Decretos Más Importantes—Tercer Año de la Victoria Nacional de Abril*.

Certain Bolivian and foreign periodicals have been of considerable use. One of these, *Labor Action*, published in New York as the organ of the Independent Socialist League, an ex-Trotskyite group, has probably published more information on the Bolivian Revolution than any other periodical in the United States. This has come principally from its correspondent, Juan Rey, a Polish

Socialist exile, who usually writes from a strongly Marxist point of view, and is in general critical of the M.N.R. regime. Of some use, too, was *The Militant,* organ of the official Trotskyite group in the United States, the Socialist Workers Party.

Of course, *The New York Times* has been invaluable for checking dates and details of specific events. Other sources include *La Prensa* of Lima, Peru, and *La Prensa* of Buenos Aires, *The American Metal Market,* and *Hanson's Latin American Letter,* all of which are more or less hostile to the Bolivian National Revolution.

Periodicals put out by one or another of the various political and trade union factions in Bolivia have also been utilized. These include *El Ferroviario,* organ of the Railroad Workers Confederation and spokesman for the pro-Siles wing of the labor movement after July, 1957; *Rebelión,* a newspaper published by the Central Obrera Boliviana in the first period of its existence; and *Intransigencia,* organ of the Peasants Confederation and spokesman for the anti-Siles wing of the labor movement after July 1, 1957. The newspaper *Linterna Minera,* organ of the Federación Sindical de Trabajadores Mineros, headed by Juan Lechín, has also been consulted.

Of the political publications, one of the most important is *Lucha Obrera,* which has appeared in two phases, first as the organ of the united Trotskyite Partido Obrero Revolucionario, and second as spokesman for the Guillermo Lora splinter of that party. *Masas,* organ of the González faction of the P.O.R., has also been used.

Notes

CHAPTER 1

1. *Report of the United Nations Technical Assistance Mission to Bolivia* (New York, 1951), p. 1. Hereafter referred to as Keenleyside *Report*.
2. *Ibid.*, p.2.
3. Asthenio Averanga Mollinedo, *Aspectos Generales de la Población Boliviana* (La Paz, 1956), p. 8.
4. Carter Goodrich, *The Economic Transformation of Bolivia* (Ithaca, New York, 1955), p. 2. Published by the New York State School of Industrial and Labor Relations, Cornell University.
5. The foregoing information is taken from a lecture of Adolfo Linares, member of the Bolivian National Planning Commission, to the Labor Seminar of the International Cooperation Administration, La Paz, July 25, 1957.
6. Louis Baudin, *El Imperio Socialista de los Incas* (Santiago, Chile, 1945), pp. 171–172.
7. José Carlos Mariátegui, *Siete Ensayos de Interpretación de la Realidad Peruana* (Lima, Peru, 1928), p. 44.

8. Baudin, *El Imperio Socialista de los Incas*, p. 393.
9. George McCutcheon McBride, *The Agrarian Indian Communities of Highland Bolivia* (New York, 1921).
10. Ciro Alegría, *El Mundo es Ancho y Ajeno* (Santiago, Chile, 1949). Published as *Broad and Alien Is the World* (New York, 1941).
11. Víctor Paz Estenssoro, "Mensaje del Presidente de la República Dr. Víctor Paz Estenssoro al H. Congreso Nacional, 1956," p. 32.
12. Keenleyside *Report*, p. 85.
13. Fernando Diez de Medina, *Thunupa* (La Paz, 1956), p. 253.
14. Keenleyside *Report*, p. 91.
15. *Ibid.*, p. 2.
16. Víctor Andrade, *Bolivia—Problems and Promise* (Washington, 1956), p. 10. A collection of speeches, published by the Bolivian Embassy.
17. Keenleyside *Report*, p. 91.

CHAPTER 2

1. Víctor Paz Estenssoro, "Mensaje del Presidente de la República Dr. Víctor Paz Estenssoro al H. Congreso Nacional, 1956," p. 125.
2. Edmundo Flores, "Land Reform in Bolivia," *Land Economics*, May, 1954.
3. *The New York Times*, May 18, 1936.
4. *Monthly Labor Review*, U.S. Bureau of Labor Statistics periodical, Washington, D.C., March, 1937.
5. Interview with Tristán Maroff (Gustavo Navarro), in La Paz, May 26, 1947.
6. Interview with Hernán Sanchez Fernandez, former leader of the Federación Minera, in La Paz, May 28, 1947.
7. *The New York Times*, April 25, 1939.
8. This information was supplied by a leader of the La Paz Jewish community who has asked that his name not be divulged.
9. Interview with José Antonio Arze, P.I.R. leader in La Paz, June 2, 1947.
10. Interview with Nicolas Sánchez, P.O.R. leader among Miners, in La Paz, June 3, 1947.
11. Translated by the author from the M.N.R. Program, as published in *El Marxismo en Bolivia—Informe en Mayoría de la Comisión Designada por el III Congreso de la Confederación Interamericana de Defensa del Continente, Sobre la Situación Interna de Bolivia* (Santiago, Chile, 1957).
12. Víctor Paz Estenssoro, *Discursos Parlamentarios* (La Paz, 1956), p. 208.
13. Interview with Víctor Paz Estenssoro, in La Paz, August 21, 1956.
14. Interview with Mario Gutiérrez, candidate for Vice President of Bolivia, in La Paz, August 23, 1956.
15. Interview with José Antonio Arze, in La Paz, June 2, 1947.
16. Interview with Víctor Andrade, Villarroel's Ambassador to Washington, in New York City, November 17, 1948.

17. Interview with Víctor Paz Estenssoro, in La Paz, August 21, 1956.
18. Alberto Ostria Gutierrez, *A People Crucified: The Tragedy of Bolivia* (New York, 1958), p. 81.
19. *The Militant*, May 7, 1951.
20. Harold Osborne, *Bolivia: A Land Divided* (London, 1954), p. 63.
21. *Isthmania*, news magazine, Guatemala City, May 28, 1951.
22. Ostria Gutierrez, *A People Crucified*, p. 96.
23. Interview with Víctor Paz Estenssoro, in La Paz, August 21, 1956.
24. Ostria Gutierrez, *A People Crucified*, p. 93.
25. Interview with Víctor Paz Estenssoro in La Paz, August 21, 1956.
26. Ostria Gutierrez, *A People Crucified*, p. 98.
27. *Ibid.*, pp. 99–100.
28. Keenleyside *Report*, p. 3.

CHAPTER 3

1. *Labor Action*, New York, February 9, 1953.
2. *Intransigencia*, La Paz, August, 1957.

CHAPTER 4

1. From the Agrarian Reform Law, published in *La Revolución Nacional a Través de sus Decretos Más Importantes—Tercer Año de la Victoria Nacional de Abril* (La Paz, 1955), p. 44.
2. Abraham Maldonado, *Derecho Agrario* (La Paz, 1955), p. 312.
3. *Ibid.*, p. 315.
4. Víctor Paz Estenssoro, *Discursos Parlamentarios* (La Paz, 1955), p. 12.
5. Interview with Nuflo Chávez, Minister of Peasant Affairs, in La Paz, July 11, 1953.
6. Luis Antezana, *Resultados de la Reforma Agraria en Bolivia* (Cochabamba, 1955), p. 11.
7. Maldonado, *Derecho Agrario*, p. 325.
8. *La Revolución Nacional a Través de sus Decretos Más Importantes—Tercer Año de la Victoria Nacional de Abril*, p. 46.
9. Interview with Edmundo Flores, Mexican U.N. Adviser to the Agrarian Reform Commission, in La Paz, July 30, 1954.
10. Víctor Paz Estenssoro, "Mensaje del Presidente de la República Dr. Víctor Paz Estenssoro al H. Congreso Nacional, 1956," p. 33.
11. Carter Goodrich, *The Economic Transformation of Bolivia* (Ithaca, New York, 1955), p. 30.
12. Interview with Edmundo Flores, in La Paz, July 30, 1954.
13. Paz Estenssoro, "Mensaje del Presidente de la República Dr. Víctor Paz Estenssoro al H. Congreso Nacional, 1956," p. 34.
14. *Ibid.*

15. Interview with Celso A. Reves Patiño, Member of Consejo Nacional de Reforma Agraria, in La Paz, July 17, 1957.
16. Paz Estenssoro, "Mensaje del Presidente de la República Dr. Víctor Paz Estenssoro al H. Congreso Nacional, 1956," p. 34.
17. *La Revolución Nacional a Través de sus Decretos Más Importantes— Tercer Año de la Victoria Nacional de Abril,* p. 47.
18. Maldonado, *Derecho Agrario,* p. 336.
19. *Ibid.,* p. 337.
20. *Ibid.,* p. 336.
21. *Ibid.,* p. 337.
22. *Ibid.,* p. 338.
23. Interview with Juan Flores Oblitas, Director General of Cooperatives, in La Paz, July 19, 1957.
24. Antezana, *Resultados de la Reforma Agraria en Bolivia,* pp. 24–26.
25. Interview with Nuflo Chávez, in La Paz, July 11, 1953.
26. Antezana, *Resultados de la Reforma Agraria en Bolivia,* p. 7.
27. *Ibid.,* p. 18.
28. Interview with Alvaro Pérez del Castillo, Minister of Peasant Affairs, in La Paz, August 22, 1956.
29. Interview with Ernest J. Sanchez, head of Supervised Credit Section of Banco Agrícola in La Paz, July 30, 1957.

CHAPTER 5

1. *La Revolución Nacional a Través de sus Decretos Más Importantes— Tercer Año de la Victoria Nacional de Abril* (La Paz, 1955), p. 11.
2. *Ibid.,* pp. 12–13.
3. Interview with Mario Gutiérrez, in La Paz, August 23, 1956.
4. Speech by President Víctor Paz Estenssoro, published in the Ministry of Education's *Código de la Educación Boliviana* (La Paz, 1956), p. 22.
5. Luis Antezana, *Resultados de la Reforma Agraria en Bolivia* (Cochabamba, 1955), p. 35.
6. Speech by Paz Estenssoro in *Código de la Educación Boliviana,* p. 22.
7. Interview with Fernando Diez de Medina, Head of the Education Reform Commission, in New York City, October 26, 1954.
8. *Código de la Educación Boliviana,* p. 12.
9. Interview with Fernando Diez de Medina, in New York City, October 26, 1954.
10. Interview with Fernando Diez de Medina, Minister of Education, in La Paz, July 19, 1957.
11. Interview with Fernando Diez de Medina, in New York City, October 26, 1954.
12. Víctor Paz Estenssoro, "Mensaje del Presidente de la República Dr. Víctor Paz Estenssoro al H. Congreso Nacional, 1956," pp. 118–119.
13. Interview with Fernando Diez de Medina, in La Paz, July 19, 1957.
14. *Código de la Educación Boliviana,* pp. 185–190.

15. Interview with Roberto Gallardo Lozada, head of Plans and Programs of Basic Education Directorate of the Ministry of Peasant Affairs, La Paz, July 18, 1957.
16. Paz Estenssoro, "Mensaje del Presidente de la República Dr. Víctor Paz Estenssoro al H. Congreso Nacional, 1956," pp. 119–120.
17. Interview with Fernando Diez de Medina, in La Paz, July 19, 1957.
18. Interview with Robert Wilson, Advisor on Vocational Education of the I.C.A. Mission to Bolivia, in La Paz, July 9, 1957.
19. Interview with Roberto Gallardo Lozada, La Paz, July 18, 1957.
20. Interview with Alvaro Pérez del Castillo, Minister of Peasant Affairs, in La Paz, August 22, 1956.
21. Antezana, *Resultados de la Reforma Agraria en Bolivia*, p. 32.
22. Paz Estenssoro, "Mensaje del Presidente de la República Dr. Víctor Paz Estenssoro al H. Congreso Nacional, 1956," p. 120.
23. Interview with Roberto Gallardo Lozada, La Paz, July 18, 1957.
24. Antezana, *Resultados de la Reforma Agraria en Bolivia*, p. 31.
25. *Ibid.*, pp. 36–37.
26. Paz Estenssoro, "Mensaje del Presidente de la República Dr. Víctor Paz Estenssoro al H. Congreso Nacional, 1956," p. 114.
27. *Ibid.*, p. 116.

CHAPTER 6

1. Carter Goodrich, *The Economic Transformation of Bolivia* (Ithaca, New York, 1955), p. 6.
2. *Isthmania*, news magazine, Guatemala City, May 28, 1951.
3. Interview with Víctor Paz Estenssoro, in La Paz, August 21, 1956.
4. Speech by Víctor Andrade, Ambassador of Bolivia to the United States, delivered at Rutgers University, New Brunswick, New Jersey, December 19, 1952.
5. Víctor Paz Estenssoro, "Mensaje del Presidente de la República Dr. Víctor Paz Estenssoro al H. Congreso Nacional, 1956," pp. 15–17.
6. Keenleyside *Report.*
7. Comisión Económica para la América Latina, "El Desarrollo Económico de Bolivia," mimeographed, Santiago, Chile, 1957, Vol. I, p. 99. Hereafter referred to as E.C.L.A. report.
8. *La Revolución Nacional a Través de sus Decretos Más Importantes—Tercer Año de la Victoria Nacional de Abril* (La Paz, 1955), p. 19.
9. *Ibid.*, p. 20.
10. *Ibid.*, pp. 21–22.
11. Quoted by Ambassador Víctor Andrade in speech in New York City, November 15, 1952, published in *Bolivia—Problems and Promise* (Washington, 1956), p. 11.
12. Interview with Goosens Broersma, General Manager of Corporación Minera de Bolivia, in La Paz, July 18, 1957.

13. Goodrich, *The Economic Transformation of Bolivia*, p. 18.
14. Paz Estenssoro, "Mensaje del Presidente de la República Dr. Víctor Paz Estenssoro al H. Congreso Nacional, 1956," p. 19.
15. Goodrich, *The Economic Transformation of Bolivia*, p. 18.
16. Keenleyside *Report*, p. 36.
17. E.C.L.A. report, Vol. II, pp. 128–129.
18. Interview with Juan Lechín, Executive Secretary of Federación Sindical de Trabajadores Mineros, in La Paz, July 30, 1957.
19. Paz Estenssoro, "Mensaje del Presidente de la República Dr. Víctor Paz Estenssoro al H. Congreso Nacional, 1956," p. 22.
20. *Ibid.*, pp. 25–26.
21. Goodrich, *The Economic Transformation of Bolivia*, pp. 18–19.
22. Interview with Jorge Salazar, President of Banco Minero, in La Paz, July 31, 1957.
23. Interview with Joseph George, Bolivian Manager of International Mining Company, July 10, 1957.
24. Quoted in *El Marxismo en Bolivia—Informe en Mayoría de la Comisión Designada por el III Congreso de la Confederación Interamericana de Defensa del Continente, Sobre la Situación Interna de Bolivia* (Santiago, Chile, 1957), pp. 27–29.

CHAPTER 7

1. *Rebelión*, organ of the Central Obrera Boliviana, May 1, 1952.
2. Interview with Catalina Mendoza, President of Sindicato de Floristas of the old F.O.L., in La Paz, August 22, 1956.
3. *Rebelión*, May 1, 1952.
4. *Labor Action*, October 27, 1952.
5. *Ibid.*, January 10, 1955.
6. *Informativo del Comité de Unidad Sindical Latinoamericano*, Buenos Aires, April, 1952.
7. *Noticiario Obrero Interamericano*, organ of Organización Regional Interamericana de Trabajadores, democratic trade union center, Mexico, June 1, 1957.
8. *Lucha Obrera*, organ of Trotskyite Partido Obrero Revolucionario, La Paz, June 12, 1952.
9. *Rumbo Sindical*, trade union newspaper, La Paz, November 19, 1953.
10. *Eco Bancario*, bank clerk union's paper, La Paz, March 14, 1953.
11. *El Ferroviario*, organ of Railroad Workers Confederation, La Paz, July 23, 1957.
12. Interview with Edwin Moller, Secretary of Organization of Central Obrera Boliviana, ex-Trotskyite, in La Paz, July 20, 1957.
13. *La Prensa*, New York, March 8, 1958.
14. The information was given the author by officials of the company involved, who request that their names not be published.

CHAPTER 8

1. Army Decree, in *La Revolución Nacional a Través de sus Decretos Más Importantes—Tercer Año de la Victoria Nacional de Abril* (La Paz, 1955), p. 33.
2. *Ibid.*, p. 34.
3. Keenleyside *Report*, p. 55.
4. Víctor Paz Estenssoro, "Mensaje del Presidente de la República Dr. Víctor Paz Estenssoro al H. Congreso Nacional, 1956," pp. 126–127.
5. *La Revolución Nacional a Través de sus Decretos,* p. 35.
6. *Ibid.*, p. 36.
7. *Ibid.*, p. 37.
8. Paz Estenssoro, "Mensaje del Presidente de la República Dr. Víctor Paz Estenssoro al H. Congreso Nacional, 1956," p. 129.
9. Joaquín de Lemoine, President of Corporación Boliviana de Fomento, "Provecto de Migraciones," typed report, dated July 3, 1957.
10. Paz Estenssoro, "Mensaje del Presidente de la República Dr. Víctor Paz Estenssoro al H. Congreso Nacional, 1956," pp. 130–133.
11. *Ibid.*, p. 128.
12. *Ibid.*, p. 133.
13. *Ibid.*, p. 134.
14. *Ibid.*, p. 135.

CHAPTER 9

1. E.C.L.A. report, Vol. II, pp. 251–252.
2. Interview with Eduardo Hinojosa, General Manager of Y.P.F.B., in La Paz, July 28, 1954.
3. *Política Petrolera 1952–1956* (La Paz, 1956), p. 12. Published by Yacimientos Petrolíferos Fiscales Bolivianos.
4. E.C.L.A. report, Vol. II, p. 253.
5. Interview with Eduardo Hinojosa, General Manager of the Y.P.F.B., in La Paz, July 20, 1957.
6. *Política Petrolera 1952–1956,* p. 52.
7. Interviews with Eduardo Hinojosa, in La Paz, July 28, 1954, and July 20, 1957.
8. Interview with Jorge Fernández Solís, lawyer of the Bolivian Gulf Oil Company, in La Paz, August 1, 1957.
9. E.C.L.A. report, Vol. II, p. 287.
10. *Ibid.*, Vol. II, p. 288.
11. Interview with a Bolivian official who requests that his name not be printed.
12. *Hanson's Latin American Letter,* Washington, August 24, 1957.
13. Interview with Jorge Fernández Solís, La Paz, August 1, 1957.
14. *La Prensa,* New York City, April 11, 1957.

15. Interview with Ramón Claure, Minister of Transport, in La Paz, July 24, 1957.
16. *Hanson's Latin American Letter*, December 14, 1957.
17. E.C.L.A. report, Vol. II, p. 368.
18. Víctor Paz Estenssoro, "Mensaje del Presidente de la República Dr. Víctor Paz Estenssoro al H. Congreso Nacional, 1956," p. 71.
19. *Ibid.*, p. 73.
20. *Ibid.*, pp. 73–74.
21. *Ibid.*, p. 75.
22. *Ibid.*, p. 74.
23. *Ibid.*, pp. 74–75.
24. Joaquín de Lemoine, "Proyecto de Migraciones."
25. Paz Estenssoro, "Mensaje del Presidente de la República Dr. Víctor Paz Estenssoro al H. Congreso Nacional, 1956," p. 55.
26. *Ibid.*, pp. 56–57.
27. *Ibid.*, pp. 63–64.
28. *Ibid.*, p. 64.
29. *Ibid.*, p. 65.
30. Interview with Alfonso Gumucio Reyes, President of Corporación Boliviana de Fomento, in La Paz, August 22, 1956.
31. Paz Estenssoro, "Mensaje del Presidente de la República Dr. Víctor Paz Estenssoro al H. Congreso Nacional, 1956," pp. 130–133.
32. Interview with Joaquín de Lemoine, President of Corporación Boliviana de Fomento, in La Paz, July 19, 1957.
33. Interview with Domingo Alberto Rangel, member of National Planning Commission, in La Paz, July 29, 1957.

CHAPTER 10

1. E.C.L.A. report, Vol. II, p. 57.
2. *Ibid.*, Vol. II, p. 101.
3. *Ibid.*, Vol. II, p. 99.
4. Keenleyside *Report*, p. 86.
5. E.C.L.A. report, Vol. II, pp. 100–101.
6. Keenleyside *Report*, p. 87.
7. Interview with Joaquín de Lemoine, President of Corporación Boliviana de Fomento, July 19, 1957.
8. Keenleyside *Report*, p. 16.

CHAPTER 11

1. E.C.L.A. report, Vol. I, pp. 157–158.
2. *Ibid.*, Vol. I, p. 185.
3. *Ibid.*, Vol. I, pp. 187–188.
4. *Ibid.*, Vol. I, p. 198.

5. *Ibid.*, Vol. I, p. 197.
6. *Ibid.*, Vol. I, p. 215.
7. *Ibid.*, Vol. I, p. 221.
8. Keenleyside *Report*, p. 13.

CHAPTER 12

1. *El Marxismo en Bolivia—Informe en Mayoría de la Comisión Designada por el III Congreso de la Confederación Interamericana de Defensa del Continente, Sobre la Situación Interna de Bolivia* (Santiago, Chile, 1957), p. 41.
2. Interview with Sergio Almarás, Secretary General of Partido Comunista de Bolivia, in La Paz, July 9, 1953.
3. Interview with Mario Gutiérrez, Vice Presidential candidate of Falange in 1956, August 23, 1956.

CHAPTER 13

1. Carter Goodrich, *The Economic Transformation of Bolivia* (Ithaca, New York, 1955), pp. 11–12.
2. Keeleyside *Report*, p. 3.
3. *Ibid.*, pp. 3–4.
4. *Ibid.*, p. 4.
5. Goodrich, *The Economic Transformation of Bolivia*, p. 12.
6. This information was given the author by a member of the U.N. Mission who has asked that his name not be revealed.
7. *Ibid.*
8. *Ibid.*
9. Carter Goodrich, "Bolivia and Technical Assistance," in *Foreign Affairs*, April, 1954.
10. This information was also supplied by the member of the U.N. Mission who did not wish his name to be disclosed.
11. Víctor Paz Estenssoro, "Mensaje del Presidente de la República Dr. Víctor Paz Estenssoro al H. Congreso Nacional, 1956," p. 149.
12. Goodrich, *The Economic Transformation of Bolivia*, p. 21.
13. *Ibid.*, p. 31.
14. Agnese N. Lockwood, "Indians of the Andes—Technical Assistance on the Altiplano," in *International Conciliation*, May, 1956, pp. 377–380.
15. Interview with Señor Paniagua, head of Pillapi, in La Paz, August 21, 1956.
16. Lockwood, "Indians of the Andes—Technical Assistance on the Altiplano," p. 398.
17. Interview with Simón Romero, veterinarian of Playa Verde Project, at Playa Verde, July 27, 1957.
18. *Ibid.*, pp. 398–399.

19. Goodrich, *The Economic Transformation of Bolivia*, p. 21.
20. Interview with Señor Quesada, head of the Cotoca Project, in La Paz, August 21, 1956.
21. Goodrich, "Bolivia and Technical Assistance," p. 475.
22. *Ibid.*, p. 476.

CHAPTER 14

1. Introduction to Víctor Andrade, *Bolivia—Problems and Promise* (Washington, 1956), p. 3.
2. Interview with Víctor Paz Estenssoro, in La Paz, July 20, 1956.
3. Speech by Ambassador Víctor Andrade in Des Moines, Iowa, November 12, 1955, in *Bolivia—Problems and Promise*, p. 45.
4. Víctor Paz Estenssoro, "Mensaje del Presidente de la República Dr. Víctor Paz Estenssoro al H. Congreso Nacional, 1956," p. 150.
5. *Ibid.*, p. 150.
6. Lecture by Manuel Valdarrama Aramayo, to Labor Seminar of International Cooperation Administration, in La Paz, July 25, 1957.
7. Interview with an official of the Servicio Agrícola Interamericano who requests that his name not be published.
8. Interview with another S.A.I. official who does not want his name published.
9. Interview with Robert Wilson, in La Paz, July 9, 1957.
10. Keenleyside *Report*, p. 71.
11. *Ibid.*, p. 3.
12. *Ibid.*, p. 5.
13. Lecture by Manuel Valdarrama Aramayo, to Labor Seminar of International Cooperation Administration, in La Paz, July 25, 1957.
14. *Ibid.*
15. *Ibid.*

Index